THE
FIGHTING
WESSEX WYVERNS

THE
FIGHTING
WESSEX WYVERNS

From Normandy to Bremerhaven with the 43rd (Wessex) Division

PATRICK DELAFORCE

SUTTON PUBLISHING

This book was first published in 1994 by
Sutton Publishing Limited · Phoenix Mill
Thrupp · Stroud · Gloucestershire · GL5 2BU

This edition first published in 2002

British Library Cataloguing in Publication Data
A catalogue record for this book is available from the British
Library.

ISBN 0 7509 3187 6

Typeset in 9.5/11pt Benguiat.
Typesetting and origination by
Sutton Publishing Limited.
Printed and bound in Great Britain by
J.H. Haynes & Co. Ltd, Sparkford.

CONTENTS

FOREWORD AND ACKNOWLEDGEMENTS

Maj.-Gen. Ivo Thomas DSO, MC, was one of the most controversial British divisional commanders in the Second World War. Brave, thrusting, skilled in the arts of war, humourless and brutal, he led his Fighting Wessex Wyverns – the famous 43rd Division of Cornwalls, Dorsets, Hampshires, Somersets, Wiltshires and Worcesters – to one victory after another. In so doing they lost nearly 3,000 men, killed in action at the famous battle of Hill 112, the taking of Mt Pinçon, the River Noireau crossing, the forcing of the River Seine, the forlorn hope in Market Garden, the savage Siegfried line battles to take Goch and Cleves, and Geilenkirchen, the Reichwald Forest, and then the final 'Tally Ho' through the Fatherland to help capture Bremen and the Cuxhaven peninsula. It was a formidable record. I would like to think Gen. 'Butch' Thomas would have been proud of the Wyverns who contributed to the making of this book.

So, many thanks to Brig. George Taylor CBE, DSO, for permission to use extracts from *Infantry Colonel*; to Sydney Jary MC, for extracts from *18 Platoon*; to Doug Proctor for extracts from *Section Leader*; to David & Charles for extracts from Ken Ford's *Assault Crossing*; to William Clowes (Publishers) Ltd for permission to quote from Maj.-Gen. H. Essame's divisional history (1951); and to the authors of the various regimental histories including Capt. John McMath (5th Wiltshires), Peter Whately-Smith (94th Field Regiment RA), Maurice Edwards (5th Dorsets), William Gould's journal *An Infantry Signaller* (1st Worcesters). Thanks also to Maj. George Searle and Ken Ranger who lent me crucial books, Brig. Gordon Reinhold and Pat Spencer Moore for their helpful letters, and to Brig. A.I.H. Fyfe, Maj. Hugo White DL, Rex Fellows and Harry Michaels, who encouraged contributors from the Cornwalls, Somersets, Worcesters and Wiltshires. Photographs came from a variety of sources including Stan Procter, John Majendie and Maj. R.F. Hall. Douglas Goddard contributed diary and photographs.

I would also like to express my appreciation to the following: William T. Avery, Ernie Bolton, Vic Caldwell, Wally G. Caines, C.G.

Cleal, Eric A. Codling, Jim Collins, Vic Coombs, D. Davies, Leo V. Davis, T.C. Dutton, Fred Fowler, N.L. Francis, Ted Gardner, Ron Garner, Bill Garnham, R. Gladman, Bill Gould, Phillip Guppy, Col., P.G.B. Hall, David Hadow, Percy Huxter, D.E.R. Illsley, Anthony S.P. Jeans, Eric Levy, Don Linney, Albert Kings, John D. Majendie, John Meredith, John R. Newmark, D. O'Connell, Harry Peace, Eric Portway, Charles Precey, Doug Proctor, J.A. Rapp, Reg Romain, Leonard R. Smith, Norman Smith, Leonard R. Stokes, Ken Storey, S.G. Sweby, Laurie Symes, Rev. Leslie Skinner, Joe Thomas, Les Trimmer, Robert W. Thornburrow, Lt.-Col. G. Tilley, Lt.-Col. D.E.B. Talbot, B.J.V. Vigrass, Brig. C.G.T. Viner, E.N. 'Syd' Walker, Jack Webb, Freddy Wilson.

As a very young RHA FOO in the 11th Armoured Division, I helped bring down countless stonks to protect our infantry. This book is dedicated to the memory of those young Wyverns who fell along the centre lines from Normandy to Bremen.

If there are errors of names, ranks, dates and places, they are mine alone.

1

THE GENERAL

Gwilym Ivo Thomas was undoubtedly a very brave man. He was twenty-one when the First World War started and he served on the Western Front for three years after being commissioned in the Royal Artillery in 1912. Although his father was harpist to Queen Victoria and King Edward VII, soldiering was obviously in his blood, for after Cheltenham College he went to the Royal Military Academy, Woolwich.

As a young battery commander he was twice wounded and won the MC and bar and a DSO for great gallantry. In every photograph of Thomas taken during the Second World War he looked as though he had just fought the battle of the Somme. He wore high oiled boots, light-coloured riding breeches, a battle dress blouse covered in medal ribbons and his field service cap carried a faded red Major-General's cap band. In the depth of the frozen winter of 1944/5 he wore a long leather coat. In the photographed groups of Monty's generals, Thomas was always the easiest to pick out and identify. Like many regular soldiers in the period between the two world wars he became a good horseman, and polo and hunting were favourite pastimes. In that same twenty-year period he passed through the Staff College, Camberley, and surprisingly, the Royal Naval Staff College, became adjutant of a territorial gunner unit and brigade major, RA of the British 1st Division. In 1938 he was posted as GSO 1st Grade to the Plans Division of the Home Office, where he worked on the organisation of the Air Raids Precautions system. The following year he was appointed Deputy Director of Recruiting and Organisation at the War Office and became Director in 1940. He then left the WO to become a divisional commander, Royal Artillery (CRA) and then CRA of an army corps before being promoted to command the 43rd (Wessex) Division as Major-General on 2 March 1942.

Thomas commanded the Wyverns for over three years – two years of extremely tough and arduous training in England (see Chapter Two) and then through nearly a year of bitter war until September 1945. His obituary in *The Times* of Friday

1 September 1972 mentioned that 'his long tenure of this command gave him an exceptional opportunity of impressing his personality and theories of warfare upon his officers and men and this he did with marked and incisive effect'.

At the mature age of fifty-one he took his division into the brutal attritional fighting in Normandy. His experience in battle had been that of a gunner officer and most of his many brigade and divisional actions were set-piece attacks preceded by heavy artillery and mortar bombardment followed by rolling barrages. As Gordon Reinhold, then BM of 130th Brigade, now Brigadier, writes: 'How remarkable that a regular gunner should have commanded an infantry division with such consummate skill.'

In his book *Corps Commander* Lt.-Gen. Brian Horrocks commented: 'The commander of 43rd Division, G.I. Thomas, was an immensely able divisional commander though a very difficult man.' Brig. H. Essame, CO of 214 Brigade, who wrote a superb history of the division shortly after the war, noted:

> The truth is that the influence of (Thomas's) original mind and dynamic drive was so great that any account of the Division's battles would lack colour and life if he were treated merely as a highly efficient military calculating-machine. . . . It is doubtful whether any other divisional commander of the period impressed his personality and ideas of those under his command, or indeed on those above him, with greater or more incisive effect. . . . Whether the problem under discussion (in training) was the occupation of a reverse-slope position, the passage of a minefield or the layout of the Bren guns, General Thomas missed nothing. The slightest flaw in reasoning, the least departure from principle, the most successfully concealed ignorance brought immediate and – when deserved – devastating retribution. For many these were an ordeal (cloth-model training exercises), physical because they were almost invariably held in unheated huts and lasted many hours, and moral, according to the mental capacities of the individual concerned. They were essentially group exercises for not only did he expect all arms to train and fight together, he insisted that they should think as teams as well. Although quick to detect an error and to demolish a heresy, he was nevertheless always ready to listen to the comments of the younger officers. In fact his ready sympathy with them and his ability to detect potential capacity to command resulted in the Division going

overseas with a magnificent team of junior commanders imbued with his ideas and aggressive outlook.

Lt.-Col. R.W. James, the CO of 5th Duke of Cornwall's Light Infantry (DCLI), was only twenty-six when he was killed in action on the slopes of Hill 112 – half Thomas's age. Essame went on to say:

Thomas conceived war in terms of speed – speed of thought and decision – of rapid issue of orders and of quick and effective communication. On the radio he was formidable. He had a voice which seemed able to blast its way through interference from wireless programmes, Fighter Command operations, other formations' activities and even the worst splutterings and explosions of the wireless sets of the period. (And later) The Division was called upon to carry out many experiments on behalf of the War Office. Whenever a new flare, a new weapon, a new piece of equipment or a new procedure had to be tried out, the task fell to the 43rd. Thomas certainly invented 'quick lift', the drill by which a battalion group mounted on its tanks and 'F' echelon transport, made itself in a flash as mobile as a tank regiment.

In fact 11th Armoured had perfected joint tank-infantry battle co-operation well over a year before D-Day. The technique of 'Monty's moonlight', the use of searchlights at night to prolong daylight, owed much to Thomas's inventive brain.

Although he looked like a veteran of the First World War and his medal ribbons proved it, he was not refighting his 'old' trench-wars as most GOCs do (or did). Nevertheless he was a very tough and often brutal martinet with a professional, almost Teutonic, attitude to divisional command. It was Monty who was credited with the nickname for Thomas of 'Von Thoma' after the celebrated German commander who had caused us so much grief and pain in the African desert campaigns.

Gordon Viner, then a company commander with 7th Hampshires, recalls Thomas as 'rigid with little flair. The principle of surprise was not in his vocabulary.' But everyone agreed about his bravery, which often drew enemy fire and was not 'well received' by the local PBI as John Majendie recalls: 'From the comparative safety of a slit trench a lasting impression was of him standing out in the open on the edge of a cornfield on Hill 112 dressed in his usual riding breeches and wearing his general's red banded hat discussing the situation with our CO (Lt.-Col. Lipscomb) as if it was just another exercise.' Harry Peace, Adjutant 5th Wiltshires, recalls: 'A fine and imaginative soldier who drove his troops hard, in training and battle. The costs were high especially for the infantry – ruthless – even brutal.'

Gordon Reinhold again:

Thomas was a superb trainer of men comparable at his level to General Sir Bernard Paget who in Arthur Bryant's words 'like Sir John Moore who also trained an army for victory'. His exacting standards had to be met or you left! As a staff officer you would expect to be allowed one major mistake, but that was your ration! He was greatly respected and held in some awe but not feared. Indeed as we all came to appreciate his remarkable qualities a sneaking affection developed for him. At one time in 1943 a new ADC was sought and for some incomprehensible reason Evelyn Waugh (then masquerading as an ensign in the Blues) was sent down to Div. HQ. He got very drunk on the first evening and was returned to London on the first train the next morning! 'Von Thoma' was a thrusting battle commander who was always well forward in his Humber armoured car (the Ark) and getting a personal feel for what was going on. I never saw him in a flap, he always appeared calm and confident and his stamina was inexhaustible. Fears that such asceticism might produce a Monty look-alike were dispelled when reports started circulating that he was to be seen from time to time in the company of a blonde female companion around the local pub! Probably apocryphal but we all wanted to believe him to be *human* as well as our commander!

The human side to Thomas was closely observed by the young Patrick Spencer Moore, who in March 1944 had an interview for the new post of ADC. Spencer Moore was then a platoon commander, a second lieutenant with the 4th Battalion Wiltshires under Lt.-Col. Ted Luce:

At my interview at Tenterden he by no means frightened me, but was sympathetic and very decent. We agreed to give it a try for a time to see how we got on. It was driven home that I succeeded a gunner ADC who failed to book him a sleeper on an overnight train to Scotland. Thus the chop! And that the General O'Connor experience was to be avoided at all costs! O'Connor and his ADC went in the wrong direction in the desert – towards and into the welcoming arms of Rommel's lot. Not so good! My breaking-in was confined to escort duties, not any question of passing any time in G Ops room. If you stood up to him (and second lieutenant to major-general takes some doing) he would respect your views even if he thought they were wrong. I was responsible for his ARK – armoured car – radio links so that I made sure he received all messages, and made sure he got to where he wanted to go, and brought him back safely. I was not a staff-officer and was not privy to his 'line of battle'. His best friend was his CRA, Bill Heath – I think his only real friend.

'Gen. Thomas had the reputation of firing officers rather too readily but his own standards were very high,' recalls John Majendie. Two of his three brigade commanders – Peter Essame and G.H.J. Mole – were able, confident and experienced officers who stood up for themselves and survived – Essame throughout and Mole until he was unfortunately killed in a mine explosion on 14 November 1944 in Holland. But the management of 130th Brigade was changed rather frequently by the GOC:

A few months before D-Day (recalls Gordon Reinhold, then Brigade Major) Fergus Knox was replaced by David Leslie who had been GSO 1 of 51st Highland Division. This was a planned move by Montgomery to give a leavening of battle-experienced senior ranks to as yet untested formations. It was a disastrous move! He did not stand up to General Thomas the way that Essame did. I rated him a very nice chap but not a (brigade) commander. Ben Walton was an older more mature chap, liked by the Brigade and was accepted at once. A typical inter-war years infantryman, solid, basically sound. At that stage commanders were needed who had very powerful personalities indeed! (Knox) survived about a month in Normandy before being sacked by Von Thoma! His successor, Ben Walton from Monty's regiment, the Royal Warwicks, was not welcomed by the GOC either! But he did last until after Market Garden in September. Then Aubrey Coad took over. He had been CO of 5 Dorsets and was a very experienced battalion commander.

There are many stories about 'Von Thoma'. Spencer Moore recalls how before a battle he had a knack of saying

'I'm going to sleep. Wake me when they report objective taken or at a specified hour.' The nearby artillery guns lulled him to sleep. Music! He could ignore shelling. A splinter through his map board at Brigade HQ meeting left him unperturbed. One conversation at a brigade 'O' Group with G.I.T. went like this: G.I.T. to Brigadier Coad, 'Do you understand the plan?' Coad: 'Yes, sir.' G.I.T. to Gunner CO: 'Do you understand the plan?' Gunner CO: 'Yes, sir.' G.I.T. to both of them: 'Well then, fucking well get on with it,' turned his back on them and off he went.

John Majendie, a company commander with the Somersets, recalls that another nickname for the General was 'Fourpence a Quarter'. A character in Sharps Creamy Toffee press advertisements apparently was the spitting image. But Majendie writes: 'Thomas was a brilliant tactician with a very good war record, but had never been seen by anybody to smile!' And Maj. David Hadow, a FOO with 94th Field Regiment RA, remembers the GOC as 'a tough old bird. He certainly expected results, but he did not squander men's lives. He knew the value of thorough preparation, in particular, artillery fireplans before every operation. Artillery support was on a lavish scale in both attack and defence.'
Maj. Hugo White, 5th DCLI, wrote:

John Fry (who commanded the remnants of the battalion on Hill 112) said that for the last few months when posted to 43 Div. HQ he was far more frightened of the General than ever he had been of the Germans! The General required immediate answers to any question. One night John Fry was on the Div. command net when the General asked for information; John replied 'Wait one, out' while he consulted the map; immediately the cold voice came back 'One minute is too bloody long – I'll give you exactly thirty seconds!'

But he was often difficult and bloody minded. Lt.-Col. George Taylor, initially 2 i/c of the 1st Battalion Worcesters, then CO of 5th DCLI, noted in his book *Infantry Colonel* that before the battle for Hill 112: 'There had been an astonishing argument over an open wireless line between General Thomas, who wanted the attack at night, and Brigadier Essame who advocated a day assault. The general threatened to remove the brigadier.' The Worcesters then made a successful daylight attack to take Mouen, so the brigadier got his way, but the wretched Somersets also attacked during the day over 1,500 yds of open ground and were duly torn to ribbons.

Later in the filthy muddy conditions in the Peel country, winter of 1944, the Humber Ark had been well and truly bogged down, so Spencer Moore drove the General by jeep on the 'filthy roads near Brunssum. Bloody wet, foul weather. ARK abandoned. I driving, map clipped to steering wheel, 19 set head phones around my neck. Hood down. First occasion driving a jeep. (Second lieutenants aged nineteen or twenty regarded jeep driving as a personal challenge in terms of speed and roadholding.) G.I.T. afterwards, "Pat," says he, "I would rather you drive as if I was a very elderly lady – gently!" We visited everyone – sometimes company HQ – all alone in our jeep.'

When Brig. J.O.E. Vandeleur took over command of 129 Brigade near Geilenkirchen after his predecessor had been killed by the explosion of a lorryload of mines, he wrote: 'Ivo Thomas was a very forceful character and taught me a great deal during the time I was under his command. He was an extremely ingenious man and thought out clever expedients to deal with every situation. One of the most able soldiers in the field, fertile brain and was always one jump ahead of the enemy.'

It was rare to find evidence of the General's sense of humour. Just west of Vernon the General and ADC met sappers of 260 Field Company RE. Sgt. Pat Tucker stepped from his half-track and was chatting to Sgt. Alan Moore. To their surprise they saw the GOC in his scout car. 'Ah sappers, just the chaps I want. There's a blown bridge a few miles down the road. Will you go up and deal with it?' 'Yes, Sir' said Tucker, 'but what's the tactical situation up there?' 'Oh there are a few Huns about, but they are very inoffensive Huns' was the GOC's reply, and off he went. Tucker and Moore tossed a coin to see who should go and check the bridge. Tucker lost but fortunately found the Americans putting a wooden trestle bridge over the river.

The General could be infuriating. Perhaps that is a Major-General's perquisite. Essame related:

He loved to be in close contact with the action. He always wanted to know exactly what was going on. It was his nature.

He spent a great deal of time swanning around visiting his brigadiers, often interfering with their decisions as a result. A good gardener leaves his plants to grow on their own and doesn't come round every couple of days to pull them up to see how the roots are growing. Whenever he did not have enough to do he intervened in the handling not only of battalions but even of companies.

Despite Essame's protests, Gen. Thomas sacked Lt.-Col. Nichol after the Somersets lost a company at the Seine crossing. He was posted to the staff of XXX Corps. His comment: 'Thomas was a shit. He would do anything to save his own neck.'

During the fierce battle on the 'Island' to relieve the gallant paratroops in Arnhem, their commander, Gen. Urquhart, talked by radio to Gen. Thomas: '"We are being very heavily shelled and mortared now from areas very close to our positions." To my intense annoyance Thomas replied with some impatience, "Well why don't you counter-mortar them? Or shell them?" I flared up. "How the hell can we? We're in holes in the ground. We can't see more than a few yards. And we haven't any ammo." I found his gratuitous advice infuriating.'

There is no doubt that 'successful' divisional commanders need to acquire a brutal streak, and Thomas was known through much of the British Army as 'The Butcher'. At a key moment in the crucial battle for Hill 112 in Normandy, several battalions having been torn to ribbons, he ordered Brig. Essame to launch 5th DCLI, to take the objective 'at any cost'. They too were torn apart by German shellfire. As Pte. D. Davies, 'B' Company, 7th Battalion Royal Hampshires, wrote after the defeat at Maltot: 'The General earned himself the nickname of "Butcher" Thomas by his use of the units under his care and attention. The trouble is, at least to this survivor, one is left wondering just whose side he was supposed to be butchering.'

Thomas introduced the 4th Wiltshire's history with these words: 'Try to put yourself in the places of individual men. This is war at its crudest as fought by the man in the front line – dogtired, often cold and wet, sometimes hungry, yet always determined, unflinching and never giving in until the job is successfully done. It shows at its highest what ideal training and team work can accomplish . . . I was lucky to command such men.'

Like him or hate him, Thomas was one of the most controversial generals of the Second World War.

Sunday 6 May 1945. Message from Divisional GOC to all ranks of 43rd Division:

During the years of hard training at home we had two wishes, a chance to show our mettle – and to finish off the job. We have more than justified the faith which was placed in us and the high hopes with which we sailed last June. By God's help we have utterly defeated the Nazi beast and we have gained for ourselves an imperishable name. It is a good job thoroughly well done. In the doing of it every single officer and man in this wonderful team has pulled his weight. As the Commander I would like to thank each individual.

In the years to come we shall all be able to say 'I fought with 43rd Div. and 8th Armoured Brigade.'

2

FORMING UP

The wyvern was chosen in 1935 to be the sign – the emblem – of the 43rd (Wessex) Division. Brig. Essame pointed out that in both Eastern and Western mythologies the dragon is the bringer of death, and the serpent the symbol of guile. The West Saxons, who landed in the west of England in the fifth century, bore dragons painted on their shields and carved on the heads of their long ships. Later realising that a high degree of cunning is also needed to make war successfully, they blended the snake with the dragon and the wyvern was born. The winged dragon with two feet like those of an eagle and a serpent-like barbed tail became the emblem of the Wessex kings, as it was said to be of the mythical Uther and King Arthur. Alfred the Great is reputed to have refused to furl it (on his standard) and King Harold fell under it at Hastings! Ken Storey of 112th Field Regiment RA described the wyvern: 'the ferocity of a Dragon, the speed of the Eagle (legs and feet) and the cunning of a Serpent (the tail)'. However, some of the comics in 43rd Division referred to the savage heraldic golden beast as a 'Pregnant Prawn'. In the north-west Europe campaign of the Second World War the Germans had a variety of nicknames for the division, including (translated), 'the British SS Division' and 'Yellow Devils', referring to their insignia. This was known to the troops as 'Siegfried line humour'!

The Wessex division certainly had its roots in the west of England, although many 'foreign' elements were to join it during the savage campaign in Normandy as reinforcements from Berkshire, Essex and other counties. From the far west came the 5th Battalion of the DCLI, two battalions from Somerset (the 4th and 7th Light Infantry Battalions, the latter being Prince Albert's), the 4th and 5th Wiltshires, the 4th and 5th Dorsets, the 7th Royal Hampshires and the 1st Worcesters. The 43rd Recce Regiment was originally the 5th Gloucestershire Regiment, and the artillery regiments also came from the west country. 94th Field Regiment were the Dorset and Hants, 112th Field Regiment the West Somerset Yeomanry, 179th Field Regiment were the 12th Battalion Worcestershire Regiment, 86th Anti-tank Regiment RA were the 5th Devonshires, and 110th Light AA Regiment RA were the Dorset Regiment. 'The Die-Hards' was a well-earned nickname for the 8th Battalion Middlesex Regiment. The average field strength of a battalion was about 838 and rather surprisingly this infantry division was sped to war on 4,119 vehicles.

The division's most important pre-invasion date was on 2 March 1942, when Maj.-Gen. Ivo Thomas arrived to take command. FM Lord Alanbrooke, the CIGS, and Gen. Sir Bernard Paget, Home Forces C.-in-C., followed by the great FM Bernard Montgomery, all preached the gospel of training and more training, in an atmosphere of hard physical exercises and complete austerity. From 1940 to D-Day, Kent became the home of the division and the main training area was at Stone Street, north of Folkestone. The beaches near Lydd, the South Downs and the areas around Hythe were suitably inhospitable. The tangle of squalid woods and muddy lanes resembled – in some ways – the bocage country to be encountered in Normandy. In 1942 the Divisional Battle School was established at Sandwich under a series of battalion commanders (Luce, Coad and Atherton). Through it passed out the company and platoon commanders and section leaders of the division. When the Wyverns landed in Normandy they were perhaps the most highly trained division in the British Army, although other divisions might also have claimed that title.

In 1942 the division consisted of 129th and 130th Infantry Brigades with 34th Tank Brigade. In October 1943 the latter were replaced by 214th Independent Infantry Brigade arriving from the Isle of Wight, commanded by Brig. Hubert Essame. Very soon tight, efficient 'all-arms' grouping was organised. For instance 130th Infantry Brigade consisted of Brigade HQ, three infantry battalions, 'B' Company, Heavy Mortar Platoon (8th Middlesex), 112th Field Regiment RA, 233rd A/Tank Battery (59th A/Tank Regiment), 553rd Field Company (RE), 130th Field Ambulance and one SP Troop 362nd LAA Battery (110th LAA Regiment).

Eric Codling of the 8th Battalion Middlesex recalled the details of his 4.2-in heavy mortar platoon: 'We had a four man detachment. The No. 1, No. 2 loaded the mortar with the 20 pound bomb, set the range and direction on the sight, then lining this up on aiming posts set out in front. When the order to fire was given, No. 2 dropped down the barrel, bombs prepared by Nos 3 and 4 while No. 1 continuously checked and adjusted the accuracy of the aim.' He had to master the complexities of laying and firing the weapon, also fire control from a FOO post. The Middlesex regiment was a complicated unit. One company had three platoons of medium machine guns, another company had 20mm AA guns and the company of 4.2-in mortars also had three platoons. 'No. 1 was Corporal Doug Swallow, a young married man, a great chap. I was No. 2. No. 3 was John Perkins, about my age. No. 4 was Taffy Hughes, young Welshman and the driver was Codger Green, the eldest member, a TA soldier and greengrocer. No. 14 platoon commander was Capt. Pennock, an excellent officer, down to earth with a good sense of humour. The 2 i/c was Lt. 'Nobby' Clarke. The Carton-Lloyd carrier towed a trailer containing the mortar. Later Monty disbanded the LAA element.'

Cpl. William Gould, Signaller 1st Worcesters: 'Our equipment apart from the D5s (field telephones) was liable to be faulty and unreliable under stress and strain. Valves in the wireless sets would pack up without warning; batteries were heavy and rapidly expended when in constant use. They were always drifting from the signal, we had to use the 'phones if we wanted reliable communication. Our accomplishment (as signallers) with field drill, weapons and other related infantry skills were second to none.'

Maj. Bindon Blood wrote about the 5th Glosters, his Recce Regiment:

Each squadron maintained its strong individuality. The 'foundation' elements of the Regiment were the original West Country, then later-added Welsh and Scots. The ill-fated 'A' Squadron used to be Scots, 'C' a mixture of West Country and Welsh. Each added its flavour; the lazy cheerful stamina of the West, the quick liveliness of the Welsh, the shrewd sense of the Scots. The Welsh brought us 'Cwm Rhondda', the tune to which we sang so often 'Guide me O thou great Redeemer' in services, in canteen, churches, cellars, barns and orchards from Dover to Bremen.

Sgt. C.G. Cleal joined the 4th Dorsets in August 1939 aged nineteen: 'Many will say that our training, the majority of which took place in Kent with its many exercises and 36-mile route marches, was physically harder than the real thing.'

Pte. Robert Thornburrow, 4th Somerset Light Infantry with 129th Brigade TAC HQ was a driver of a 15-cwt truck reporting to BQMS 'Pop' Rogers. His mates were Toby Hayward, Chris Lever,

Sid Davis and Tom Fagan. Robert took a course in boot repairing, obtaining a Grade II certificate. Packed in a large wooden crate were lasts, hammers, knives, brads, nails, wax, strong thread for stitching, ready cut leather soles in three sizes, toe and heel irons with leather inserts and metal studs to give the boots grip.

We joined the 43rd Div. (wrote Pte. A.J. Kings, 1st Worcesters). Our training was hard but purposeful, we were being whipped into a real fighting unit. Our officers and NCOs did their job well, we were really good and we knew it. I had taken over a bren gun from John Alchurch, I reckoned I was the best there was, my reflexes were quick, my work rate was high and I was very fleet of foot. There was a certain rapport between all ranks which is difficult to describe. No one dared let our Platoon Commander down, or they were never allowed to forget it, we were behind Freddie Henry to a man. That feeling was the same for Major (Algy) Grubb.

Rex Fellows said: 'There was only one Algy – he who said of battle "It's all theatre, old boy". Nobody will ever forget the tall athletic figure, the slicked-back fair hair, the aristocratic face enhanced by the occasional wearing of a monocle and the use of a monocle, the purposeful gait and the eloquent expressive voice. He earned the title of "The Mad Major" from his men.'

Exercise followed exercise. Practice in combined arms, in loading and sailing vehicles, waterproofing of vehicles, river crossings, wood clearance and house to house clearance. Gen. Thomas kept up the intense pressure to get his division fit and trained for most of the emergencies created by modern war. Stan Procter with TAC HQ 214th Brigade recalled Operation Shudder in the bitter midwinter. He and Harry Wilde were responsible for working the two 19 radio sets in the unarmoured 3-ton command vehicle. He also trained officers of 1st Worcesters in the use of 19 sets, and went on First Aid, continental map-reading and mine clearance courses. Later on he practised with live ammo on the South Downs.

Les Trimmer joined 553rd Field Company RE before it moved to Harbledown in Kent:

I was engaged in defusing mines along the coast, St Margaret's Bay, Kingsdown, Walmer to Deal. The mines had been laid by Canadians and I had no (minefield) drawings. The Cinema

Television Co. at Sydenham made a Mine/Bomb detector which I tried out at their factory. It worked fairly well but was too clumsy and sensitive for active service use, so they came up with a version of the Polish mine detector. (Les devised his own method to defuse the mines, working entirely alone.) We also visited Mote Park near Maidstone for bridge building and field works (we dug up part of Warrior Square Gardens). We built bridges across the Thames at Pangbourne and across the Swale from the mainland to the Isle of Sheppey (at night). As an electrician I was sent to work on West Ham Power Station during the London Blitz. (Later) I rejoined my unit at Blackheath constructing radar mats close to A/A gun emplacements. The mats gave the gunners greater accuracy.

John Newmark was the 2 i/c of 'A' Company 7th Battalion Somerset Light Infantry and wrote: 'May 1944. Our training was over. The battalion was now well practised in all the necessary skills of war and ready for battle. The world was waiting for the Second Front to open up. I deemed it right to brush up my scant knowledge of French and to teach my NCOs a few elementary phrases. "Comment allez-vous?", "Merci beaucoup", "Bonjour" and "Au revoir".'

Leo Davis was a NCO with the 4th Battalion of Somersets stationed at Folkestone:

One particular 'scheme' carried out in early 1944 was the worst I ever recall. The weather was bitterly cold, it rained incessantly, we fought our way from Stone Street mostly across country through muddy fields and almost impassable tracks. Many men suffered from exhaustion. The company issued with bicycles found them clogging up completely with mud. When taken to Normandy the experience was the same and all were abandoned a few miles from the coast. I recall a complete platoon blown up on Dymchurch beach on a demonstration of the Hawkins 77 antitank mines used as anti-personnel grenades.

'We must have been a well trained Division. One scheme followed another with little time to get cleaned-up in between. All the activity (remembers Corporal Eric Levy, 8th Middlesex), almost crossing the Channel to France, nearly getting drowned during a landing at Selsey Bill, may have been part of a build-up of a second invasion force that was in Kent and Sussex ready to strike after the Normandy invasion.'

Operation Blackcock on the Yorkshire Moors was the last large-scale exercise before the final months of waterproofing, inoculations, checking of stores and inspections. Monty inspected the division on 4 February at Rye, as Pte. Robert Thornburrow recalls: 'Snow fell from an overcast sky, a grey winter's day and a speech from a frail-built man in battledress and beret stirred the hearts of everyone present.'

'In Eastbourne, we alternated', wrote Maj. Bindon Blood, Recce Regiment, 'between the town life of individual training – wireless, tank recognition, cafés and cinemas – and the windy downs of "Snap Hill" where we loosed off a lot of the taxpayers' ammunition. On the crest of the Downs we looked away to the sea, to Blackcap, to the misty Weald or the sweet Cuckmere valley sending up its smoke to the quiet autumn sky. . . . At night the Eight Bells of Jevington would fill up.'

A grand inspection is remembered by Sid Stopp with 94th Field Regiment RA, who was stationed near Northiam in East Sussex:

About three weeks before D-Day a regimental sports day was held in the village recreation field. We were told that a VIP would be visiting but for security reasons not told who it would be. In the afternoon several escorted cars pulled up outside and who should get out but Winston Churchill accompanied by the prime ministers of Canada, Southern Rhodesia and General Smuts from South Africa. They walked round the field (which was roped off) talking to everybody including the local people. To make the day 218 Battery did a crash action display. In Northiam there is a plaque on the gatepost of the field stating 'Four Prime Ministers entered this field on 12 May 1944'. They had made a stately progress through cheering troops in Wittersham, Brede and Battle.

In June 1944 Brig. Essame's HQ was near Battle Abbey and as Stan Procter, 1st Worcesters, recounts: 'He gave us a pep talk before we sailed for Normandy. It went like this. "We are going over the water tomorrow. Some of you will be blown to pieces but that doesn't matter. But I want you to understand that if anyone deserts, he will be courtmartialled and he will be shot" – very comforting.'

Capt. R. 'Henry' Hall, who was then a platoon commander in

the 4th Dorsets, recalls how 'the Battalion gave a huge Ball in the biggest Hotel in Bexhill and my wife attended. I was confirmed in Canterbury Cathedral with many other soldiers at that time. My wife was there and we said "Good-bye" after the service as we both knew I was to take part in D-Day.'

On 3 June Gen. Montgomery briefed all senior officers in the division at 12 Corps HQ (under Lt.-Gen. N.M. Ritchie) in Tunbridge Wells, and a few days later the GOC briefed all divisional officers at the Ritz cinema in Hastings. By now the purpose of Operation Overlord was made clear and map reading 'exercises' of the Normandy countryside revealed names thereafter indelibly printed on the memory – Caen, the rivers Odon, Orne and Noireau and the sinister Mt Pinçon. The division was concentrated around Battle, Hastings and Rye with Divisional HQ at Tenterden. Codeword 'Mary' on 12 June signified notice to move, and on the next day the Wessex Wyverns marched their troops to Newhaven, and waterproofed guns and 3,300 vehicles to the London docks.

Bill Avery with 4th Dorsets headed for London docks: 'Some of the lads having their final drop of beer with farewells (no breath tests in them days otherwise we would have been short of a few drivers). The Met. Police escorted the convoy. They knew how to ride their motorcycles on those tarred wooden blocks and tram lines.'

L/Cpl. Ron Garner was in the Intelligence section of the 5th Wiltshires and heard the news of D-Day while in hospital suffering from shingles: 'I had a great desire to get back to my battalion as soon as possible, not because I felt a hero, but because I was afraid the men I knew would go without me, and I would be sent over with a new unit. . . . On 9 June the maps came in – thousands of them – all of France, large scale and small scale, all wrapped in brown paper and sealed. Each bundle had code letters instead of the usual numbers. These maps were quickly distributed to companies.' On the 11th Ron went to the little Baptist church in Hawkhurst to attend his last service in England, and on the 13th 'I was paid in French money, to the rate of 200 francs a man in special currency . . . the need for security was great and drastic steps were taken to see there were no leakages. All kinds of amusement were laid on in the marshalling area. There were two cinemas with a different show each night, tombola was organised, brains trusts were in full swing. For those so wishing the Padres of various denominations were available giving lectures, services and help with queries from the men.'

The senior chaplain, the Revd I.D. Neill, had built a team whose physical and spiritual help in the Normandy battles undoubtedly contributed to the troops' morale. Gordon Reinhold: 'Later on the regimental Padres were marvellously brave in getting bodies recovered after an engagement, often under hair-raising circumstances.'

So the Wessex Wyverns set off to bloody war – young virgin soldiers, the vast majority of them under twenty-one – led by their tough, brutal leader, 'Butch' Thomas. As Rudyard Kipling wrote:

> Then it's Tommy this, an' Tommy that, an' 'Tommy 'ows yer
> soul?'
> But it's 'Thin red line of 'eroes' when the drums begin to roll
> The drums begin to roll, my boys, the drums begin to roll
> O it's 'Thin red line of 'eroes' when the drums begin to roll.

3

DISASTER AT SEA

The 5th Glosters, the reconnaissance regiment RAC of 43rd Division, moved from the 48th Division with its blue parrot sign to join the Wessex Wyverns in November 1941. After years of frenetic training – exercises Great Binge, Tiger, Harlequin and Porpoise – the regiment eventually moved its armoured cars and carriers from Eastbourne to the dirty and dusty marshalling area at West Ham on 13–14 June 1944. Apart from 'B' Squadron still in Eastbourne, the whole regiment embarked on MT 41. 'A' Squadron and part of HQ Squadron were given No. 5 hold, 'C' Squadron and the rest of HQ Squadron, No. 4 hold. Most of the vehicles were stowed in three holds forward of the bridge, but some were placed at the bottom of holds No. 4 and 5 aft, which were planked over to form sleeping quarters. After anchoring off Southend Pier, the convoy finally sailed through the Straits of Dover during the night of 19 June. On arrival off the little village of Ouistreham a storm hindered disembarkation. MT 41 rode out the storm until, early in the morning of the 24th, a landing craft came alongside with orders to move to another and safer beach to unload. Each night enemy planes had flown overhead and dropped flares and mines. Fishing for silver corpses killed by the constant shelling, cooking on Tommy cookers and poker and pontoon schools enlivened the boredom. At 0830 hrs the ship's engines started up. Nearly all the men were still asleep in the holds or on deck and the officers either in the cabins beneath the bridge or on the boat deck.

This is Maj. Ben Vigrass MBE's narrative of the sinking of the *Derry Cunihy*:

> On Sunday 18 June '44, the Regiment embarked on the ill-fated ship, *Derry Cunihy*. I went on board, before the Regiment, at about 1200 hrs, to take over rations for the voyage, which consisted of 215 fourteen-man packs (containing tins of excellent Christmas pudding, which the officers and men thoroughly did justice to, and 3,000 tins of delicious soup).

The following accommodation was allotted on the *Derry Cunihy*. Officers shared cabins with Ship's Officers; A Sqn. plus ½ HQ Sqn., No. 5 hold; C Sqn. plus /2 HQ Sqn., No. 4 hold.

Both holds were very crowded and in the stern of the ship. Vehicles were mostly in the forward hold, but some on the forward and well decks. The rations for the voyage were stacked in No. 5 hold with a sentry on guard. I went down to this hold every morning about 0730 hrs to see if the number of packs were correct, as they were not under lock and key and any man in the hold could have helped himself to a pack if the sentry was not on the alert.

The voyage to Normandy was very smooth and the officers had a space on the upper deck towards the stern of the ship. I remember one evening while anchored off the Normandy coast (we couldn't land when we arrived owing to rough seas) a number of officers were trying to do a cartwheel over a spar. Col. Lane-Fox said, 'I bet Ben will go over.' On hearing this I got up from where I was lolling on the deck and did a cartwheel over the spar like a bird.

I don't believe that any one of our officers heard the following conversation on the morning of 24 June '44. I slept in a cabin on the port side of the ship towards the stern and very nearly opposite was the gangway going down to the engines. The engineers' cabins were alongside mine. The SQMS of the ship used to bring me a cup of tea at 0700 hrs every morning. I awoke on the morning of 24 June and no tea had arrived. I looked at my watch and it was about a minute or two past 0700 hrs. Just then the Chief Engineer of the ship called out to the other engineers in their cabins, 'Come on, we are going to start the engines, we are going to move.' He said this a couple of times. A moment later I heard the engineers going down to the engines. A few seconds after I heard the engines start and simultaneously with the starting of the engines a violent explosion.

The radiator in my cabin fell on top of me as I lay in the berth. I then heard the Chief Engineer say to the others down with him in the engine room, 'Come out, it's hopeless,' and with that they all scrambled up the gangway and past my cabin. The SQMS rushed into my cabin. I was still lying on my berth. He said, 'Come on, Sir, the ship is sinking.' Now all this, from the time I heard the Chief Engineer calling the others to the time the SQMS rushed into my cabin to say the ship was sinking, happened in the space of the most, three minutes, I should say.

I got up, dressed, blew up my life saver, put it on and left my cabin with my pack and haversack, which I always kept ready packed for a move. I entered the passage, turned to the right towards the stern of the ship. I could only go about a yard, because from there to the poop was under water or nearly so. An ammunition lorry on the well deck was in flames and contents were exploding. I saw men on rafts and others waiting to get on rafts as the deck went under water.

I couldn't do anything here, so I proceeded back along the passage, to my action station forward. There wasn't a soul about, but when I reached the forward deck, there was Col. Lane-Fox and Maj. Kinnersley. I then went back to my cabin and rescued my greatcoat and rejoined the Colonel and 2 i/c. I believe we were the last three people on the ship.

The stern half sank rapidly; in a matter of seconds No. 5 hold was under water. Part of No. 4 hold remained above water for about twenty minutes. The men of 'A' Squadron and HQ Squadron in No. 5 hold had little chance of escape. Sgt. Pavey of 'A' Squadron was asleep in his hammock when he found himself under water and sinking fast. He gripped the edge of the shattered hold at the moment the whole of the stern sank, and managed to pull himself to safety along the ship's rail. Sgts Wright and Ross were carried by the rush of water into an escape hatch and through it to safety. The sea was soon full of struggling figures and floating debris and patches of oil began to spread. MTBs, landing craft and even rowing boats appeared very quickly and rescue work began. A large Motor Gun Boat came alongside and one by one the wounded were taken aboard. A truck on deck caught fire and the fire soon spread to the patches of floating oil in the hold and small arms ammunition caught by the flames popped and spat in all directions. A depth charge was dislodged accidentally from the MGB and fell alongside the wreck but mercifully failed to explode. As Anthony Scott narrated: 'The most impressive thing about the tragic scene was the calmness and discipline. There was no vestige of panic and very little noise. Wounded men disregarded their hurts and struggled to help less fortunate comrades. There were many deeds of bravery.' SSM Barr of 'A' Squadron plunged into the sea from the bows and towed a number of rafts back to the stern helping several men in the water to safety. Sgt. Drake of 'C' Squadron found a rope, looped one end into the hold and pulled several men out of the water. Tpr. F.M. Greener of 'C' Squadron rescued his comrades and was later awarded the George Medal. The MO, Capt. J.M. Ellis, and the padre, the Revd J.E. Gethyn-Jones, worked desperately, helping the wounded and encouraging the men. Sgt. Law of the Mortar troop, though wounded, worked on to rescue others. The majority of the survivors were then taken to a large depot ship, the *Cap Tourain*, a French liner.

Sgt. Pavy and a few others were rescued by an American trawler and were scrubbed with stiff brushes to remove their coating of thick diesel oil. All through the day and night, surgeons, doctors and orderlies from the depot ship and neighbouring ships of the Royal Navy tended the 150 wounded aboard the *Cap Tourain*. The CO, Lt.-Col. Lane-Fox, and the adjutant called the roll from the ship's bridge. One hundred and eighty-nine were missing, including nine attached from RAC and REME. 'Looking back on the grim day,' the Revd Gethyn-Jones remarked later, 'one realises that three factors prevented a major disaster from becoming the extinction of a Regiment. The first was the wonderful discipline of the men and their efforts to help each other; the second, the promptness and skill of the Royal Navy; the third, the favourable weather.'

Working non-stop for the next three days, a large number of vehicles and equipment were salvaged from the wreck despite shelling by enemy guns during the day and the Luftwaffe sowing more mines during the night. The survivors landed near Lion-sur-Mer and Gen. Thomas visited the regiment at Pouligny and promised every help with a quick re-organisation. Maj. Scott-Plumer returned to England to find reinforcements and came back with a new 'A' Squadron from the Green Howards 161st Recce Regiment. And Maj. Carter with 'B' Squadron arrived on 28 June. By much hard work the regiment was ready for action again by 30 July.

In the close fighting around Caen and the battles of Cheux, Mouen, Vernon, Maltot and Hill 112, the Divisional Commander pointed out that they would not have been needed in their usual mobile role.

4

NORMANDY LANDINGS
'The Debris of War'

Most of the division landed in Normandy by sunset on 24 June having been delayed four days by severe storms which caused most people acute *mal-de-mer*. The turn-around was slow of the myriad LSTs, LCTs and supply ships of all kind carrying precious cargoes of men, supplies, tanks and other vehicles. The landings at both Courseulles-sur-Mer open beaches and at Mulberry Harbour pontoon piers were unopposed and peaceful apart from occasional Focke-Wulfe sorties and the constant danger of parachute and floating mines. The beachmasters were by now – D+18 – highly experienced and the CMPs had marked efficiently the Wyvern routes inland, as well as the more sinister 'Danger – Mines', *ACHTUNG – MINEN*, with skull and crossbone minefield signs.

Few units knew of the terrible disaster that had befallen the Recce Regiment (See Chapter Three) or indeed of the heavy losses sustained by the assault divisions pushing out of the bridgehead after D-Day.

John Majendie wrote of Lt.-Col. W.S.C. Curtis, CO of 4th Battalion Somersets: 'known as "Scatty Jack" to the soldiers, brave (1918 MC), with quick brain and even quicker temper. Not as fit as other members of the battalion. Once said to his batman "Gudge, Battalion route march, tomorrow make sure my staff car is ready."' Curtis was an immediate casualty when he sustained injuries by jumping rather impetuously from his landing craft, plunged into the swirling seawater and sadly was sent back to hospital in England, never to lead his troops into action. Lt.-Col. C.G. Lipscomb (Lippy to the regiment) then commanded the 4th for the rest of the campaign.

Reg Romain, A/Tank Platoon 5th Wiltshires wrote:

Embarked at Tilbury Docks in London with our 6-Pdr A/Tank guns and Carden Lloyd Carriers and sailed for the Normandy beaches on an American liberty ship called *Fort Romain* (I wondered whether that was a good or bad omen) and arrived at the beach head in a heavy gale – after lying up for quite a while, we disembarked via the Mulberry Harbour pontoon bridge at Arromanches, then drove to our assembly area at Sommervieu and our platoon camped in an orchard. At that time Sgt. Short was in command of our gun sections (two guns) and I was 2 i/c as a Corporal with No. 2 gun. My carrier driver was Reg Carter who was a long service TA man.

'We sailed that evening at 1630 hrs, 18 June, a lump came into a good many throats as we steamed out in convoy in a small LCI and watched the Sussex cliffs till there was nothing to be seen but a distant skyline. At dawn on 19 June outside Arromanches (recalls Maj. Anthony Jeans, 4th Wiltshires) we witnessed the amazing sight of the Navy in action, shelling shore targets, while inside the Mulberry Harbour the small craft were doing the gigantic job of unloading the supply ships.'

When Sgt. Norman 'Smudger' Smith with 18 Platoon 5th Wiltshires and his mates Bert Portis and Chalky White landed at the damaged Mulberry Harbour, he wrote: 'It seemed to me the biggest catastrophe that ever was – all that Technology and training went up in smoke (so to speak) with one good storm, I bet Mr Churchill was laughing his socks off – so he could say "I told you, it wouldn't work."'

Pte. O'Connell and his carrier platoon and 500 men of the Somersets took ship aboard the 10,000-ton liberty ship *Will Rogers*. 'We were detailed to man the guns after instruction from an American. There were six or twelve-pounder guns plus the Oerlikons. My job was to lift the ammunition to the Gun Platform from the magazine below.' The fresh air was preferable to the fug below in the holds. He learnt to play poker on the way over and on arrival admired 'the Rodney and Nelson Battleships have a belt of shooting.' His heavily loaded carrier got stuck in soft sand but was quickly pulled ashore by a bulldozer. He remembered 'to drive on the Right in truly Continental style' to join up with 'S' Company.

One of the Duke of Cornwall's officers who arrived via the SS *Biarritz* waded ashore laden with forty-eight chocolate bars only to have them eaten by cows in the concentration area!

There was a heavy swell off the beaches and as we scrambled down the nets on the side of the Troop Carrier, the landing craft was rising and falling about 20 ft. We had to let go and jump on when the LC was at the highest point! When landing on the beach, the RN idiot who was i/c my boat had great difficulty in steering a straight course for the beach and eventually ended up on a sandbank 50 yds from the waterline. We lowered the ramp and I (Capt. R.H. Hall, 4th Dorsets) as commander of the boat tested the depth of the water – and with a cry 'Never mind it's my mother-in-law's birthday' jumped in. There was a great laugh from my platoon and we all waded waist deep to the beach. Stanley Couchman, our Adjutant, landed with a sandbag full of bars of soap tied to his pack with a large label attached reading 'Vouley vous coucher avec moi pour un piece de savon'.

'The bell finally tolled in mid-June when we finally sailed for the Normandy beaches in a large ferry called the *Canterbury*. Outside the Mulberry outer harbour on 22 June, we had to jump into the surf and in small groups pressed forward through the village of Mont Fleury where destruction was on every hand with broken vehicles and shattered tanks in abundance,' wrote Cpl. William Gould, 1st Worcesters. Albert Kings: 'after wading along for about 50 yds we saw the first sign of death, a dead sailor was half submerged in the water. My stomach lurched, I felt sick inside, was I sorry for myself or was it concern for the sailor, I don't know.'

On arrival off Normandy Bill Avery recalls: 'we had to stay offshore for a few days due to the weather. Our rations getting short also no fags. Albert Meddins and I stood by the ship's crew who were smoking their precious fags. As they blew their smoke, we breathed it in (just like the Bisto Kids).'

At the concentration area north of Bayeux the order was that all bicycles were to be dumped (recalls CSM Laurie Symes of 7th Hampshires). First order was 'Sarn't-Major, Get the lads to dig a bloody great hole and bury those sodding bikes.' This order was later rescinded, just make a big heap. Bicycles were coming in all the time from other companies in the brigade until a considerable heap was formed. Several hundred I would say, so ended our 'Tour-de-France'. Perhaps Monty thought that cycled infantry could not take on Mk IV tanks?

Don Linney, 8th Middlesex, saw 'what looked like a procession coming along the street, turned out to be a large group of locals, escorting a number of women who had had their hair cropped short. These women had been "going" with the Germans and some of them were carrying babies in their arms. Deserted farm houses provided eggs, hams, potent home-brewed cider and occasionally a small cask of fiery Calvados.' Don found a small wind-up gramophone with one English record – Artie Shaw playing 'Begin the Beguine' on one side, 'Deep Purple' on the other. The record was played until it was nearly smooth.

That day . . . 18 June 1944. The marching troops of the 4th Bn Somerset Light Infantry in which I (Doug Proctor) was a section commander in 18 Platoon 'D' Company, embarked at Newhaven on the Steam Packet *Ben Macree* – a steam ship which had seen better and happier times plying her trade between mainland Britain and the Isle of Man. After an incredibly turbulent Channel crossing we were anxiously awaiting to disembark on the tenuously held beach-head. . . . The weather had taken a turn for the worse – the near gale-force winds made disembarkation an impossibility for the time being. As far as the eye could see, there were ships, ships and more ships. Barrage-balloons floated high in the sky, playing their part in keeping enemy planes at bay. The RAF undeterred by the fierce weather continued to fly and few German planes managed to penetrate the protective screen. . . . Our time was spent trying to help and encourage those who were suffering most (from the misery of sea-sickness). Nervous tension and apprehension ran high at our approaching baptism into combat. As NCOs, Chunn and I had to mask our own feelings of fear in order to boost the morale of our section, not an easy task. . . . For four days and nights we were tossed and rolled unmercifully by the wind and sea.

On his arrival at the beachhead on a dirty channel boat, SS *Biarritz*, John Newmark was expecting a dry landing. 'I was disappointed. We had to walk ashore waist deep and squelch our way across the beach (Courseulles-sur-Mer) to a sandy track that led inland. The beach of course was littered with the debris of war: smashed landing craft, smashed boats, smashed vehicles and houses fronting the beach destroyed. It gave us an idea of the struggle it must have been to capture the beach and of the sheer futility of war, yet for some it provided an element of excitement and exhilaration.'

Syd Walker, 59th A/Tank Regiment: 'After being stuck on the ship for three days we landed on the beaches on the 18th. We got off into the landing craft, then the silly clot of a seaman steered us on to a sandbank. Yes, stuck fast! On the order "start up, we will drive off". Thump, thump, thump off we drove (the gun and quad), fingers crossed down the ramp. Halfway there the bloody driver stalled the engine.' Syd and crew waited for hours for a recovery truck to tow them in. 'We was all on the roof. "No use" said Charley the Troop Sergeant, "we will wade ashore." "Sod that," I said, "I can't swim." The answer? "Now is the time to learn."'

Most of the invasion force of 2nd British Army probably expected a fairly riotous and enthusiastic welcome. The Normans had suffered German occupation for four years. We had just bombed and destroyed most of their towns and villages near the coastline. They might have thought 'Better the devil we know'. Anyway Sgt. Leo Davis, 4th Battalion SLI, having been sick aboard the *Ben Macree* for five days wrote: 'We marched into a little town, possibly Arromanches, or Ryes. We were amazed at our reception. Instead of a welcome from the civilians watching us, the looks they gave us were hostile.'

Ron Garner, 5th Wilts, thought: 'This is a strange country, desolate and cheerless reminding me of the impressions I had of the last war – peculiarly enough, the French people in this part of the country didn't seem to acknowledge us as liberators – they didn't seem to care whether we had come or not. Perhaps it was because it was a farming area, where the Germans were seldom seen and seldom worried the people.' Ron visited the local café in Sommervieu. 'Only ersatz coffee, coffee made from burnt wheat was available for sale, but there was a great demand for this horrible liquid with no sugar. It was just a fact of getting something outside any rations which was such a draw.'

The short drive through the Normandy countryside similar to Kent (wrote Eric Codling, 8th Middlesex), evidence of invasion near the road. Knocked-out tanks and other vehicles abandoned guns and ammo littered the road and fields. Roadside graves both Allied and German with makeshift mark of rifle stuck in the ground and steel helmet placed on top indicated the bridgehead had been dearly paid for. For us a sobering thought. Our carriers were dispersed in a large meadow under large trees growing in the thick wide hedgerows. Our first sight of the infamous 'bocage' in which we were to suffer badly in the near future. Absolute priority on arrival was to get the cooker working and cook for ourselves a really good hot meal. Rations issued for the first two days were the individual 24-hr parachute pack – dehydrated meat, porridge, tea, biscuits, chocolate, chewing gum and sweets, all in a small cardboard box.

Vic Coombs, 5th Wilts: 'Bayeux was out of bounds at this stage because of snipers and resistance in the town. This did not register with us young lads, as having won a load of French francs on the Derby we were determined to spend it and enjoy ourselves.' At the Café Normandie in Bayeux, Vic got drunk on wine, 'the first and last time I had any alcoholic drinks in France'.

5

ACTION AND FIRST SMELL OF DEATH

Early in the morning of 25 June, Gen. Thomas held his first operational 'O' Group for his division at Divisional HQ at Sommervieu. Brig. Essame recalled: 'There were notices everywhere with the CMP briskly controlling and checking the scores of participants from all arms. The layout of the HQ had been practised during training in England.' The key players were the GSO I, Lt.-Col. H.F. Meynell, the AA and QMG, Lt.-Col. J.B. McCance, and the IO, Capt. G. Matthews. Operation Epsom was to start on 26 June with 60,000 men and 600 tanks, backed by 700 guns and the Navy. As part of VIII Corps under Lt.-Gen. O'Connor, who had been brilliant in the desert, but who had spent the last two years in an Italian POW camp, 43rd Wessex with 15th Scottish and 11th Armoured were to attack on a 4-mile front towards the wooded banks of the River Odon between Rauray to the south-west and Carpiquet aerodrome to the north-east. Initially 43rd was in reserve following up behind 15th Scottish, and 214th Brigade (Brig. Essame) was to take responsibility for holding Cheux, halfway between Rauray and St Mauvieu, and 129th Brigade (Brig. Mole) was to relieve the Scots in St Mauvieu. The concentration areas were to be Brecy and Rucqueville. The weather was very hot, the roads were dusty, crammed with traffic and the corn was high in the fields.

Maj. E.G. Godfrey MC, historian of the 5th DCLI, wrote: 'Around Rucqueville was pleasant gently undulating countryside of ripening cornfields (an ideal haunt for snipers), orchards, pasture and high thick hedgerows and deep rutted lanes. Compact small villages and the old, larger farms were massively built, favouring the defence, handicapping guns and armour.'

This was to be Monty's third major effort to capture Caen by surrounding it from the south-west and south.

The divisional artillery were the first units to get into place. BSM Fred Fowler's diary of 24 June recounts:

Recce with digging party for fire gun position in orchard, enemy reported less than a mile down the road towards Tilly. Terrific gun fire going on from a line on our right. Dug in all day, during it an armour-piercing shell sailed over trees on our flank, retrieved same, used for paper weight. Met guns at RDV at 2400 hrs on Bayeux–Caen road. Tremendous amount of traffic about, guns firing everywhere sky permanently alight with their flashes, fair bit of AA over the beaches. Guns (94 Field) arrive, taken them to GP, no trouble, beginning to rain.

The 5th Wiltshires were to relieve the Royal Scots of 15th Division,

. . . who had attacked and taken a village called La Gaule, near Cheux (wrote Sgt. Reg Romain). We moved off and the distant sounds of war became nearer and more intense – the lazy howling of the naval shells became cancelled out by the field artillery, both British and German, then the sharp cracks of 25-pounders and 88mm guns, superseded by Spandau and Bren gun firing as we moved into the battle area. We lost quite a few men by the carpets of mortar bombs that dropped around us and we were becoming excited with the atmosphere of battle. From Brecy we travelled through St Manvieu Norrey, then left the road to sweep across country to La Gaule. My first sickening sight of death in the fighting was to see two of the Royal Scots infantrymen straddling the barbed wire fence as we entered the village. (A few minutes later under a flurry of mortar bombs Reg dived into a disused German slit trench. It was a latrine hole.) I came out quicker than I went in – smelling – and fighting mad.

'Our company suffered its first casualties after turning a corner and coming face to face with a Tiger tank. We lost a Platoon Commander and driver,' recollects Cpl. Don Linney; and Cpl. Eric Levy of 8th Middlesex remembers:

We were ordered to crawl forward to a hedgerow and dig-in – there were some trenches or dugouts already there – complete with occupants. Hitler Youth Panzers who had to be 'winkled out' – evil-looking characters – more like animals than human beings. We set up our Vickers gun, and our tanks came forward from behind us, over our head. 'Get that bloody gun out of the way.' No Vickers gun and its accessories was ever dismantled so quickly and dragged into a hold. The three man gun team were praying that the sides of the slit trench did not cave in.

On the third night of arrival at dusk 'stand-to', Cpl. Stan Procter and 214th Brigade HQ signals section were visited by the Brigade Major W.J. Chalmers, 'who told us to get down behind the hedgerow banks and in the nicest sort of way said "kill as many as you can" – which for troops not really trained as infantrymen was to us a novel suggestion.'

'We were now getting the first smell of death, not just soldiers but dead cattle – it was awful – that SMELL stayed with me long after the war. Also the smell of the de-lousing powder the Germans used,' remembers Sgt. 'Smudger' Smith.

'The whole of this period 26–29 June was one of the most trying periods I went through. We were shelled pretty consistently the whole time,' wrote Maj. Anthony Jeans, 'C' Company CO 4th Wiltshires, 'we were there and night was absolute hell. None of us could have had more than one hour's sleep in twenty-four and the Boche was expected to make his big effort at any moment to push us back into the sea. We had three shell-shock cases, two wounded.'

Boy Barrett of the Wiltshires launched into verse.

> I'm a good old British Tommy
> And I fight in every war
> I don't use the aeroplane
> Neither use the oar
> The good old rifle does me well
> I shoot a lot of Hun
> If I don't catch the rest of them
> I make them fastly run.

That seemed to show the right spirit!

6

CHEUX

A Terrifying Cat and Mouse Game

Throughout 26 June 15th Scottish encountered bitter resistance from elements of 12th SS (Hitler Jugend) Division and 21st Panzer Division. Through minefields, an avalanche of shells and mortar bombs – now under drizzle and low cloud the gallant Scotsmen fought and died. By the time Operation Epsom was over they would have suffered 2,331 casualties. 'The furious Scotsmen', as the enemy called them, took the villages of La Gaule, St Mauvieu, Le Haut du Bosq and Cheux. During the night, bicycles abandoned, 43rd Wessex marched through deep mud into their first battle. 5th Wilts took over from the Royal Scots in La Gaule, 4th Wilts moved into St Mauvieu and in utter confusion 5th DCLI entered Le Haut du Bosq on the outskirts of Cheux. But the 2nd Highland Light Infantry and 9th Cameronians withdrew, taking their 6-pounder A/Tank guns with them. Maj. George Taylor, then 2 i/c of the Worcesters in support of the Cornwalls, wrote: 'I watched the DCLI move off led by their CO Lt.-Col. J.W. Atherton, a tall, lean ex-lawyer. I wished him luck as he went by. He replied sombrely: "I'll need it, George." In less than two weeks I would have his job with Atherton and his successor both dead.' The village streets of Cheux were a solid mass of traffic under constant mortar and artillery fire, with snipers in many houses. George Taylor again: 'For the first time the men were experiencing their first whiff of battle. The night reverberated and flashed to the continual firing of the guns and in the half-light of dawn, they were greeted by the sight and smell of dead cattle with their bloated bodies, and burnt-out tanks, both British and German. Rough hewn crosses by the wayside marked the graves of the fallen – this was no exercise in Kent.'

Now the divisional artillery were in action supporting the Wyverns and the Scots moving into the shattered Norman villages. BSM Fred Fowler wrote in his diary for 26 June:

Fired first rounds at 7.30 a.m., continued firing all day. Fired biggest barrage ever known! Moved to another position, occupied by Canadian infantry just out of the line, saw many knocked out tanks, ours and Jerry. Bought some cigs from Cannooks, still wet; tracks to gun positions, almost impossible. Ammo truck hit just in front of us, burnt for hours. Moved again to St Mauvieu. Dug in an orchard, meet Desert Rats, Prowse, Essex etc., firing continuous. Mortaring in front near one of our batteries, trouble from a sniper located in trees, shot him. Big field ambulance in our front shelled. Strafed by HE, and AA from our own guns, terrific tremendous air bombardment on our right, hundreds of bombers – ours. Bill Houlton was killed here. Recce party to Cheux dug in for two days. Tremendous amount of firing, hundreds of rounds per gun, battle here is pretty grim. Occasional shelling. Command Post hit, nine killed including Lt. Hill, BSM Crouch, two quads burnt out. Cheux village is a shambles. Had first bath in cow manger, very good too. Attacked by night by bombers, not so good, no casualties.

Pte. Tom Perry of the Worcesters heard 'the noise came first. I was sure that a thousand gates on rusty hinges were being opened, the sound amplified a million times. I tried to claw myself below ground. The aptly named "moaning minnies", those multi-barrelled mortars. Trembling like a leaf, every shell Jerry had in France seemed to be dropping in our company area. If I get out of this lot, I'll live for years.'

Eric Codling's (8th Middlesex) mortar carrier shed a track in 3 in of liquid mud near the burning village of Marcelet. 'We were surrounded by drunken French Canadians pressing us in the most belligerent manner to mugs of rough cider.' (The Canadian troops had relieved 15th Scottish.) Eric and his mortar crew were lost and 'relieved to hear that lovely West Country English being spoken. We had come too far forward, no mortars could fire this near to the infantry! Our lack of experience allowed us to take unbelievable risks, like standing up to watch the nearby track being mortared or taking great pains to dig the mortars in, and then sleeping on top of the ground!'

Syd Walker's 'L' Troop (333rd Battery) was also dug in. 'Then bang, bang, airburst. We were amazed, there coming across the field from the back of us was a Panzer. Well we had a go to turn the gun around. By this time five of our troop had been wounded by the airburst. I got this lump of iron in my left hip, placed my field dressing on it, and Sergeant said "into that Red Cross station", which I did.' Two days later Syd with his Blighty was back in hospital in Wakefield.

Still on the 26th the 4th Wiltshires heading towards Cheux were due to relieve the 7th Battalion Royal Scots Fusiliers in St Mauvieu. They found the village distinctly not taken. It was a nightmare relief in pouring rain. The Scots were using captured Spandaus which added to the confusion. Supporting tanks had their hatches closed down as a small number of SS infiltrated back into the village. Total disorganisation, as everybody fired at everybody else.

A mile or two away Eric Codling's Middlesex mortar platoon was under fire. Jack Matthews, the wireless operator, was wounded by a piece of shrapnel which 'carved a parting across Jack's skull, a rapid blighty'. Jack had lost his precious silver Diehard cap-badge. 'He leapt out of the carrier to search in the undergrowth, leaking blood over himself and the countryside in generous quantities.' The same day Eric was 'shaken, using a thick hedgerow as a latrine, to discover that the mound of soil which he squatted beside had a pair of jack boots protruding from the far end. Our Somerset LI neighbours captured a young lad from the Hitler Youth SS Div. We were amazed at his arrogance as he approached his captors, combing his blond locks, only minutes before he had been sniping at them from trees until his ammo ran out.'

As the Cornwalls filtered into ruined Cheux and started to dig in, Maj. A.F.C. Kitchen, OC 'C' Company, made a recce to an orchard on his right flank and found it full of Germans, so he formed a defensive flank to cover Battalion HQ from that direction. At 0900 hrs 'B' Company were making themselves at home in another orchard and heard the rumble of tanks approaching down a sunken road. Capt. H. Jobson, 2 i/c 'D' Company, related what happened next:

The wireless was working to battalion headquarters and life seemed to be a little better and more like an exercise around Folkestone. During the course of the morning I was walking back to company headquarters having flushed a German sniper from a farm building. Cpl. Ronan and I both had a fresh egg in our hands and life seemed better than ever. About 10 yds up the road we were surprised and glad to see six nice big tanks trundle up the road and turn into Company Headquarters' orchard. 'Always nice to have armour in support – pretty decent guns on them – funny camouflage they have. My God! German crosses on their turrets!' This last observation was too awful to be ignored and violent evasive action was taken by the two of us. At the same time Maj. (John) Fry (commanding 'D' Company) also made the same discovery and gave one of his characteristic shouts. One tank went on for 50 yds, and knocked out a whole troop of 17-pounder anti-tank guns just coming up (from 333 A/Tank Bty).

Cpl. Ronan and myself soon found ourselves in Sgt. Hicks' mortar pit. After a brief 'pow-wow' it was decided that he, Sgt. Hicks with his PIAT and with Cpl. Ronan's help, should start shooting up the tanks from the back. I went off and organised the three PIAT teams from the three platoons. On returning I had the pleasure of watching Maj. Fry and Ptes Jeffries and Parrish being chased all round the orchard. Each time a tank moved it was necessary for them to move also. Funny to watch, but not for them. The rest of the Company Headquarters were in their slits with the tanks actually on top and around them. Next two German dispatch riders came down the road and Maj. Fry and I had the honour and pleasure of killing the first Germans to enter the battalion area. The German tanks then started to edge forward and knocked out the two 6-pounder guns in 'D' Company area, wounding most of the crew. Battalion Headquarters was their next objective. It was a nice hull-down shoot for them at about 50 yds range. Very soon there were soft vehicles and carriers brewing up and much activity was seen by the Battalion Headquarters ditch. Our 6-pounders replied despite the fact that they were under direct fire. Lt.-Col. Atherton was killed in a gallant attempt to keep one gun firing. He was acting as loader as the rest of the crew was knocked out. At this time I met Capt. (David) Willcocks, the Intelligence Officer.

We lay in a shallow ditch in an orchard under the barrel of an 88-mm gun with the tracks of the tank not 2 ft from us. Prayers were said amongst other things! Four PIATs were hitting the tanks up their backsides and the Germans did not like it. One fled, hit three times by the PIAT in No. 17 Platoon . . . he got away badly hit and the crew well shaken. Sgt. Hicks knocked out another one at short range. Two more went round the corner and were worried by Capt. Blackwell of 'C' Company who led a PIAT party. He knocked one out and the other turned itself over in its excitement to escape. Sgt. Willison's 6-pounder accounted for another when to his own surprise and everyone else's the Panther brewed up at about 100 yds range.

The hunting of the crews was the next phase and exciting sport it made. Four prisoners were captured and about nine Germans were killed.

Col. George Taylor wrote after the action: 'In their first action the DCLI accounted for five tanks manned by battle hardened SS crews in less than half an hour in an action fought at speed and with great ferocity. They lost twenty men killed and wounded and their CO was among the dead. Maj. John Fry suffered the humiliation of being chased round the orchard by one of the Panthers leaping in and out of the slit trenches, in the terrifying cat and mouse game.' So Maj. Dick James, a twenty-six-year-old Territorial took over the Cornwalls and Capt. Blackwell was awarded the MC and Sgt. Hicks the MM. The news spread quickly round the division.

By the evening of the 26th, 15th Scottish had made a small salient 3 miles deep and 2 miles wide in the German defences – the bloody Scottish corridor. The Worcesters were now in Cheux, 5th Wiltshires in La Gaule, 4th Wiltshires mopping up in St Mauvieu and Marcelet and 4th SLI were dug in near La Gaule. The Germans, mainly young fanatical Nazi youth aged eighteen or nineteen, fought brilliantly from well-defended positions. They left snipers and 'stay behind' parties so that one could never be sure that a village or hamlet was 100 per cent cleared. A German soldier appeared in front of a Worcester position with his hands up, then suddenly threw a grenade – so he was promptly shot. Another two 'surrendered' and 'D' Company were spandau-ed as they pulled them in. Snipers in chimneys and trees were, fortunately, often bad shots, but brave. Nevertheless few prisoners were taken. A mortar bomb fell on a Worcester's 'O' Group of 'A' Company, killing Maj. P.J. Riddle, Capt. Dingley, Lt. Hulme and Lt. Wye – a real disaster – and a 'B' Company carrier was blown to pieces killing its four occupants.

Meanwhile 11th Armoured Division fought their way across the River Odon.

7

WORCESTERS TAKE MOUEN

'One of the Slickest Attacks of the War'

The division was now ordered to take responsibility for the 3-mile line between Colleville, south-east to Tourville and south to Baron, although the 2nd Highland Light Infantry were still meeting severe opposition around Colleville. So on 29 June 214th Brigade and 129th Brigade were in action most of the day.

One of the key objectives was to be the capture of Mouen, a small hamlet a mile or so to the east of Colleville. Stan Procter wrote: 'I was in Signals on the Brigade Commander [Essame]'s command vehicle. He was ordered to attack Mouen at dusk but he told the General that he thought this was too risky. Nevertheless the General insisted. I remember the Brigadier pacing up and down outside the CV for some time, then he climbed back to the wireless set and sent his orders (to 1st Worcesters), "We attack at dawn."' Essame, with Lt.-Col. A.R. Harrison, CO of the Worcesters, had made a recce just north of Colleville. He decided that a night advance through the Highland Light Infantry of 15th Scottish with the enemy still in possession would be unsuccessful. A dawn attack on Mouen from the north over the open cornfields had a better chance. No tank support was available. Backed by two medium regiments and the three Field Artillery regiments, the Middlesex 4.2-in mortars at 0800 hrs started a moving barrage, mixing smoke with HE. Although defended by a 'Boche' company with dug-in tanks used as pillboxes, the attack was completely successful. Led by RSM Hurd brandishing a shovel, the Worcesters advanced with two companies up in very open formation, about 8 yds between the men. So often the British infantry were caught in the open bunched up, a prime target for Spandau and moaning minnies. Maj. A.J. Gutch, Lt. Richards, Lt. Peter Hall and Lt. Brigider were wounded and Sgt. Stupple, a veteran from Tobruk, was awarded the MM. RSM Hurd captured the enemy HQ house in the village with its Nazi flag which he proudly presented to the GOC, who kept it in his caravan. By 1100 hrs the mediums had destroyed several of the enemy tank-pillboxes, and PIATs knocked out others. A line of concrete electricity pylons led in a straight line through the cornfields to Mouen, which lay in the midst of apple orchards, gardens and small fields. The usual enemy DF fire fell on the right flank where the Worcesters would have been if they had attacked by night! Amidst the wrecked tanks, mortars and other equipment, the Germans fought on, and the last survivors were not eliminated for several days.

C Company was to spearhead the diamond formation for the attack. My company commander (Johnny Gutch) and I (wrote Peter Hall) agreed we should keep as close behind our artillery barrage as possible – perhaps risking casualties from our own guns. We would descend upon the enemy stunned by the weight of our artillery shells. This tactic paid off handsomely. The only casualty was ME! An almighty crash about 20 yds to my left and I felt a great smack on my left arm, buttock and shoulder. A big wham. And then no pain. The adrenalin was flowing and we stormed on.

Later Peter Hall passed out and was evacuated to a hospital in Surrey, but he rejoined the Worcesters later in the campaign.
Pte. Albert Kings recalled:

While moving up (towards Mouen) 'B' Company suffered our first casualties. The company carrier was blown up killing four men including Atwood the driver and Pte. Tuck, the OC's batman. We were now in range of enemy mortars which were very active and casualties were becoming most frequent. Our battalion was to attack and capture Mouen. We were called out of the protection of our slits and formed up ready for the attack. I had a feeling in my guts as if it was tied in a knot, a feeling that was to be repeated many, many times over whenever an attack was under way. I was not feeling very brave now. I would dearly have loved to have been able to go home. One of my mates said he couldn't stop his knees from knocking. . . . I was in good company. The order came 'On your feet – Move.' The attack was on, strangely enough I was feeling better – the adrenalin was working – I was ready to fire at anything that moved. Our support was marvellous.
The Artillery was pounding the enemy then lifting up 100 yds every four minutes. Jerry was not idle. Air bursts were

exploding overhead. We hated them. We couldn't somehow crouch close enough to the ground. We came into a field next to the first buildings of Mouen; several Scottish soldiers were lying dead across the field. This strengthened my resolve to hit back. When about 40 yds from the building, a machine gun opened up from an upstairs window. My reaction was instant. I whipped my (Bren) gun up and fired a burst across the window. Whether I hit anyone or not, I did not know nor did I care. On rounding this building we came on Cpl. Poade, a popular NCO. Kenny was badly wounded . . . the whole thing seemed very confusing. The attack was a great success. To survive was purely a matter of luck. Good friends died at Mouen including a fellow Bromsgrovian, L/Cpl. Lewis.

The lessons learned, according to Maj. D.Y. Watson, the regimental historian, were surprise, no armour, a lot of smoke, deceptive heavy MMG fire to the left flank aimed at Carpiquet aerodrome, good battle drill procedure (everyone knew where they were going), advance in depth (8 yds apart) to reduce casualties and finally when enemy positions were obscure, the CO gave the company commanders their objective but let them fight company battles to get there. As Gen. Thomas said that evening: 'one of the slickest attacks of the war'. The 7th Somersets then came through and dug in round Mouen and discovered the rough charms of the local calvados! The local cows, abandoned by their owners, came up to the slit trenches to be milked.

8

THE ODON 'DEATH VALLEY'

Wiltshires and Somersets in Action

On the 27th and 28th 4th Wiltshires were ensconced in the hamlets of Bouliesse-le-Peron, an old SS Battalion HQ, and Marcelet. Capt. D.I.M. Robbins with his Gunner FOO, Capt. T. Greenshields of 94th Field, took a section of carriers as a fighting patrol into Carpiquet village and aerodrome. They reported 'no signs of life' – a brilliant deception by the well-disciplined, well dug-in German troops with hidden tanks. On the way back in the evening they were involved in a spirited fire fight with no casualties. That night the Wiltshires were relieved by the Coldstream Guards. A Canloan officer, Lt. W.I. Smith, took part in several patrols around Verson, to check on two bridges across the Odon and encountered Tiger tanks. On one occasion he said: 'I felt as if I were standing naked in Piccadilly Circus with everyone staring at me.' Farmers who stayed put amidst the battles plied troops with chickens, eggs, even geese and vegetables, and Lt.-Col. 'Lippy' liberated some well-bred white rabbits to mingle with their country cousins. Many riflemen from the West Country took pity on the ownerless cows, so fresh milk was plentiful.

The 2nd Guards Brigade now took over responsibility for St Mauvieu from 129th Brigade, who were ordered on 29 July to clear a square area of orchards and woods between Tourville and Baron – roughly 1 mile in depth and length. 4th Somerset Light Infantry under Lt.-Col. 'Lippy' Lipscombe would be on the left and 5th Wiltshires on the right under Lt.-Col. Neville Kenrick. Ahead around Hill 112, 11th Armoured Division, the Black Bull, were fighting a savage battle well across the River Odon. The first two objectives were the main Caen–Villers Bocage road, and, half a mile ahead, the River Odon, which in this hot midsummer was barely a stream. Pioneers built makeshift bridges for carriers and anti-tank guns. In front of the Somersets the stream ran between high sided rocks, in effect a gorge, to be nicknamed Death Valley. The advance took place under heavy mortar fire, but by nightfall the 5th Wiltshires were on the slopes near Baron where their CO was wounded in his HQ by a moaning minnie which sliced off a finger.

'In a cornfield (near Brecy) from each platoon of the battalion we were attached to, came the murmur of the Lord's Prayer – it was really uncanny – one could only assume that their CO had requested that his subalterns gather their men for a few quiet moments before moving off to the start line,' wrote Cpl. Eric Levy, 8th Middlesex. As Ron Garner, 5th Battalion Wiltshires remembers: 'Our padre the Revd Douglas held a short service in the field followed by a short Communion, both well attended.'

John McMath, the regimental signals officer, wrote:

The battalion was shelled for thirty-six hours, trenches were dug down to 5 or 6 ft and we had seventy-three casualties in the first two days around Baron. Seventeen ORs killed, two officers and fifty ORs wounded and four missing. Pte. Roper, a signaller in 'D' Company, whose partner was killed, had his own foot blown away, manned his telephone and twice when the line was cut by shellfire, crawled unaided more than 100 yds to mend the break. He held out for four hours before being evacuated, and was later awarded the MM.

Sgt. 'Smudger' Smith, 5th Wiltshires, dug in his 18 platoon

. . . in a large indentation in the woods on the left flank. We were digging through RED SOLDIER ANTS that had been there for a hundred years . . . and could they bite. I would take my chances being shelled by Tiger tanks, rather than digging through RED SOLDIER ANTS' NESTS. We were all bitten something rotten. (Later) The ground was covered in bodies; the company carrier after a direct hit burning in the hedgerow. Many poor lads lost their lives there. A German shell landed at the side of me, I lost half of my hearing then. I was cut with shrapnel, back and front. My pack on my back was shredded. In daylight I found the muzzle of my rifle had been blown off and sealed up.

Ron Garner, Intelligence section:

Our objective had been won, we had cleared the woods between Mouen and Baron, crossed the Odon and the battalion set up a defensive position over this bridgehead. We came under incessant attacks from the 'Sobbing Sisters'. This name was very demoralising and soon the name was changed to 'Moaning Minnies'. All through the night casualties were brought into the RAP, a large hole 12 ft deep, 12 ft square covered by tarpaulin and protected on three sides by carriers . . . slit-trenches had a roof to provide head-cover made from tree trunks, doors from bombed houses, etc. . . . Two of our snipers, Cpl. Lever and Cpl. Skelding, were killed outright from a direct hit on their slit trench. Ambulances only came when called for. Pete Rogers, one of the section reserves, died at the RAP after a seven-hour wait. Harry Rice was evacuated from shell-shock and burst eardrums. Other casualties were Johnny Fairbrass, the battalion barber, Harry Weaver, our tailor, Morgan, an old soldier and 'B' Company runner, Bob Mills, 'S' Company clerk – they were all killed. Maj. McLintock was badly wounded in the arm and was evacuated.

Sgt. Reg Romain's anti-tank gun was in a paddock 200 yds from the church in Baron: 'Our field of fire was limited because of the tall corn. The German tanks were reluctant to come over the hill during daylight, so we shifted to an orchard near the track to the Caen–Esquay road. We were stationed there for a few days with German patrols and sniper infiltration all the time.'

Meanwhile still on the 29th 4th Somersets on the right flank were entrenched along the road to Fontaine Etoupefour, also under heavy fire. John Majendie, OC 'A' Company, wrote:

The country between Cheux and the Odon is very close, a lot of orchards, small fields, not the bocage but still very close, it was necessary for the rifle companies to advance on compass bearings. After crossing the Caen/Villers Bocage railway we came under a particularly nasty concentration of artillery fire. L/Cpl. Stanley my company clerk was killed beside me. I was slightly wounded but Adj. Norman Burfield bore the brunt of blast from one of the shells. (Later) We finally got down into the valley of the Odon river named initially by the soldiers 'Happy Valley', then for obvious reasons, 'Death Valley'. The Somerset and Wiltshire salient was 2 miles deep and a mile across. The Germans were on three sides of us and could fire on us with a variety of mortars, artillery and that unpleasant weapon the Moaning Minnie or Nebelwerfer.

Battalion HQ and the RAP were in a farm and when one of the

farmer's cows was killed by a shell, he butchered it and his wife cooked a lot of meat for 'A' Company and Battalion HQ. 'We had a visit on one day from the Divisional Commander. With a certain amount of glee it coincided with a fairly heavy stonk of mortar shells and he was forced to make a very hasty retreat into his armoured car.'

There were three small bridges across the River Odon, one at Fontaine Etoupefour, the farm bridge near John Majendie's Battalion HQ and another at Tourmauville. So 260th Field Company RE, under Maj. W.A. Vinycomb, at dawn on the 30th under intense mortar fire, constructed or reinforced the farm bridge with logs and stones from a nearby quarry. The slate below the grass in Death Valley prevented digging. The 2 i/c was killed, three other sapper officers wounded and vehicles were blown up. John Majendie again: 'The REs were trying to widen the farm bridge so that tanks could cross, under heavy fire; they suffered many casualties and the small bulldozer they were using tipped over into the river.' The sappers also discovered the first Rieger mines, which had to be disarmed. Majendie had a healthy respect for the German snipers. 'Very brave young Germans who strapped themselves into trees. When they were spotted and fired on, they were killed or wounded. There was no way to come down, they merely hung there in the trees.' Sgt. C.G. Cleal 4th Dorsets shot a sniper. 'Something fell from the trees. One of the lads returned, exclaimed "Sarg! you got him, he's dead – aren't you going to see for yourself?" "No" I replied. My stomach turned over. I had killed a human being in cold blood.'

At midnight on the 29th the 7th Somersets were being relieved by the Welsh Guards south of Cheux. John Meredith wrote:

The trenches were dreadfully overcrowded and heavy shelling by mortars on the Battalion HQ caused twenty-one casualties, including the IO Lt. Macey, Sgt. Long, the Welsh Guards CO and 2 i/c. The Somersets' CO was badly shaken by the blast but led the battalion back through the night into Mouen. The 4th Dorsets had left their concentration area on the 26th between St Gabriel and Vienne-en-Bassin, to relieve the Canadian de la Chaudière regiment back at Putot-en-Bessin. Maj. P.J. Riddle left to join the Worcesters and was immediately killed in action.

From 30 June until 7 July the division remained in action in the Odon bridgehead.

9

ODON BRIDGEHEAD,
30 JUNE TO 7 JULY

The whole divisional area was under fire, from Carpiquet aerodrome to the north-east, from the far side of Hill 112 and from the west. But the two brigades up in front – 129th and 214th – bore the brunt. Montgomery's Operation Epsom had drawn no fewer than seven German divisions into furious activity. Three Panzer divisions, 1st, 9th and 10th, were now putting pressure on the Wessex Wyverns. The divisional artillery was in action all the time. BSM Fred Fowler, with 224th Battery supporting the 5th Wiltshires, wrote in his diary: 'Recce move to Mouen and dig in, mortared all day. Dozens of dead cattle, stench is awful. Three burnt out Mk IVs on position, battle still very grim. . . . Open position in cornfield, we cover Verson and 112. Still very hard battle. Mandie Clarke killed on 112. Shelled again and strafed, lots of prisoners coming in, SS and Panzer Grenadiers.' The divisional artillery were on call for their own infantry battalion, for their own brigade, their division and their corps. Troop, Battery, Regimental, MIKE, UNCLE and YOKE targets meant that up to a range of 13,500 yds 94th, 112th and 179th Field Regiments could pinpoint their 25-pounder guns anywhere on their front and their neighbours' front. The CRA Brigadier, G.W.E. Heath (and above him the CCRA), could wave a magic wand and, adding in Corps and AGRA medium and heavies, deploy several hundred guns on to a single target. They were probably, apart from the Russian front, the biggest and almost certainly the quickest defensive or offensive fire plans of the war.

Maj. Le Quesne, FOO supporting 5th Wilts:

While we were waiting for the sappers to make a bridge over the Odon, some Tigers broke through in our rear and for a time a free for all took place between them and our anti-tank guns. The anti-tank (wireless) net was bang on our frequency and we could hear them saying 'See that Tiger in the corner by the hedge?' 'Yes, but I can't get a decent shot yet. I'll wait till he moves.' All this was punctuated by rounds of solid shot bouncing on the slopes and then screaming away into the distance.

Capt. R.K. Kerr, another FOO with 94th Field Regiment RA, was known as 'The General'. He *did* look like the GOC! He was constructing an OP at Baron on the flank of Hill 112, on his hands and knees, laboriously with an entrenching tool. After ten hours' solid work two PBI asked him what it was for! 'The General' had a remarkable command of language – the abuse was unrestrained!

On 1 July 94th Field Regiment had their twenty-four 25-pounders in action at Le Mesnil-Patry. Part of their war diary reads: 'O643 Amn. very short – reported to HQRA. 0740 hrs 190 rounds per gun delivered by RASC; 1119 Uncle target scale 4 (fired) on enemy approaching Grainville; 2140 Victor target on Verson. Reported enemy M.T. choc-a-bloc.' The next day Capt. Harry Woods, FOO with 5th Wiltshires, in the forward edge of the wood south of the Odon could hear the Boche approaching through the corn. Uncle target No. 150 was called down for several hours by the divisional artillery as well as two medium regiments. By 0800 hrs 94th Field were out of ammo but the 'cousins', 112th and 179th Field Regiments, responded and sent over supplies.

Philip Guppy was a maintenance fitter for the quads that towed the limbers that fed the hungry 25-pounders of 468 Battery, 94th Field Regiment RA:

> For four days and nights there was no let up. I was surprised with all the firing, the guns being so hot did not blow up. Around Hill 112 we lost our Capt. Wilson along with others. (On 2 July 468 Battery ran out of ammunition.) For the first time the guns were quiet, a SOS was sent out for supplies. Two other regiments came to our aid and immediately four counter attacks were broken up. . . . Although I did not seem to be frightened with the guns firing at us, the bombs, machine guns, mortars etc. I did fear the snipers hidden in the trees. You knew when you heard the crack of a solitary rifle that one of your mates was now dead. I saw several snipers hanging in the trees.

Eric Codling spent much of the week with 8th Middlesex in Tourville: 'Our Brigadier (Essame) a veteran of the First World War said the conditions were similar to the very heavy artillery fire and trench warfare of '14–'18. We constructed some very deep and strong dug-outs. 4.2-in Mortars really came into their own as artillery ammo was in short supply due to the bad weather and storms in June. Our mortar bombs broke up the incessant counter attacks.'

John Majendie:

Nobody at the time could understand why during the course of Operation Epsom, 8th Bn Rifle Brigade and 23rd Hussars (of 11th Armoured Division) had established positions up on Hill 112 very much out on a limb while we were still in Death Valley. On 29 June they received orders to withdraw back into the Salient. Although under fairly heavy fire they were not in danger at that time of being ejected from Hill 112. But forty years later the Official Secrets Act revealed that the Army Commander, Gen. Dempsey, had received from (the very secret) ULTRA transcript, messages indicating the Boche were about to launch a very heavy counter-attack from the west of the Salient. So Dempsey withdrew his leading elements back behind the River Odon.

The Wyverns were now responsible for Epsom. On 2 July the divisional artillery broke up four counter-attacks, which came storming in on 129th Brigade. In the Odon 'Box' the 5th Wiltshires were in the forward area round Baron, the 4th Somersets left forward in the orchards north-east of Baron and 4th Wiltshires on the wooded spur east of Tourville. 214th Brigade stayed in the area Mouen–Verson. The 4th Wiltshires found it difficult to dig in the rocky valley commanded by Hill 112, and discovered some enemy who had infiltrated in civilian clothes and were sniping them from the rear. Their gunners were praised for their counter battery and DF plans. Everyone cheered the Typhoons attacking dug-in Tigers on Carpiquet aerodrome.

Sgt. 'Wally' Caines was Battalion HQ Signals Sergeant with 4th Dorsets, and kept an interesting campaign diary:

2 July. The Bn was to be relieved by 1 Worcesters. A few shells fell in the area, unit suffered several casualties, some badly wounded. The medical services were excellent. One could see wounded being brought in by the stretcher-bearers, who would sweat in streams after their strenuous slogging to and from the RAP, a hundred yards away from Tactical HQ. One could hear

the wounded moaning, sometimes crying with pain as they passed by. The boys would walk alongside saying 'Cheer up, mate' and stuff a lighted cigarette in their mouths. A cig always helped soothe the pain; this was well known to all. The Padre held a burial service and the Bn dead were put to rest.

During this week there was a wide no man's land on the left of the 214th Brigade sector between Mouen and Carpiquet airport, a distance of 2 miles. The village of Verson was 'piggy in the middle' and patrols from both sides sought to dominate. At night mortar teams would sally forth protected by an infantry screen, advance, set up and blast away at pre-arranged targets and then withdraw at speed before the German counter battery fire arrived.

Brig. Essame was in his element. Pte. D. O'Connell of the 7th Somersets, wrote: 'I drove our Brigadier into a village in no man's land and he proved he was no backstreet driver because he had all the nerve in the world when confronted with some Germans. To us in the carriers he was always affectionately called "Twinkletoes". He wasn't tall but he had all the guts and go and we admired him for it.'

On 3 July Lt.-Col. R.G.P. Besley, CO of the 7th Somersets, was wounded by a mortar bomb and his batman Pte. Chapman killed, so Lt.-Col. G.C.P. Lance took over command. Aggressively he decided to occupy Verson, to take some prisoners of war of the Adolf Hitler regiment, and also to send 'D' Company into Jumeaux. Maj. S.C.W. Young and three Canloan officers, Lts Tharp, Jones and Mercier, all led platoon, even company, patrols into and through Verson to keep the enemy guessing. Tiger tanks dug in on Carpiquet aerodrome were reported and positions identified. And 7th Somersets were very active sending patrols from Haut de Mouen to Verson. When Capt. W.H. Goudre, OC A/Tank platoon, and Pte. W. Napper ventured into Verson, they were greeted with cherry brandy by the French civilians still there. But on their return a mortar bomb burst above them and the body of the nearby Capt. Hedges was not seen again; he had been standing by the carrier. Later a memorial service was held for him. He turned up in England eventually, minus a leg. 'Thanks for the memorial service – the rest of the body is doing very nicely,' he wrote.

After four days in Colleville, the 5th Cornwalls under Lt.-Col. R.W. James were marched through the night of 3 July to Verson, then to Fontaine Etoupefour, where they dug in. Capt. Bill

Gorman, the adjutant, describes the advance to this strongly built stone village clustered round the chateau and church:

> The battalion left Colleville at midnight: there was no moon and it was very dark. At first, the advance went easily, with men moving in single file over the open heath and at a steady pace. All was quiet, except for the shells from both sides that swished overhead through the still July night. Occasionally, a salvo would fall unpleasantly close, and those nearest ducked involuntarily as the deadly splinters whined menacingly into the distance. But what had started off as a pleasant night time stroll deteriorated into a nightmare as the Cornish men reached the railway track. In places the rails had been torn up and jagged fingers of twisted steel bit into unwary ankles; shell holes pitted the track, and bodies littering the banks looked like a grotesque, lurking enemy.
>
> Broken telegraph poles had fallen across the rails. But worst of all was the wire. It was everywhere – telegraph wire, railway wire, signal cable, all tossed up on the track like tangled knitting wool. And in the darkness men stumbled, sweated, tripped, and cursed their way forward, now more concerned with the obstacles in their path than with the sudden flash and burst of falling mortar bombs or the tracer flying in thin pencil lines above.

Near Verson the ordeal ended, and the battalion paused for a while to reorganise. They began the descent into Fontaine Etoupefour. Entrance into the village was an eerie experience. By now there was a pallid moon, and in the dim grey light the place looked like a ghost town.

The relics of battle were there, a derelict tank with one track spread out behind it like a giant entrail; broken ammunition boxes, a twisted gun, shattered houses and shell splattered walls. The men moved in cautiously, but no one, friend or foe, was there to greet them. By dawn they were dug in and concealed.

Surprised prisoners brought in next day confessed that patrols had visited the village twice in the night and were completely unaware that, under cover of darkness, a whole battalion had taken up residence there. But by 8 July the Cornwalls had a draft of sixty men, including several Canloan officers, to bring them up to strength.

Sgt. Wally Caines, 4th Dorsets, wrote in his diary:

4 July. Bn organised a bath house in each Coy area. I felt really lousy and was literally stinking after having spent days and nights in filthy trenches without a proper wash. 5 July. Relieve 11th Armoured unit. Our line system not working for over two hours, a junction box was faulty, shells had cut the line in several places. Several fighting patrols went out during the night to put out of action several SP guns. One patrol suffered heavy casualties having bumped a strong enemy outpost, several were killed on both sides, some badly wounded. Pte. Stroud, a newly classified signaller, was one of the casualties. 7 July. Sgt. Northover and three members of the Intelligence section were sent out to establish a FO post escorted by two snipers and to keep wireless contact. No report received. At 1400 hrs Pte. Sibley, one of the snipers, returned running like hell, sweating like a bull. The whole of the section had been trapped by the Germans; all were wounded except for the two snipers, and were captured.

Maj. Anthony Jeans wrote:

I had to take over from Tim Braithewaite of 4 SLI astride the route 'Headache' which ran from the village of Tourville to the Old Mill at the bottom of Hill 112. I found him in good heart but very tired. They had had a pretty good dusting and suffered a number of casualties. They were completely overlooked from 112 to their front and from Caen and Carpiquet on their left. The Boche used to send patrols down from Hill 112 every night to within 100 yds of their positions. They got little rest from continued shelling and sporadic LMG fire.

By 4 July the 4th Wiltshires had already suffered ten KIA and forty-seven wounded, and reinforcements of one officer and sixty-two ORs arrived from RHUs.

'On the night of the 6th 'A' Coy, 4th Wiltshires were given the task of attacking and clearing up any Boche in the small farmstead (called Chateau Fontaine) in the chateau and orchards around it,' remembers Anthony Jeans. 'Attack most successful, they cleared the position, took a prisoner, but unfortunately (Maj.) Donald Tiechman and a number of his men were killed or wounded in the show.' He knocked out a Spandau with a Very pistol but was ambushed and killed trying to rescue a wounded man. He won a posthumous MC. 'A' Company was reduced to ninety men and lost five KIA and six wounded, but accounted for ten of the enemy.

The following night Anthony, with 'Smasher' Baldwin, took out a patrol to the crossroads at the foot of Hill 112, and heard a man breathing heavily. Pause for thought. It was a little owl flying from tree to tree!

All the division saw the massive bombardment of Caen. At 2150 hrs on 7 July, 460 heavy bombers in two waves dropped 2,350 tons of high explosive on top of the town. Troops climbed out of their slit trenches to cheer the Lancasters. As Eric Codling mentioned in his diary: 'We did not know that the devastation caused by the bombing was to prove a bigger hindrance to the Allied advance than to the Germans in the coming battles to take the city.' But John Majendie commented: 'Most chaps in the army those days used to be rather rude about the RAF, referring to them as the Brylcreem boys, but I've never since then had anything but praise for Bomber Command. I've never seen anything like the AA fire that went up at the 400–500 heavy bombers. Unfortunately a lot of them were shot down.'

It was just as well that the division did not yet know about Operation Jupiter.

10

OPERATION JUPITER

The Killing Grounds

By the evening of 9 July most of ruined Caen was in the hands of the British and the Canadians (who had painfully gained Carpiquet airfield at the second attempt. The first attempt on the 4th had been repulsed by the enemy's concrete pill-boxes and dug-in tanks.) The British I Corps had lost 3,500 casualties in the savage fighting during Operation Charnwood. The British 59th and 3rd Canadian Divisions lost over 1,000 each, and eighty tanks had been knocked out. However, Meyer's 12th SS Panzer Division had been almost annihilated. The Wyverns had also suffered in the last two weeks fighting. Lt.-Col. George Taylor, CO of the Cornwalls wrote:

> We began to get a number of medical cases officially termed 'battle exhaustion'. Some of these were undoubtedly men whose minds had been disturbed by intensive shellfire. But others were the weaker brethren who lacked the necessary strength of will to keep going, when exhausted by lack of sleep and tested by shelling and mortaring and all the other unpleasantness of war. . . . Later I made it a rule that exhaustion cases were only to be evacuated to B Echelon (transport lines) where our good Doctor Dickie Williams treated them with sleeping pills and in a few days they were back with their Companies. I emphasised the value of sleep before battle. We developed a drill to ensure this (battles are often fought by tired men). Battle exhaustion cases became rare.

Twice postponed because of the delays in capturing Caen, Operation Jupiter was to be a classic set-piece attack to secure the high ground between the rivers Odon and Orne. 'He who holds Hill 112 holds Normandy' was the German tactical doctrine, according to Gen. Hauser.

If all went well the final objective would be Feugerolles-sur-Orne, but to get there four key 'bastions' had to be secured. From north-east to south-west, a distance of 2 $\frac{1}{2}$ miles, were the village of Etterville, the area of Les Dauns and Chateau de Fontaine, and of course Hill 112. A thousand yards to the south-east was the village of Maltot, in a valley close to the River Orne. Until now 'Death Valley', along the River Odon, had been overlooked by the artillery and mortar observers in Carpiquet airport. But the enemy still held the high ground east of the Orne with excellent observation of Hill 112 and the ridge above Maltot.

Hill 112 is a 10-acre plateau, sloping on three sides. There is no cover on top apart from a copse surrounded by some hedges. Standing cornfields gave some cover to friend and foe. After the bombardments from both sides, the Germans called Hill 112 the 'Wood of half trees', and the British named it 'Crown of thorns'. The 10th SS Frundsberg Division was already ensconced on top of Hill 112, while the 277th Wehrmacht Infantry Division was on the western side around Evrecy, and a Hitler Youth unit was holding the north side. Behind Hill 112 and Maltot, in the village of St Martin, was the newly arrived 102nd SS Heavy Tank Battalion of 11th SS Panzer Corps, equipped with 56-ton Tiger tanks. The enemy had two brigades of Nebelwerfers ('Moaning Minnie' mortars), in addition to their divisional artillery, and had observation points all along the commanding ridges. It looked like being a nightmare to attack against this opposition.

Gen. Thomas was responsible for Operation Jupiter and he was given massive resources. 46th Brigade of 15th Scottish together with the 4th and 31st Armoured Brigades were under command. There was also immense artillery back-up, including two Army Group RAs, the guns of 11th Armoured and 15th Scottish, and the Wyvern divisional artillery.

Initially 129th Brigade on the right and 130th Brigade on the left were to capture Hill 112 and the road leading north-east for 1 mile to Chateau de Fontaine. The second phase was for 129th Brigade to hold the south-west flank to allow 130th Brigade to capture first Etterville and then Maltot. The Scottish 46th Brigade were on the left (northern) flank occupying Verson. When Etterville had been captured, the Scots would occupy and hold it. 214th Brigade, which had suffered in 'Death Valley', were in reserve with Brig. Essame's HQ in Fontaine Etoupefour. He pointed out that 130th Brigade, which so far had been in reserve, now had the major role in Operation Jupiter. If all went well 214th Brigade with 4th Armoured Brigade would pass through 130th Brigade and tackle the River Orne bridges.

A huge artillery and mortar barrage of 100 guns covering a 2-mile advance line would give the advancing troops cover. Typhoons had been promised to take out specific targets.

This account of the appalling two-day battle that ensued is mainly made by the young soldiers who took part in it. After several days of overcast weather the morning of 10 July dawned bright and clear. As Lt.-Col. George Taylor wrote:

> the stage was now set for the whole division to swing into action. The fighting of the next few days was to reach a standard of sustained ferocity equalled only perhaps by the Reichswald and Siegfried campaigns months later. The two brigades deployed in the fields along the road from Fontaine Etoupefour to Baron as the dawn bombardment started. 129th Brigade placed 5th Wiltshires on the right, 4th Somersets in the centre and 4th Wiltshires on the left. 130th Brigade plus 5th Dorsets prolonged the line to the east. At 0500 hrs the three battalions in line set out through the waist-high cornfields, each supported by Churchill tanks of 31st Tank Brigade spraying BESA tracer all the time. For a while all went well, resistance seemed light and soon five battalions were in action – from right to left, 5th Wilts, 4th Somersets, 4th Wilts, then 4th Dorsets and 5th Dorsets.

11

THE 5TH WILTSHIRES

'Sitting Ducks'

John McMath, the regimental signals officer, wrote in the battalion history:

'C' Company advanced up Hill 112 and despite mortar, shelling and small arms gained the top astride the Caen–Esquay road but were pinned down by dug-in Tigers and machine guns firing from Esquay (to the south-west). CSM Smith in a Bren gun carrier bringing up ammo saw a tank shooting its way along the road towards the prostrate company, grabbed a PIAT, ran through the cornfield, fired it from the hip and knocked out the tank, for which he received a merited MM. There were dug-in well-defended enemy artillery OPs on the hill, constructed many months before. Hill 112 was always intended to be the main German defensive position (south of Caen). Eventually 'C' Company were rescued, withdrawn in Baron. During 'Jupiter' we suffered 120 casualties with 26 ORs killed, 21 missing, and 4 officers and 68 ORs wounded.

Cpl. Vic Coombs, with 'A' Company, recalls:

Hill 112 was very sad for me as I lost a few of my good friends. On reaching the top of the hill, I remarked to my officer about a wood in front of us and suggested we should reconnoitre it. This was turned down. I then found a wire running through the corn. I traced this and came upon a German sergeant, directing gunfire from a hole in the ground. I took him prisoner and back to my officer who immediately had him dispatched to the rear for questioning. One of my friends, Ted Wilkins, was then killed by a shell from a Tiger tank which came from the wood to our front.

Sgt. Reg Romain with the A/Tank platoon wrote:

We received orders to form up for an attack to secure the advantage of Hill 112 so that the 5th Cornwalls could go through to capture the woods on the reverse slope. We formed up behind 'D' Company. The enemy spotted us, started to shell and mortar our 'start line'. (Reg spotted a hole and jumped into it) . . . for a bit of cover, we were fast becoming 'battle experienced', only to find a dead Jerry soldier lying in the bottom. The smell was awful so I immediately came out again. I shall never forget the moment I watched our men go forward into the hell of tank fire, mortar, machine gun, shells, you name it, Jerry was slinging it. We were just 'sitting ducks' taking everything that was thrown at us. We had 'limbered up' our (A/Tank) guns ready to get forward as quickly as possible. The attack had broken down on the Caen–Esquay road over the brow of the hill. Our forward troops were digging in on our side of the summit. Our section sergeant had been forward with Company HQ and returned with map references for our new gun positions whilst the forward companies were consolidating. We left our start line position and proceeded up a well-used track on the left of Baron to take up a defensive gun position on our side of the hill – a bad anti-tank position. We dug the gun in as well as defensive slit trenches. When it became dark a runner came round saying the troops would get a hot meal when the 'A' echelon vehicles had come forward. It always amazed me that except for extreme circumstances when we relied on compo packs, our 'cooks' always produced some kind of hot meal. . . . (Later that night) We heard the German panzers come over the top of the hill down into Baron, some tanks milled around on the hill and their comrades were shouting orders at each other. (Reg ordered No. 3 on the gun to fire off 2-in mortar flares but only two out of the dozen ignited.) We formed a tight circle round the gun. At first light we could see where the tanks had come in during the night, milled around on top of the infantrymen's slit trenches – burying them alive.

Reg Garner, with the Intelligence Section, wrote in his diary:

On our maps was marked a high point about a mile to our front, 112. This was our objective. 'D' and 'B' Coys gained their first objectives and dug in. 'C' Coy then moved forward but came under heavy machine gun fire when about 150 yds from the main road. . . . At 1700 hrs the Brigade put in a diversionary action to cover the withdrawal of 'C' back to the position held by 'A'. The casualties included Lt. Litrizza, the Signal Officer, and Lt. Keeling, the IO, both wounded. The next day was rather quieter. RE stores were brought up and our positions strengthened. We had the support of Typhoons which attacked MG posts immediately to our front. By the 15th we were firmly dug in and nothing short of a hurricane could shift us. Supplies of beer were got through – one per man.

Capt. Harry Peace was the adjutant of 5th Wiltshires:

After Lt.-Col. Neville Kenrick was wounded on 1 July, Maj. 'Pop' Pearson, the 2 i/c took over, was promoted to Lieutenant-Colonel. He had been Brigade Major of 130 Brigade, a regular officer in the South Lancashires. He was about 6 ft in height, spare, with a sandy complexion, a clipped moustache and thinning hair, and he sported a walking stick. He had a strong sense of humour, a lively imagination and inventive frame of mind. The 5th Wilts were not in good shape. The approach to the front of Hill 112 near Baron had not been without incident and for the first time, the reality of the horror of the battle fields had been encountered, by rotting corpses of men and cattle, the ghastly stench of death, for which no amount of training could be a preparation. Stonks from the frightening 'moaning minnies', the fear of snipers – fanatical members of the SS Youth who stayed concealed to pick off selected targets. On reaching their objective the Bn had dug in – but not deep enough. With Carpiquet aerodrome still in enemy hands giving good observation, well-directed mortar and artillery fire rained down. That night of 13 July an enemy counter-attack was duly frustrated by overwhelming fire from our own artillery directed largely by a gallant FOO from 94th Field Regiment. What wonderful support they gave throughout. The 5th were dirty and dishevelled. Orders had been given by higher command that water was only to be used for drinking. Some officers and NCOs had covered up their badges of rank for fear of snipers. 'Pop' countermanded the orders about water and encouraged all ranks to wash and shave. He indicated he was not in favour of badges of rank being concealed. He moved Bn HQ to more comfortable quarters in a farm building with thick walls. Every evening he visited the leading troops and talked to them about how the battle was going, to convince them that they were not there just to be shelled and shot at. He plucked a red rose and put it in the webbing of his helmet like a knight of old bearing his lady's favour. The red rose was a favourite of his beloved wife and also the flower of his much loved South Lancs regiment.

'D' Company held on to Hill 112 for the rest of that terrible day and through the night. The Tiger tank that came through our lines running over one of our trenches, caving it in, withdrew thinking that we had ALL been wiped out. As daylight approached (Sgt. 'Smudger' Smith, 18 Platoon 5th Wilts, recalled) we thought how did we survive that, there were bodies everywhere. Later that day a German Spotter plane flew over, dropped some leaflets telling us London and most of the Big Cities had been bombed with their secret weapon Doodle Bug or Buzz Bombs. They advised us to surrender and save any more bloodshed. Later 'Dolly' Grey, our CQMS, brought up a dixie of hot stew in his carrier. The first I had seen for a long time. He made so much dust coming up. Bombs fell around us. Our four lads, the CQMS and carrier driver all piled into the same slit trench knocking the dixie over. . . . With tongues hanging out we watched the stew soaking into the dirt.

Brig. Essame summed up the situation:

On the extreme right flank, 5 Wiltshire had gained its objectives on our side of the hill. 'C' Company were ordered to advance to the crest and then fall back to positions prepared for them on the reverse slope. Despite mortar, shell and small-arms fire, they gained the top and got astride the Caen–Esquay road only to be pinned down by intense fire. . . . On the right the carrier platoon closed with the enemy. Only with great difficulty and loss was 'C' Company finally extracted.

12
THE 4TH SOMERSETS

'The Battalion Which Had Landed No Longer Existed'

The battalion plan of attack was to be in three phases: (1) 'B' and 'A' Companies to capture the line of the road Evrecy–Etterville; (2) 'D' and 'C' Companies to pass through them to the plateau on Hill 112; and (3) A line of Observation Posts to be set up on the plateau.

'The Somersets plan seemed a sensible one: the two leading companies each with a troop of tanks were given the limited objectives of dealing with the enemy outpost positions on the forward slope: the two reserve companies also with tanks would leap-frog through to capture the small diamond shaped wood,' wrote Col. George Taylor of the Cornwalls. The attack started at 0500 hrs and the advance of 1,500 yds over open country under enemy observation meant casualties were very heavy. The company commanders of 'A', 'B' and 'C' companies were wounded. At the end of phase 1 the battalion was simply too weak to continue: 3 officers and 13 ORs were killed, 9 officers and 100 ORs were wounded and 67 were posted missing or POW – a total of 192. Col. Taylor saw them:

they attacked with great courage but the carnage was fearful. Bursting shells and mortar fire decimated their ranks but they hit back with every weapon available to them. But the Somersets' casualties were so heavy that the plan to capture the orchard with the reserve companies was abandoned. The problem was that for a short time too many men had been exposed under tremendous artillery and mortar fire, a plan based on First World War French tactics, when the first wave would capture a line of trenches and shelter in them.

'I was throwing grenades into dugouts where the Germans were hidden,' Capt. Perks said, 'then I was wounded in the side. A splinter I think. A violent tank battle developed on the northern slopes, I had anti-tank guns, but by this time there were not enough men to man them. The corn was so high that we couldn't use the gun sights. We aimed by guesswork. Soon three German tanks were in flames and a fourth was beating a hasty retreat with smoke pouring out of the turret.' By 0900 hrs the Somersets had reached the line of the Etterville road and could see the stone cross of the Calvary.

John Majendie was commanding the support company which consisted of the Carrier Platoon, the Mortar Platoon, the A/Tank Platoon and the Pioneer Platoon. While arranging all the battalion vehicles and the start line, his old pair of school braces broke, but luckily his trousers didn't fall down. He had sausages for breakfast at 0315 hrs on 10 July:

We attacked with two rifle companies up 'A' & 'B', with 'C' & 'D' behind them, then a squadron of tanks, then all the various armoured vehicles in the middle of that box. At about 5 o'clock our guns, 3-in mortars and 4.2-in mortars opened up behind us. Anybody there will agree that the battle for Hill 112 was saved from being a disaster by our own artillery, who fired 43,000 rounds during the first twenty-four hours. I advanced with my Pioneer Sergeant, two Pioneers, my batman and my runner behind the second of the right hand companies. A lot of stuff was coming down from ahead of us, and small arms fire; and vehicles were hit, and started to burn. I remember a group of terrified thoroughbred horses from a stud farm galloping across the fields to our right. Also a tank commander with his microphone still round his neck, with his head missing. The walking wounded were starting to come back asking for the RAP, then a steady succession of carriers or jeeps loaded with stretchers. Now we all carried, whatever one's rank, a rifle and bayonet. We went on this attack with fixed bayonets. When anybody went down (wounded or killed) into the unharvested tall corn about waist height, the rifle was stuck in the ground with a steel helmet hanging on top of it to indicate he was there. Edward Trottman, CO of 'A' Company was hit fairly early on by machine gun bullets which ricocheted off the silver whisky flask he had in his breast pocket, wounding him in arm and leg. He was evacuated stinking of whisky because his flask had burst, and was worried that people would think he had been drinking it! Col. 'Lippy' was in his Bren gun carrier with his IO, Gordon Bennett (later Dean of Truro Cathedral). The CO threw a hand grenade at a German armed with a Panzerfaust (equivalent to our PIAT) and the IO gave him a burst from a sten gun and dealt with him. The CO turned to his driver, said 'Drive On'. The driver was sitting beside him with a hole in his head, stone dead.

Of John's little group of six, one was killed, two wounded, which 'was about average'. They kept passing Somerset and Wiltshire wounded. 'One soldier was standing by his wounded mate wrapped in a blanket and looking not at all well, saying to him "Would you like my chocolate ration?" A big sacrifice in those days. . . .' The attack ground to a halt about 300 yds from the point of 112 along the line of the main road: 'The strength of about a hundred in the rifle companies were down to twenty or thirty with Platoons which should have been thirty-six men consisting in some cases of only four or five.' Clifford Perks, the A/Tank Platoon Commander, later to become Mr Justice Perks, was hit in the arm and said 'I know it can't be anything bad as it hurts too much and they always say a bad wound doesn't hurt.' John Majendie again: 'He was a tower of strength, wouldn't allow himself to be evacuated and was awarded the MC. I found the CO and asked him how things were going. He said "Well, Lance Wardle, OC 'C' Company, Charles Stewart commanding 'B' Coy and Edward Trottman commanding 'A' Coy are all wounded, would you like to take over 'A' Coy?'

John Majendie commented: 'The CO was "Lippy" to all ranks, respected and admired throughout the battalion, always firmly in control and when required up in front. A very brave man, or possibly one of those lucky individuals who are fearless.'

Pte. Vic Caldwell was in 7th Platoon, 'A' Company:

We were dug in an orchard and the attack was to begin at 0500 hrs just as it was beginning to get light, our artillery had been softening up the front for some time and we moved off. Everything was coming at us, Nebelwerfers, rifles, LMGs, etc. We hadn't got very far when the cries rang out for stretcher-bearers and the shouts of men in pain who had been hit. We all went to ground in the standing ripening corn which was waist-high – just to move would disturb the corn which would bring down a hail of LMG on you and whip off the tops of the corn.

The platoon sergeant, G. Brewster, was now in command of 'A' Company, as Maj. E. Trottman and all the platoon officers were casualties.

Leo Davis was initially LOB (Left Out of Battle) at Hill 112 with thirty others:

> We were suddenly marched hotfoot to rejoin the battalion which was suffering heavy casualties. We were rushed up the slopes of Hill 112, directed towards Bn HQ, on the other side of a hedge. Before crossing the hedge I was a signal corporal. On landing in the trench I found I was acting Signal Sergeant. On contacting the few signallers remaining I found our casualties were appalling. Fifteen men were left of one (rifle) company. We were shelled unmercifully. Casualties mounted. The cries 'stretcher-bearers, stretcher-bearers' were piteous and almost continuous. Mending telephone lines to companies, broken by mortar and shellfire, meant journeying out into open cornfields. . . . How the rifle companies suffered.

Sgt. Hole with the Mortar Platoon:

> It is difficult to describe the attack itself but it was more as one imagines a battle to be, than any other I have seen. At daylight the whole scene was illuminated by burning carriers and tanks. Flame throwers were in action. The enemy using Nebelwerfers was mortaring the advancing troops. Practically every weapon was in action – rifles, grenades, phosphorous, LMGs and tanks, and the casualties were extremely heavy. Our mortars fired some 5,000 rounds during the battle.

Pte. Robert Thornburrow's diary, *What's in a War* related: '4 SLI lost over 200 men to take and hold a piece of high ground – just a number on a map and now the Division was nicknamed the "Yellow Devils" after the two-legged dragon with erect wings and barbed tail. And the shortage of water, but an issue of yellow hand soap!' Near Mouen with Brigade TAC HQ he met Pte./Driver Darbyshire, 'blackened, unshaven face who blurted out "Bob, it's me, Darby, I've deserted, I just couldn't take anymore, it's bloody murder up front," in his north country Lancashire accent. Next day he was seen amongst a group of deserters in a barbed wire compound, next door to a much larger one holding POW.'

But Operation Jupiter was not yet over for the Somersets as Cpl. Doug Proctor wrote in *Section Commander*:

That night and all the next day we held fast suffering under intense German mortar fire. Snipers were making life very difficult. Late on the 11th a plan – born no doubt out of desperation – was decided upon. The Cornwalls had failed to capture the forward slope (of Hill 112) in a battalion daytime attack, a night attack by one company might succeed. At 0100 hrs on the 12th, 16 and 17 platoons commanded by Sgts Oxland and Partridge led our advance to infiltrate quickly forward, then rush the German positions. (The Germans were alert, waited behind barbed wire defences and 'D' Company was fully exposed. They) inflicted on us their murderous attack with small arms and mortar bombs. The signal was given to withdraw. We moved back quickly to our defensive positions – a very chastened company indeed. The brigadier was ill-advised to have authorised it in the first instance. During the attack a young section leader was scrambling through the barbed wire and a bullet exploded his phosphorous grenade carried in his pouch. Entangled on the wire, ablaze, he begged for someone to shoot him as quickly and mercifully as possible. This was done by a compassionate but appalled officer.

The Churchill infantry tanks of the 7th RTR, supporting the Somersets, were no match for the opposing Tiger tanks or their supporting 88mms, as Maj. Joscelyne reported: 'Lt.-Col. Gaisford was blinded in one eye and Maj. Fleming killed in his tank. "C" Squadron suffered terribly, losing six tanks. . . . The Somersets were decimated.' The surviving Churchill tanks pulled back down to hull-down positions.

'Surely the long 1500-yds approach called for a *night* attack?' wrote Col. George Taylor in his book *Infantry Colonel*.

During the week of Death Valley and the attack on Hill 112, the 4th Somersets, out of a strength of 845, suffered 556 casualties, and between 26 June and 14 July 4th SLI received 19 reinforcement officers and 479 ORs as replacements.

13

THE 4TH WILTSHIRES

'Like a Combine Harvester'

In *The Maroon Square*, the campaign history of the battalion, it is recounted that:

> their objective was the area of the road junction on the top of the ridge of Hill 112 but east of the summit top. The battalion advanced at 0500 hrs in extended order in the Division's first set piece attack through waist high corn with red poppies against dug-in SS in elaborate deep dugouts in the centre of a web of roofed over crawl trenches, leading to weapon pits with Spandaus. The SS tried to cut off the Wiltshire riflemen from their supporting Churchill tanks of 31st Tank Brigade, by enfilading them with Spandau crossfire. Maj. Parsons noted that on their left 5th Dorsets were level as they cleared Les Dauns, but on the right 4th Somersets had diverged a little. The SS wounded had a nasty habit of throwing hand grenades at stretcher-bearers. Carriers were the ideal vehicle from which to fight standing up, to see the enemy in his holes in the corn. It was a confused soldiers' battle with many individual actions, flushing out SS in dugouts, verifying the 'deadness' of corpses, watching for hidden snipers or bypassed Spandau teams or mortar postions. Lt. J.P. Williams was shot by SS as enemy raised their hands in surrender, some of them wearing Red Cross armbands. Cpl. Frank, one of the stretcher-bearers with 'B' Coy, tried to succour Lt. Williams who died in a few minutes. Frank was attacked by two wounded SS men so he had to shoot them. The Churchills with their BESA MG, penetrated two belts of Spandau teams but enemy counterfire caused 20 per cent casualties.

Maj. J.E.B. Duke, BC 224th Battery 94th Field Regiment, wrote:

After fourteen days of continuous battle day and night it seemed hard to believe that we were ever going to get out of the Odon valley where we were overlooked by the enemy from three sides. After a night of orders and careful preparation at the gun position, I snatched a few hours sleep before joining 4th Wiltshires in their forming-up area, an orchard on the lower slopes of the hill. The barrage was terrific and we got as close as we safely could to the opening line. Eventually we all started forward, the infantry in full battle order and behaving as calmly as if on an exercise back in Kent. We quickly ran into heavy mortar fire and found many wounded men crawling in the standing corn and dead German SS anti-tank gunners lying round their guns. Bombadier Nobbs was soon able to report to RHQ on his wireless that we had reached the first objective and Gunner Cox got a German Spandau and opened fire on some enemy infantry who appeared over the hill. A tremendous relief to see at last over the hill and to get some shooting on a wide range of targets. Tom Greenshields and John Fletcher, the troop commanders, were both carrying out some very effective shoots. John was in a Churchill tank with the leading company. Having finished my task of firing a smoke screen to blind Maltot and Mary-sur-Orne, I was returning down the hill when a German counter-attack led by three Tigers came over the crest. An 88mm shell from one of these hit my halftrack and I was wounded in the left arm and the truck was badly knocked about. Bombadier Bird my driver-Ack put a tourniquet on my arm and drove us to safety.

John Duke lost his fore-arm but rejoined the regiment later in Germany.

The FOOs constantly ranged the battlefield looking for targets. Capt. R.A. Lowe took temporary command of 'D' Company Wiltshires. A small triangular field lined with tall double hedgerows, south of the battalion objective of the road fork was known as 'Lowe's Triangle'. Counter-attacks came in and two tanks were knocked out by a 6-pounder A/Tank gun or PIATs. It was a long hard day for the Wiltshires, shelled and mortared all day, a bitter day's fighting. Two officers and nineteen ORs were KIA, and another six officers and sixty-nine ORs wounded; ninety-six casualties during the day. 'But the battalion had gone through the SS entrenched in the standing corn like a combine harvester,' wrote Maj. Parsons. Maj. Anthony Jeans, CO of 'C' Company, remembers:

We reached our objective with comparatively few casualties. Our position was the line of a partly sunken track running from the western cover of the trees surrounding the Chateau Fontaine area and running parallel with the Caen/Maltot/Evrecy road. 'B' Coy was to our immediate front, 'D' a little further forward and 'A' to our left area. Roger Prideaux' batman Pte. Truckle marched a prisoner back to rear Bn HQ. Truckle gave the order 'March', whereupon the Boche started off at the double. The more Truckle shouted 'March' the faster the Boche went till the last we saw of them was the Boche 50 yds ahead going well, and poor old Truckle panting along in full equipment shouting 'Walk you bugger, walk!' Another very big red-haired Boche who was severely wounded asked for help and water. Sgt. Smith of 13 Platoon went to tend him only to have an egg grenade thrown at him. Fortunately the swine was too weak to throw it properly. It fell only a few feet from him, doing Sgt. Smith no harm, but wounding the Boche again.

At the end of the attack I was personally engaged in getting myself underground (digging in) when I felt a bump and burning pain in my tail-end. I thought that CSM Webb who was digging his trench just behind had found the sight of my tail sticking up too much of a temptation for him, and had given me a wallop with his entrenching tool handle! Actually a sniper had found the temptation too much for him, and had popped one into my seat. It was not serious but a source of amusement to others!

After dark Anthony encountered two Tiger tanks in the middle of the Company position not 20 yds from his truck. No PIATs could be found, Anthony lost his two 77 grenades and felt a Sten was not adequate: 'They cruised off towards the Somersets where they were both brewed up by their 6 pdrs.' The Wiltshires had a firm rule that slit trenches must be at least five yards apart: 'This I am sure saved us many casualties.'

Brig. Essame summed up:

On the left flank of 129 Brigade 'D' Coy 4 Wiltshire had fought their way through the corn as far as the wood and gained their final objective but, a further 300 yds into the main enemy position, became involved in a desperate battle with Spandaus sited in enfilade. Casualties mounted, Maj.

Coleman was wounded, Capt. R.A. Lowe took over and 224th Field Battery (Maj. J. Duke, Capts Greenshield and Fletcher) brought DF to prevent a counter-attack. The Worcesters arrived at 0200 hrs and the Wiltshires went back into reserve for a spell.

14

THE 5TH DORSETS

'Our First Full-scale Battle'

During the night of 9/10 July the battalion moved by route march to an assembly area at Mouen where breakfast was eaten. At 0345 hrs they set off again – 2 miles east – to Fontaine Etoupefour where they met up with a squadron of 9th Royal Tanks. At 0455 hrs the Corps artillery unleashed their barrage and smoke screen on the left flank. The Brigade plan was for 5th Dorsets to seize the high ground around the Chateau de Fontaine. When the Chateau was secure, the 4th Dorsets were to pass through and capture Etterville, a small village on the left, a mile away due east. Finally 7th Hampshire with two companies of 5th Dorsets would take Maltot and a small triangular orchard a little to the east of the village. The advance started at 0500 hrs. Les Dauns on the right was quickly taken by 'C' Company (Maj. Newton) and on the left 'D' Company (Maj. Roe) and after some fighting 'Horseshoe' road was taken. Soon however both forward companies were in difficulties. 'C' Company was in trouble in the area of the Chateau, and 'D' reported a platoon missing. Maj. John Roe was wounded and the company was suffering heavy casualties, so Lt.-Col. B.A. Coad went forward to see for himself. But by 0615 hrs the remains of Chateau de Fontaine and the farm nearby had been captured. Maurice Edwards, their adjutant, wrote:

> The start line was some low ground in the village of Fontaine Etoupefour. A dry bright sunny morning with the Corps and Div. artillery making the most tremendous row. As Adjutant I was with Bn HQ and we moved off after the two leading companies. As soon as John Roe ('D' Coy) reported Horseshoe Wood clear, I was to establish Bn HQ in the wood. I can remember walking quite slowly through a field of corn – barley or wheat – with the amazing noise of shells passing overhead – smoke, mortars, tank guns, and every other gun within 5 miles seemed to be directed just ahead of the leading companies. We soon found

our first casualties, many dead lying in the corn. Remember this was our first full-scale battle which we had all trained for, for nearly five years, so we all knew each other pretty well. It was quite a shock to find bodies so soon after the start line. A White scout car with a 22 set linked to Brigade followed me and some signallers as part of the I section. RSM Horton accompanied me carrying a Bren gun. We were soon at Horseshoe Wood and started to dig in and generally set up HQ. Soon after there was the most tremendous stonk of shell or mortar fire which burst in the trees above us so we quickly left the wood and re-established Bn HQ just clear of the trees. [Maurice Edwards also described his CO.] 'Aubrey Coad was a really first class fighting CO who came to us from commanding the 43rd Div Battle School. He refused to set up an attack until he personally had at least one look at the ground. His O Groups were a model of clarity and everybody knew exactly what should happen.

At 0800 hrs 'A' Company (Maj. G. Tilley) and 'B' Company (Maj. P.S. Godrich) moved forward in the second phase of the attack with the 7th Hampshires. 'B' soon reached their objective of the triangular orchard but no news was heard of 'A' Company, who were in fact firmly established east of Triangle orchard. The supporting tanks were suffering casualties from 88-mm guns away to the right, so 'C' Company were ordered to put in an attack on a small wood. The three Tiger tanks hidden there caused severe casualties so 'C' Company were withdrawn. 'B' Company were counter-attacked by tanks before they had dug in, Maj. Godrich was semi-blinded and was evacuated. Capt. 'Crasher' White, wearing a soft cap and brandishing a bamboo cane, led two sections of the anti-tank platoon to support the forward companies and was not seen again. Brig. Leslie ordered the battalion to be withdrawn to the reverse slope in front of the Chateau. During that bloody day the 4th Dorsets suffered 208 casualties – 2 officers and 41 ORs KIA, 9 officers and 113 ORs wounded and 43 ORs missing. They were up against the 10th Panzer Division, many of whom had been killed, with eighty prisoners taken together with important maps and documents. Pte. Exley, a signaller with 'A' Company, under heavy fire pulled two crew out of a burning tank and brought them back to safety. He and Cpl. Murray, also of 'C' Company, were awarded MMs. Maj. Newton and Lt. Wetherbee of 'C' Company won MCs.

Maurice Edwards wrote:

In the first attack early in the morning it seems that the enemy let the leading platoon of 'D' Coy under Lt. J. Hayes go past and then opened up with their MG – he and almost all his platoon were killed. Of the second attack, Maltot on our left was to have been taken by 7 Hants but the attack failed so 4 Dorsets were ordered to attack. They had a very bad time. Our carriers were sent to assist 4 Dorset. I'm afraid Capt. White and his carrier crew were all killed or wounded. Our flank was exposed owing to the failure to take Maltot and Hill 112 was still in enemy hands. I know we felt somewhat exposed. Enemy armour together with infantry tried to dislodge us but as always our supporting gunner 112 Field Regt gave us magnificent support and we stayed put.

220th Field Battery, commanded by Maj. R. Tomlinson, were always ready by day or by night to return with interest any shells which landed in the area.

The Chateau had been the HQ of the 2nd Battalion 22nd Frundsberg Panzer Grenadier Regiment. Although at 1815 hrs the 5th Dorsets signalled that the Chateau de Fontaine was in their hands, the Waffen SS soldiers went on fighting to the end. Days later individual snipers, superbly well hidden, were taking their toll and needed to be flushed out.

For the next eight days the battalion maintained its position at the Chateau, which came to be known as the Fortress. In the face of intense mortaring and shelling, Maurice Edwards recalls: 'One day Gen. Ivo Thomas the Div. Cdr. raised a cloud of dust in his armoured car on one visit (to the Chateau) and was soundly cursed by the troops. He returned on foot to apologise! Each cloud of dust immediately produced a heavy stonk. Those eight days were some of the longest I can remember.'

15

THE 4TH DORSETS

'Trapped Rabbits at Harvest Time'

Brig. N.D. Leslie, CO 130th Brigade, launched the 4th Dorsets from the outskirts of Fontaine Etoupefour against Etterville. Maj. G.L. Symonds, commanding 'B' Company, wrote:

> Etterville was a small village in the high undulating land south of Caen between the rivers Odon and Orne surrounded by trees and cornfields. At 0620 hrs Col. Cowie gave the long awaited signal to go by having L/Cpl. Butt sound the charge on his bugle. The battalion rose to its feet as one man, many cheered. It was a wonderful experience.
>
> I was the leading platoon commander in 'B' Coy (noted Capt. R.F. Hall). We advanced with our Maori Totem pole shouting the Maori war cry. The totem was a 6-ft holly stick with a brass jug that we had pinched from a local pub in Dorset and the whole platoon had scratched their names on it. On top of the holly pole was the skull of a cow! The war cry, a modified 'Waka', was 'Tee na ta toga ta cora cora commity commity yaaaaa.'

Hall and Joe Symonds had been on an exercise on Salisbury Plain with a Maori Battalion and drank in a local pub with their officers! *Ça explique.*

Joe Symonds: 'We were very close to the barrage, still in excellent formation. About four fighters (Typhoons) came over, presumably a little late, dropped two bombs in the middle of my company, a number of casualties including Sgt. Fowler were killed. Three of our No. 88 sets were put out of action . . . mopping up was done by 'C' & 'D' companies. The enemy began to shell and mortar us very heavily.' Brig. Essame wrote: 'The troops went forward with great dash with a squadron of tanks (and flame-throwing Churchills) on the left flank, and entered the long straggling village of Etterville. Casualties at first were light.

About seventy prisoners were taken and the battalion started to consolidate.' R.F. Hall again :

> As soon as we were dug in on the northern outskirts of the village, we stuck our Platoon Totem in the ground. Many Tiger tanks were swanning around and one silly one blew our Totem to pieces with a shell. Immediately my anti-tank chap stood up and knocked out the tank with his weapon (PIAT) which was not supposed to do any damage to a Tiger tank. We made short work of the tank and its crew. We had many casualties.
>
> I could see 'A' Coy under Maj. Upton on my right with his Crocodile flame-throwing tanks in action, looking irresistible (recalled Joe Symonds, who while digging his slit trench was wounded by a shell at 0745 hrs). Maj. Gay, OC 'D' Company, was also wounded and Capt. Baker, OC A/Tank platoon, had one leg smashed but drove his carrier back to RAP with wounded aboard. The RMO, Capt. Thompson, was awarded a MC for courage in looking after the many wounded under heavy shellfire. The only approach for vehicles was by a sunken lane which became blocked by the carriers, many soon in flames. The RAP overflowed with casualties, could not be evacuated as no ambulance could reach the village.

Sgt. Wally Caines on his motorbike was scooting round the countryside checking up on the battalion signals – wireless and telephone line cable:

> German POWs rolled in. They looked exhausted and terrified. One German crawled out of his foxhole, seen walking to his captors with his hands up and shot dead through the back by one of his own comrades. Just before HQ reached Etterville, a hell of a barrage came down upon us, several were wounded. We were split up having to take cover. We then became somewhat disorganised. After some terrible minutes dodging shells and mortars, the odd few of us decided to remain until the barrage eased up and then move on. Shells were still raining down like hailstones. The battalion's casualties were pouring into the village church besides many Germans lying around wounded. Everyone was told to dig in for their dear lives' sakes. The MO and his stretcher-bearers were working like niggers to dress the wounded. Our very brave Padre volunteered to find a German MO to attend their wounded.

An hour later to our astonishment he returned with an enemy MO (Doktor Moeferdt) and both worked alongside dressing the wounded. Wireless communication was excellent, all rifle companies were through by wireless. (Smoking endless cigarettes, taking swigs from his waterbottle, Wally dug non-stop for two hours.) Two Bren gun carriers loaded with 3-in mortar bombs received a direct hit, burst into flames, did that lot go up with a bang. The company runner said to me 'I must stay with you, Sergeant, you have plenty of courage.' Yes, perhaps I have, I thought, but little did he know how really scared I was.

Orderly Room Sgt. C.G. Cleal, with Battalion HQ, remembers:

lying in the dew-drenched grass waiting for 'first light' and the order to 'GO'. Countless thoughts – a lot about home – went through my mind. (Later) We DID reach Etterville. As we passed beside the church we were greeted with a barrage of shells. The thick walls surrounding the church seemed to bounce outwards and then fall back into place. Dug-in Tiger tanks continued to pump shells into the church (the Regimental Aid Post) killing several of the wounded as they lay on their stretchers. The CO (Cowie) was only about 20 yds away directing operations over the R/T from his carrier.

Cpl. Chris Portway had a skirmish with two Grenadiers in a churchyard and threw a grenade at them in the church itself. He noticed that the chateau round which his section dug in was painted with huge red crosses and was pleased 'because the Germans don't usually shell hospitals'. His CO appeared to him to have lost control, as he met him among the ruins and asked pathetically: 'What's happening, Corporal?'

Brig. Leslie's original plan was for 9th Cameronians of 46th Brigade (15th Scottish) to take over Etterville some time after 0800 hrs, but because of the intense shelling and fighting going on in the village, the handing over took place about midday. By early afternoon the highly critical situation of 7th Royal Hampshires in Maltot was belatedly recognised (see Chapter Sixteen). Maj. H. Whittle, OC 'B' Company, wrote:

7th Hants had tried and failed to take Maltot. At 1600 hrs the attack began with our squadron of Churchill tanks in support but owing to the position of 7th Hants, no artillery support initially. The ground was flattish, fields with high standing corn. Approaching the village we came under very heavy MG and A/Tank fire. The enemy had a large number of tanks and SP guns dug in in concealed positions in the orchards and woods surrounding the village. We suffered heavy casualties, many of our tanks knocked out. All our A/Tank platoon group were destroyed before they had a chance to go into action. Rifle companies and carrier platoon reached objectives by 1645 hrs. Next two or three hours very unpleasant. We had failed to knock out the majority of the dug-in tanks. The few Churchills remaining with us were withdrawn, the fighting going on all the time. Bn HQ lost contact with the rifle coys. At 2030 hrs a small party including the CO, Bn HQ, parts of 'B', 'C' and 'D' Coys and Carrier platoon dug in on the northern outskirts of Maltot. We were under heavy direct fire from several dug-in tanks. But extremely accurate artillery support put down by 112 Field Regiment helped us. The CO reluctantly gave order to withdraw through the 7th Somersets who took up position in area of Horseshoe Wood. The attack on Maltot accounted for the whole of 'A' Coy of whom not one member returned and for two-thirds of the other three companies. Maj. Upton, Maj. Connor and Maj. Dawson commanding 'A', 'C' and 'D' Coys respectively, were all missing. A large number of the missing were taken prisoner during the night. Battalion strength that night was five officers including the CO and less than eighty ORs, excluding LOBs and echelons. Later we were reinforced by a large contingent from the Essex Regiment including some officers who went 'en bloc' to form a completely new 'A' Coy. Capts Roper and Letson were promoted to Major and took over 'C' and 'D' Coys. I took over 'S' Coy.

Sgt. C.G. Cleal: 'During the advance to Maltot we were pinned down in standing corn, some of which was burning. We were like trapped rabbits at harvest time. Every time we made the slightest movement we were greeted with a burst of machine-gun fire. It was frightening to hear the bullets hitting the corn above my head.'

We formed up again to go into Maltot to assist the 7th Hampshires (wrote Bill Avery, 4th Dorsets). The CO went forward on foot, then with Fred Harris we went forward through the cornfields with the Adjutant's radio truck. The corn being waist high and being covered by German machine gun crossfire, the lads were keeping their heads down. Later when the order came to withdraw we were told to leave the bikes, so as not to draw any more fire. When we reached Rear HQ we were met by the QM Capt. Titterington with hot drinks, etc.

One way or another Bill managed to write off a large number of motor-bikes!

Brig. Essame wrote:

Lt.-Col. H.E. Cowie, the CO, arrived at the HQ of 7 Royal Hampshire on the outskirts of the village just behind his leading companies. Here he found that Lt.-Col. D.W.G. Ray had been wounded and was being evacuated. Too late Lt.-Col. Cowie learnt that what remained of the 7 Royal Hampshire was now being withdrawn. Meanwhile his two leading companies, expecting to take over from the Hampshires, advanced straight into the enemy position and were surrounded. The troop of (233 A/Tank Battery) guns was quickly knocked out. Enemy tanks worked round to the rear of the remainder of the battalion which lay out in the fields exposed to fire from every direction. The position had become desperate. . . . In Maltot the battle had now reached a climax. The position was hopeless. Lt.-Col. Cowie was therefore given permission to withdraw what remained of his battalion. Five company commanders having been lost, there was some disorganisation. As the day declined the survivors collected in the area of 5 Dorset and 7 Somerset around Chateau de Fontaine.

Sgt. Wally Caines recalls: 'Neither us nor the Hampshires stood an earthly chance of securing the village. It was I'm afraid a great disaster.'

Capt. R.F. Hall, having lost his Maori Totem pole, wrote:

We were completely surrounded by Tiger tanks. We got out by either ignoring their tanks or dodging under their fire. We found a heavy angle iron, immobilised one tank by stuffing it in its tracks. To cover our withdrawal a barrage much heavier than El Alamein. The whole Divisional artillery plus two AGRAs! Peter Steele Perkins our Battery Commander, gave the order: 'Gunfire until I tell you to stop.' The CRA eventually stopped it because the guns were getting too hot and were running out of ammunition.

Sgt. Jim Stephen, 'E' Troop 129th Battery 86th A/Tank Regiment (5th Devonshires):

We pulled out of line having suffered 60 per cent casualties, two of our M 10s have been destroyed, the other two sustaining minor damage in the attack on Etterville and Maltot (10 July) in support of 4 Dorset's E. Tp. Co. Lt. Wimpey had been taken to an Advanced Dressing Station for treatment of shrapnel wounds to his neck and arm leaving me in command of what was left of the troop as Troop Sergeant.

4th Dorsets had forty-eight members of the battalion killed in action on 10 July and nearly 300 wounded or taken prisoner. C.G. Cleal recalls: 'I was a member of a burial party involving eleven members of the battalion. My task was to remove identification, pay books and personal belongings. This was a harrowing task. I stuffed the belongings in my pockets and haversack. The sickly smell of death accompanied me for days afterwards. It was all the more wretched when snatching a hasty meal of stew.'

16

THE 7TH ROYAL HAMPSHIRES

'A Cat and Mouse Game in Maltot'

Brig. Essame wrote:

The time had now come for 7 Royal Hampshires to capture Maltot. This battalion supported by one company of 5 Dorset and one squadron of 44 Royal Tank Regiment now advanced in the gap between Etterville and Chateau de Fontaine. It was 8.15 a.m. (three hours after the attacks by 5 Dorset and 4 Wiltshire); with the barrage moving ahead they reached the crest and, passing over, moved down towards the orchards and houses of Maltot in the hollow. At this stage there seems to have been some loss of direction and control. The barrage moved on leaving the infantry exposed. Intense fire from mortars and 88s came down on the advancing companies. However the battalion entered the village and reported that it was in their hands. In actual fact, they had merely superimposed themselves on top of a very strong enemy defended locality. Many Tiger tanks lay concealed in the orchards and dug in on the outskirts.

Maj. Gordon Viner, CO of 'A' Company, recalls:

Although we were eager to be tested and our morale high, the battle proved to be violent and difficult to achieve, ending with heavy losses and failure to succeed. From the moment we crossed the start line and advanced down an open forward slope with artillery and armoured support, it was clear to me that to capture and hold the village was going to be a tough task. I was relieved to capture the first hedgerow and get a foothold in the village but to advance further proved negative as the village was heavily defended by numerous Tiger tanks and well-trained SS (Hitler Youth Panzer) troops, both well concealed and dug in. I can remember coming face to face with one tank which fired over our heads from a well-defended hilltop. The 7th Battalion held on to its initial positions and fought back against continual counter-attacks for about three to four hours but any further advance was impossible. During an attempted reinforcement by 4th Dorsets, the 7th Battalion was subjected to an intense artillery barrage for about half an hour – FIRE FROM THE FRONT OF US AND FIRE FROM THE REAR OF US – but we stood firm. Eventually the Dorset attack failed and both battalions, now in a hopeless situation, were ordered to withdraw. I personally lost a great many gallant comrades including my batman Pte. Hayes (killed) and my second-in-command Capt. Harry Collier (wounded). In spite of our losses the 7th Battalion's morale remained high.

Lt.-Col. D.E.B. Talbot, who subsequently commanded the Hampshires, wrote a campaign journal:

Maltot, marched off 0330 hrs – Mouen 0500 hrs – startline 0800 hrs. 'A' & 'B' Coys reached their parts of Maltot with little opposition. 'C' met heavy opposition from dug-in tanks, reached road in Maltot. The MO Lt. Waddell killed attending to Adjutant's wounds and the Bn Signal Officer Lt. Manley was missing. 0915 hrs Maltot village reached, hand to hand fighting in the village, three Tiger tanks entered village from south-west. The Bn 6-pdr A/Tank guns in position unable to fire under heavy MG fire. 0955 hrs gained ground 400 yds south of Maltot, attempted to dig in, and hold the village. Tiger tanks and infantry were counter-attacking from the south-east and south-west. Our own supporting tanks stood off just north of the village under fire from 88-mm guns. 1015 hrs CO Lt.-Col. D.W.G. Ray was twice wounded, evacuated to RAP. Maj. R.J. McPhillips, 'C' Coy CO assumed command. The FOO was to bring down fire on enemy concentrations in both directions – impossible due to other RA commitment. (In fact 112 Field Regiment also suffered heavily and had two FOOs killed at Maltot, and the Battery Commander, Maj. J.H. Penrose, wounded. The confusion may have been due to both Hampshires and the relieving Dorsets being in and around Maltot at the same time so targets were difficult to pinpoint.) 'B' Coy was broken having gone forward 800 yds south-east of Maltot. At 1035 hrs the CO was back with his wounds dressed and ordered new defensive positions to be taken up NW of village but amidst heavy mortaring and shelling. Maj. Penrose, the FOO, constantly ordering (but not receiving) RA fire. The situation was acute with serious shortage of ammunition. The CO was now seriously wounded. Casualties were eventually taken back to CCP at Verson and at 1530 hrs withdrawal to area just west of Verson where the remnants of 'B' and 'C' Coys were combined under Capt. Braithwaite. Each company strength was down to seventy to eighty.

In the early afternoon Brig. Leslie ordered 4th Dorsets to reinforce but they made no impression on very strong SS troops. During the battle twelve supporting tanks were knocked out and only two of the battalions 6-pounder A/Tank guns survived.

My company – 'D' – formed up for the attack on the reverse slope in front of Chateau de Fontaine waiting for the OFF (recalls CSM Laurie Symes). I was in the company Bren gun carrier which was loaded with the company's reserve ammo. Neither myself or my driver gave a thought at the time what would have happened to that lot, if we had been hit by an 88. The whole company had their tails up for this attack and were eager to go. I looked up the slope to see Maj. Eastwood, our company CO up front with his walking stick and whistle. When the time came, off we went through the standing corn. (Later) I went forward into Maltot on foot to find my company. That journey was a bit hairy, brewed up tanks and dead and wounded everywhere. I found some of the lads, the platoons were mixed together by this time. We realised we were in trouble from German tanks in dug-in positions, so eventually we were given orders to withdraw. A lot of brave men came out of Maltot that day and a lot were left behind.

Sgt. Jim Stephens of 59th A/Tank Regiment recalled in his diary how three of their SP M 10s with 17-pounders supporting the Hampshires and the Churchill infantry tanks were soon put out of action. Sgt. Jimmy Burnell's SP gun was hit a few yards beyond Etterville by a mortar bomb which landed in its open turret – killing Dick Greenwood, eighteen-year-old Phillips and the cockney Jim Burnell. The troop commander's gun was hit by an 88-mm shell near Maltot and a third SP gun's turret was jammed by fire. The two surviving guns withdrew. Of twenty men in the troop six were dead, four wounded and one a POW.

Nineteen-year-old Pte. D. Davies of 'B' Company wrote:

Our briefing was that the village of Maltot was lightly defended, thus there would be no need for artillery or aircraft support but there would be some tanks with us. We were roused at 3 a.m. – hours before necessary as usual for an 8 a.m. attack. At 6 a.m. we moved up to the start line – the edge of a large open countryside, rolling plain covered with wheat about hip-high. Two Churchill tanks were waiting for us and after a long wait we set off up the long gradual slope – two companies up and two behind. It was a bright clear morning and the tanks running at either side were beating flocks of small birds into the air ahead of us. Caen could be seen a few miles away on the left (east) of us, visible as a thick pall of smoke. On our right the other company advanced in line with us, but I could not see any tanks with them or with the Dorsets further over. One tank was hit by an 88 shell almost immediately and instantly burst into flames. The crew did not bail out. The other tank took out the 88 with two well-placed shots. Our pleasure was short-lived as we walked into a very heavy barrage of Moaning Minnies, the effective multi-barrelled mortars. 'B' Coy was particularly hit by the mortar fire and only seven men were left active of 15 Platoon. Lt. Friend was injured. I was the only man left in my section. Maj. J.J. Tomkins came up to steady us and with other Company HQ men formed a new, depleted platoon. The other platoons had also experienced casualties. As we continued the advance we came under machine gun and rifle fire from well-placed and camouflaged slit trenches. The Germans would keep hammering us until we got close then would scamper back on hands and knees through the wheat. We caught a number of them and disposed of a few by lobbing grenades down the trenches. We were maddened by the slaughter caused by the Moaning Minnies and were for a brief moment out of control. Again Maj. Tomkins steadied us down and we continued the advance over the ridge of ground to the north of Maltot. We looked down at grey stone houses on either side of the road about a mile away with a church prominent over to our right – towards the west end of the village. We came under more heavy machine gun and rifle fire as we moved down the slope and suffered more casualties. Our tank was peppering the defensive positions dug in the rear gardens of the houses and took a pot shot at another dug-in 88. As we got closer the

Germans left their positions and ran back to the houses with us firing like mad at everything that moved. At this point Maj. Tomkins spoke over the phone to the tank commander: 'I'm rushing the village now. Make your way to the other side. See you there.' He then yelled for us to charge – us for the village itself with him, and the other platoon under Sgt. Lane – for the wood to the left (east). We chased the remaining enemy troops out of the gardens killing a few on the way and rushed through the alleys to the road and on to the other side. The village looked deserted and the houses undamaged, ground floor windows were boarded up but glass was intact in some of the higher windows. The church also was undamaged. On the south side of the village in the rear gardens we were met by a Mark IV tank which blasted us with heavy MG and explosive shells. Maj. Tomkins yelled for us to charge the woods about 50 yds away to our half left. For about an hour – though it could have been much longer – we played a cat and mouse game with the Germans, each side taking pot shots at anything that moved. At some time in the afternoon I was hit by shrapnel from two hand grenades, knocked out for a while. It was evening when the Germans finally rushed us and took five prisoners, three of them wounded. I can remember in my misery staring at all our dead. I spent the next six weeks in a German military hospital then transferred to a prison camp near Halle in Saxony and was there until freed on 13 April 1945 by the 1st US Army. . . . We were not as well armed as the enemy. His tanks were much superior. In the hospital the German soldiers told me they called our tanks 'Tommy Torches'. His light machine gun belt-fed in my view was much more effective than the Bren. The German soldier, good as he was, was not that marvellous – he was better armed in the essentials.

Davies also criticised the intelligence about Maltot: 'lightly defended, no Panzers . . .'.

Lt. Douglas Goddard, CPO, 112th Field Regiment (West Somerset Yeomanry), kept a diary:

7 July, St Mauvieu. Went out to Cheux to collect timber for roofing of gun-pits. A distressing sight, complete shambles. Pathetic to see all personal belongings in wrecked houses, amazing – glass and china intact. 8 July. Fired large and lengthy

fireplan during the night. Airburst HE shells enemy's most unpleasant weapon. Wonderful sight to see rocket firing Typhoons in action. Built myself (Command Post) a grand little house of corrugated iron and earth down here in this 10-ft pit. Quite secure. Amazing how 40 per cent of Jerry shells are dud. 10 July. Barrage went forward, first part of attack successful. 4th and 5th Dorsets took objectives. 7th Hants went on to capture Maltot. Heavy enemy counter-attacks with tanks held until about 1600 hrs. We fired like mad in support – directed by Maj. Penrose from village. He was wounded. We had to withdraw. Infantry suffered heavily in Maltot. Our casualties – Blinco and Robinson killed. Capt. Atkins wounded and prisoner. Bollo shellshocked and evacuated. I was due to act as OP officer in the tank in which Capt. Robinson was killed. He had joined us as reinforcement the day before. Such is the irony of war.

On that awful bloody day, the Hampshires had 226 casualties: four officers and twelve ORs killed, a further nine officers and fifty-one ORs wounded, and another five officers and 145 ORs missing – either POW or KIA. Lt.-Col. Ray was wounded for a third time and died later of his wounds. They had run head on against the armoured battalion of the 21st SS Panzer Grenadier Regiment and the 10th SS Reconnaissance Regiment, backed by Tiger tanks from the 102nd SS Heavy Battalion and mortars of 8th Werfer Brigade.

17

THE 7TH SOMERSETS

'A Colony of Rabbits'

Brig. Essame explained:

For the battle on the left flank 130 Brigade under Brig. N.D. Leslie had been given an additional battalion – 7 Somerset Light Infantry on loan from 214 Brigade. During the morning this battalion had forced its way through the congested bottleneck of Fontaine Etoupefour and dug in beside 5 Dorset at Chateau de Fontaine. Here Lt.-Col. B.A. Coad had quickly grasped the seriousness of the situation in Maltot and organised the defence of the reverse slope.

The RMO, Capt. Marshall, wrote in the regimental history produced by Capt. John Meredith:

The period 10–13 July was the worst period of the campaign for the RAP. We left Verson on the morning of 10 July in our usual position at the back of the Bn column. The whole of 'S' Company's transport had to come in ahead of us and we were held up just before crossing the bridge over the Odon. At that point a salvo of shells dropped, aimed at the bridge. When we arrived we found one DR on the road – killed outright – so we laid him in a barn just off the road. Now our attention was drawn to the river itself where we found two RE officers thrown into the river each with a badly broken leg. We got them out, getting rather wet in the process (it reminded me of battle courses) and we sent them away in my ambulance. Then we found another ambulance just by the bridge badly damaged, splintered, without its driver. One of the casualties inside had been very badly hit; the others shaken but not more than that. My ambulance had gone so I sent a DR back for another and we heard later they had got these casualties safely away. Meanwhile I moved on with the RAP slowly. At the top of the next hill we had an uncomfortable few minutes in ditches and slit trenches

while three or four Messerschmitts wandered around but did
not attack us.

Pte. D. O'Connell was a carrier driver in 'S' Company:

We dug in around Bn HQ who were in a building called Chateau
de Fontaine. We faced from the Germans on Hill 112 the heavy
shelling from every calibre of gun reminiscent of the 1914–18
War and barrages. Every blade of grass seemed to be targeted
by German shells and bullets, attacks by their infantry came by
day and night. Noise was earsplitting and those that didn't seek
a slit trench were either dead or wounded. Our artillery
answered back nobly and it was the boast of our 3-in mortars
that they gave as good as we got with a few more bombs
chucked in for good measure. Our lot was fraught with fear,
danger and death every time we moved from our slit trench.
Move we had to, there were wounded to be picked up and
taken to the RAP. The Red Cross flag was still targeted by MGs
firing from the slope. The author Edgar Allan Poe couldn't have
described that hell on those slopes.

Capt. Marshall continues his story:

We had reached the farm buildings around Chateau de
Fontaine, dug in positions in the meadows. Mortar and shell fire
was devastating. Col. Lance (who had won a DSO in Africa) was
killed by a shell from an 88mm while sitting in his jeep, the
Gunner BC Maj. Mapp was killed, the Adjutant Capt. A. Scannell
wounded and evacuated. A steady stream of wounded was
arriving at the RAP. Maj. Young and Maj. Chalmers shared
command of the Bn with that of their own coys. Snipers were at
their worst. Shortly after Col. Lance was killed, Maj. Young's
Coy was clearing some farm buildings. A shot whistled
unpleasantly close. Maj. Y. turned to Pte. Lace (Bn sniper) with
'That's the fifth shot that basket has fired at me, we must get
him.' They found him hidden in a junk-heap in the middle of a
duck pond! They found another not more than seventeen years
old, who had buried himself in the mud of a wet ditch – only his
head, arms and rifle were free, even these covered with slime
and weeds. Another was burned out from a hayrick set on fire
by a German shell. Several days after the occupation of
Chateau de Fontaine, snipers were still being found. One had

barricaded himself in a room on the first floor of a barn while a platoon of 'D' Coy occupied the ground floor. They got him with a Bren gun burst fired through the closed door when he refused to come out. The enemy trenches in the area were full of German dead, passed over by the leading troops, and the usual scene of mutilated farm animals all around. Air was rancid with the smell of dead animals and flies.

Maj. Young recalled: 'We sit like a colony of rabbits around our trenches not daring to venture far away in the evening sunshine.' Lt. John Howarth, OC carrier platoon, changed trenches with his batman to be nearer the telephone and was killed by a direct hit on his 'new' trench. As Pte. O'Connell put it:

Our officers were dwindling through death and wounding and it was rumoured that we only had one or two officers left in the ('S') Company. Our own officer had been killed and it was left to our sergeants to look after us. The toll of dead from the German shelling and attacks had risen considerably and our graveyard increased in the same measure. We had lost all our top officers and it was a case of stick it, and stick it, until someone made a breakthrough or retreated. Our cemetery or graveyard was shelled by the Germans out of hatred or their morale breaking. . . . We did take only a few SS prisoners, that explains what a terrific defence that they had put up. It wasn't only in defence that these merchants excelled. They attacked and knew how to attack and die when they faced our guns, tanks and defenders. They seemed to have the best equipment as well.

The German tanks were lined up to our front and took periodic shots at our 17-pounder unmanned gun which two German planes had just attacked, knocking all the crew out (recalls Pte. Len Stokes, 'B' Company). I had to get out of my trench to see to 'bodily functions'. They probably thought I was a gun crew member and fired a shell which hit a tree branch above me. The blast blew my steel helmet back, the chin strap nearly breaking my neck. I was then ordered to take a verbal message to Bn HQ as radio contact had been lost. (Len had been fired at with a phosphorous shell and eventually arrived at Battalion HQ) in an outer farmhouse – they had just been very heavily shelled with many casualties. The first person dying from chest wounds said 'Don't worry about me, see to the badly wounded.' Capt. Goldy found me, said he had assumed command of the Bn. Our CO had been killed, also the CO and 2 i/c of the Regiment relieving us. I was glad to get out of that terrible shambles.

Brig. Essame wrote in his history:

From Etterville to Chateau de Fontaine the infantry and 17 pdrs of 59 Anti-Tank Regiment stood firm. Thanks to the courage and initiative of Lt.-Col. B.A. Coad, Maj. Newton and Lt. Wetherbee of 5 Dorset (who had joined 7 Somerset around the Chateau), what was rapidly developing into a very ugly situation remained under control. Four of five Tigers were knocked out. The Divisional artillery put down a storm of defensive fire and the counter-attack when it came was beaten off with heavy enemy loss.

18

THE 1ST WORCESTERS

'A Hole To Go To?'

Later in the afternoon of that fatal 10 July, Brig. Essame moved 1st Worcesters through Miebord into the cornfields south-west of the Chateau de Fontaine, where they dug in, linking up with 4th Wiltshires on their right. The positions were on the left shoulder a few hundred yards short of the crest of Hill 112.

Then began a war of attrition when we made no further progress, when for a fortnight we made no added impression upon a determined enemy for we were subjected to a most devastating bombardment day and night from shells and mortars (remembers Cpl. William Gould). We had many direct hits on slit trenches and my own slit was torn round the edges leaving two shocked and deafened inmates. My companion was withdrawn for several days recovering from a bad attack of nerves.

Stan Procter went forward in the brigadier's White scout car (the unarmoured 3-tonner Command Vehicle was full of mortar fragments) to Fontaine Etoupefour, then into the chateau grounds. He transferred his radio set into a dugout, dodged phosphorous bombs and was adjacent to the Gunner truck that was bombed, killing the BC and his driver. Amidst the concentrated shelling he had letters delivered to him from his girlfriend in England and found in the garden pears, strawberries and currants, 'nice change to our diet'. He once took shelter under a Sherman tank and admired its protective steel belly. On another occasion he was caught in the open by a stonk in the farmyard, and went flat on the ground just as Gen. Thomas drove up in his Ark and shouted at him: 'Haven't you got a hole to go to, Soldier?' And Pte. Albert Kings found life 'on and around Hill 112 very trying. It seemed as though we were never out of action. I remember a chap being evacuated with the shakes. He was unable to stand, trembling uncontrollably. This was a condition I myself was to experience later. I was lucky we had a short spell of LOB and I was able to regain control of myself.' The Worcesters dug in and were mortared for days. Lt. Spicer and their FOO, Capt. Shaw, were both killed, Capt. Radcliffe and Lt. Bennett both wounded. When 'A' Company's locality near the chateau, deemed unsound tactically, was abandoned, it drew thereafter even heavier fire – an argument for dummy positions. Maj. George Taylor, the 2 i/c of the Worcesters was transferred and promoted to lieutenant-colonel as the new CO of the 5th Duke of Cornwall's Light Infantry.

19

CORNWALL HILL

'Hold Your Fire until You See the Buggers' Eyes'

On 4 Somerset and the two other battalions of 129 Brigade (4 and 5 Wiltshires) now fell the full blast of the (enemy) counterstroke at the crisis of the battle in the afternoon (recalled Brig. Essame). They stood firm and as events proved saved the Division from disaster. . . . Without complete possession of Hill 112, the prospects of retaining Maltot in the face of the enemy's bitter resistance were small indeed. Disquieting reports of the rapid deterioration of the situation on this flank (i.e. Maltot) now began to reach Maj.-Gen. Thomas who throughout had moved between the TAC HQ of the two attacking brigades (129 and 130).

Pat Spencer Moore recollects: 'Battle for Maltot, GOC had long session with Brig. Leslie. Brigade staff told me Leslie turned down offer of a liaison officer taking him down on motorcycle to see for himself as to situation. Tracks and lanes heavily congested with Brigade and support vehicles: utter chaos.' By about 1500 hrs it was clear to the GOC that only a completely fresh attack on Hill 112 could stabilise the battle – perhaps even win it – or perhaps incur even more shattering losses? It was a gambler's throw by Thomas. The only problem was that he was gambling with the lives of hundreds of his well-trained but completely green young soldiers. It must have been a terrible decision to take and perhaps earned him the nickname of 'the Butcher'. The only uncommitted battalion were the 5th Cornwalls, now commanded, as they had been for the last two weeks, by twenty-six-year-old Lt.-Col. R.W. James. Maj. Godfrey MC, the historian of the Cornwalls, wrote: 'Maj.-Gen. Thomas decided the hill (112) must be captured at all costs and the FIFTH remained available to do it.' The battalion had been well placed to watch the early stages of Jupiter from their positions around Fontaine Etoupefour where they had been in close contact with the enemy for the last two days and nights.

Lt.-Col. George Taylor was at the crucial meeting held in Chateau de Fontaine by the GOC and his three brigadiers:

> Brig. Essame told Dick James of the decision to put 5 DCLI under command of 129 Bde (from 214 Brigade) to help secure the top of the hill. The attack was to be pushed home as the light faded supported by tanks of 7 RTR. Zero hour was fixed for 2030 hrs. We were to learn, in the grim and bloody days to come, that the time allowed (for planning a battalion attack), two hours, should be at least doubled in times of war, against a strong defensive position. Two assault companies 'C' Coy right (Capt. Blackwell), 'B' Coy left (Maj. Vawdrey), would provide the initial thrust, with 'A' (Maj. Roberts) and 'D' (Maj. Fry) in close support. An extensive fireplan was laid on to soften up the defences.

The objective was the crest of the hill and the wood, a large orchard about 150 yds wide and 250 yds long, beyond it. An advance of about 800 yds would be through the positions held by the 4th Somersets. The tanks were late in arriving and thus supported the rear companies instead of the forward ones. On the right, rapid progress was made but on the left 'B' Company came under heavy machine gun fire and Maj. Vawdrey was killed. Maj. Roberts quickly deployed his 'A' Company and Lt. Doug Ritchie with 9th Platoon silenced the enemy machine guns as 'B' Company continued the advance, sadly depleted in numbers, now down to forty. The enemy retreated from the small orchard on the flank and Lt. Carmolli, a Canloan officer, caught up in the excitement of battle, took his platoon of 'D' Company beyond the objective, down into the valley, and all were killed, wounded or taken prisoner. But Maj. Bob Roberts, 'A' Company CO, wrote later: 'No one who saw it will ever forget their courage and determination.' He and Maj. Fry decided to hold the line of the hedge running roughly halfway through the wood and bring in the survivors of 'B' Company. With the light fading, the Germans retaliated with shell and mortar fire and a counter-attack came in. The companies had little time to dig in and the A/Tank platoon lost a complete crew, and a 17-pounder gun was put out of action.

Said Maj. Bob Roberts: 'We had no difficulty in repulsing the infantry, the fire discipline being first-class and both companies giving the Boche absolute hell. It was grand to hear the section commanders shouting out their orders: "Hold your fire, chaps, until you can see the buggers' eyes." It did fearful execution.' About midnight the Germans came again with armour and infantry, raking the wood with machine gun fire from east to west, while their riflemen tried to infiltrate round the right flank. L/Cpl. Jack Foster, Signal Platoon, who won his MM there, wrote: 'In action at Hill 112, 5 DCLI held their positions in the wood against constant counter-attacks and shelling sustaining very heavy casualties. Our firepower was so reduced by this, that the position would have been over-run were it not for the protective fire of the 25-pounders behind us who inflicted just as many casualties on the enemy.' Maj. Bob Roberts: 'The CO – Col. James – was magnificent. He set an outstanding example to everyone by his personal courage . . . we were still rather green, but for him, I don't know what might have happened.' A German Tiger tank got to within 15 yds of Battalion HQ so Maj. Roberts and Sgt. Hill hit it with a PIAT and the tank retired – hurt. Other tanks manoeuvred all over the battalion area, came over the crest of the ridge and started to move down the northern slope. Col. James climbed a tall tree to direct the artillery fire. During the night a telephone cable had been laid back to Brigade HQ by the signal officer, Lt. Stock, Sgt. Gould, Sgt. Frank Grigg and Pte. Foster. At dawn a squadron of Scots Greys' Sherman tanks came up to drive the enemy out of the southern edge of the orchard. At first light they drove out the Germans and silenced several machine guns, but came under murderous fire from 88-mm guns and mortars, and quickly had five tanks brewed up.

George King commanding 7th Platoon also acted as an OP, and with his colonel corrected the fire of the supporting gunners on targets only 150 yds away, but almost immediately Sgt. Douglas Hill and George King were killed.

Maj. Roberts was arranging the evacuation of the wounded and trying to organise the arrival of a relief company of the 1st Worcesters when the news filtered round the battle-weary men, 'The CO's had it.' Lt.-Col. James had been hit in the neck by a burst of machine gun fire, as he was in a tree directing artillery fire. No fewer then twelve counter-attacks had been delivered and repulsed.

When the colonel was killed alongside me (wrote Signaller Jack Foster) it was my duty as one of his signallers at the time to report to rear HQ, that as far as I could see there were no officers or senior NCOs left unwounded to command the battalion. Never was anyone more welcome then . . . when Maj. John Fry, having handed over command of 'D' Coy, made his way through the wood to the command post to take over the Bn. He rallied the survivors and organised their defensive fire to best effect. It became obvious that very soon there would be nothing left of us, if the remnant of the Bn was not soon withdrawn.

Someone shouted 'Retreat, retreat':

One theory (wrote Col. George Taylor) was that it was a German. The night before, Lt. Greenacre commanding a platoon of 'A' Coy encountered a German soldier who, speaking in good but improbable English, said to him, 'Hello, British tommy, is "A" Company here?' At 1100 hrs men began to drift to the rear and the contagion spread. A considerable number reached the position behind held by the 4th Somersets, where the latter's Lt.-Col. C.G. Lipscomb, with the help of the Cornwall officers, Roberts, Gorman the adjutant, and Willcocks the IO, rallied them.

John Majendie, 4 Somersets:

Lippy was outstanding in many difficult situations and none more so than when the remnants of 5 DCLI after a terrible time in Cornwall Wood on Hill 112, came back into our positions. He rallied them and sensing a crisis drew his pistol and shouted 'I'll shoot the first Somerset who goes back.' And an honest private soldier in my company told me, years later, 'When I saw the DCLI coming I put on my small pack and if they'd gone I was going with them.' The Somersets watched as the groups of unshaven and exhausted Cornwalls trickled back through their positions.

Brig. G.H.C. Mole now placed Col. 'Lippy' in control of the situation on the hill. Majors Roberts and Fry got the remnants of the Cornwalls back to their original positions on the top of Hill 112, reorganised into four rifle companies, each of them about platoon strength. Lt. R.H. Bellamy moved out a 17-pounder A/Tank gun under cover of a smoke screen to fire at enemy tanks working round the left flank. Capt. Gorman was ordered to report personally on the position to Brig. Mole (NO liaison officer was sent from Brigade HQ). Maj. Roberts, who had been wounded, recalled: 'To give some idea of how depleted the Bn had become, just before I was wounded I made a tour of the companies and the effective strength was 126 although many wounded were still lying where they had fallen or been hit in the slit trenches – some were still firing, though very weak for loss of blood and fatigue.' By 1500 hrs the strength was down to about a hundred men. Capt. Gorman, the adjutant, reported to the brigadier that 'the position was untenable and further delay in withdrawing the survivors would lead to the final destruction of 5 DCLI.' One would not have expected the GOC to visit a front line battalion in such desperate straits, but it is surprising that Brig. Mole did not do so. The wood was still being swept by an intense storm of mortar bombs and shells. Enemy SPs in close support of their infantry raked the area with MG fire and solid shot. There were five or six undamaged PIATs but few bombs for them. Maj. John Fry sent a signaller, Jack Foster, back to Brigade HQ with another request that the remnant of the battalion be relieved or at least be allowed to withdraw over the crest of the ridge. As George Taylor wrote: 'There was nothing more the Cornwalls could do. Flesh, blood and nerves have their breaking point and that had nearly been reached. Maj. Fry realised the survivors were on the point of being overwhelmed.' What did Brigade HQ do? They asked (or ordered) Maj. Fry to return to explain the situation. Presumably the brigadier was scared to admit a failure. Presumably the GOC was scared to admit a failure to his Corps Commander and so on. Maj. Fry was literally between the devil and the deep blue sea. He had served with the old 1st Battalion Cornwalls before joining the 5th. He knew the consequences of allowing a battalion to be completely destroyed and the heavy responsibility for a commander who orders the evacuation of a position without orders.

Shortly after 1500 hrs he gave the order to withdraw and in the words of the Cornwalls' historian, Maj. E.G. Godfrey, 'in doing so he saved the 5th Bn from annihilation'. The plan was shouted to each company (of the three companies only about sixty men were left unscathed): 'We will clear out of this when the smoke comes down. Each man for himself. Keep well separated.' Shrouded by smoke the survivors withdrew, and Maj. Fry was the last man to leave that fatal wood. The officers of Battalion HQ – Bill Gorman,

David Willcocks, Max Stock, Lt. Birchenall and Capt. Stokoe, the mortar platoon officer, rallied the dazed and depressed Cornwalls. Brig. Essame wrote: 'It had been a magnificent struggle fought against overwhelming odds', but of course he made no comment or criticism of brigade or divisional 'management'.

Sgt. Reg Romain, 5th Wiltshires, wrote: 'The attack for the woods over the top of the hill went in by the DCLI had eased our position a bit – but we soon learned that they were having a hell of a time trying to take it – in fact, in the end it failed. I remember a lot of their dead and wounded being transported back through our lines on stretcher-bearers.'

In all the 5th Cornwalls suffered 320 casualties in eleven hours of bitter fighting. They only lost one man captured but ninety-three were killed and buried on the hill where the Divisional War Memorial now stands. Their opponents, 21st Lorried Infantry Regiment and 22nd Armoured Regiment of 10th SS Panzer Division, and elements of 9th SS Panzer Division who arrived on the afternoon of the 10th, sustained losses on a comparable scale. Their companies were reduced often to five or six effective men, and they lost eight of their ten tanks.

John Majendie, 4th SLI, wrote:

Throughout that day the DCLI had a terrible time. They were under constant fire from mortars and from the tanks which had come up from St Martin on the reverse slope of the hill. (Later) What was left of the Bn started to return. They came back through my company and I'm not saying this in any derogatory way but they were in a pretty sorry state; but they were spoken to by my CO (Lipscomb) and they reformed and very gallantly went back into Cornwall Wood and Clifford Perks our A/Tank Platoon Commander, went back with them to give advice on their very diminished anti-tank protection. Again later on in the afternoon it was quite impossible for them. They were about down to Company strength – their casualties were increasing all the time and they again retired back into our battalion position and dug in just to the left of my company as a composite company.

Peter Whately-Smith, 94th Field Regiment, wrote:

As darkness fell our troops had a very precarious hold on the hill. The infantry had had a gruelling time all day and there wasn't much let up at night. There were constant calls for DF tasks. At 0215 hrs 468 Bty reported an attack by infantry and tanks. At 0500 hrs 218 Bty reported another. So it went on all through 11 July. 5 DCLI was put under command of 129 Brigade and occupied the orchard on the hill. Here they suffered an enormous amount of killed and wounded and several enemy tanks got through to the rear. As evening drew on things quietened down gradually and at 2135 hrs the CO (Lt.-Col. Bishell) signalled from Brigade HQ 'Situation appears to be that 4 Som. LI and remainder of 5 DCLI (approx 200) are on 120-metre contour with 5 Wilts on their right up to Baron church.' Capt. Peter Wilson had been killed by a mortar bomb and a troop command post dug 6 ft deep in an open field took a direct hit from a 105mm shell and killed eight people.

George Taylor was immediately promoted from 2 i/c 1st Worcesters to command the Cornwalls and wrote in his book *Infantry Colonel*:

The little orchard (wood) spanned an area of just 300 sq. yds of which 5 DCLI held one half. At one time there were 350 Cornwalls in this small space. Surely it would have been better to have tried to hold it with just one rifle company and anti-tank guns, backed up with tanks positioned on the northern slope. As casualties mounted, reserve platoons could have been fed in during lulls. The Panzer Grenadiers suffered very heavy casualties. We could have perhaps won this battle of attrition but this is hindsight.

The remnants of the Cornwalls withdrew to positions behind the 4th Somersets and two days later were relieved by 4th Dorsets.

20

'THAT'S ONE FROM US'

The Support Arms

To the 179th Field Regiment, once the 12th Worcesters, fell the sad honour of losing three commanding officers during their campaign. Lt.-Col. G.L. Pethick was wounded on 27 June on a reconnaissance. Lt.-Col. W.D. Blacker replaced him on 3 July and was killed by mortar fire on 11 July. The 2 i/c, Maj. Sir J.E. Backhouse and Capt. G.C. Robinson were both wounded, and Maj. R.G. Mapp, another battery commander, was killed. On 10 July the guns of 179th Field Regiment never stopped firing and in one recorded fifteen minute period fired 1,800 rounds (seventy-five rounds per gun) in response to SOS calls from the infantry of 214th Brigade. At one stage Sgt. W. Trevis for several hours directed the fire support of the 7th Somersets, for which he later received the DCM. Padre Wilson buried many friends that day. Bombadier S.A. Rooney saw a 3-tonner hit by a shell; the next one alongside was filled with ammunitions, so he got in and drove it away. Later he was awarded the MM. Ken Storey was a gunner/signaller in 217th Battery, 112th Field Regiment RA:

> On 10 July I was the wireless operator in the Battery Command Post. From early morning we had been firing regimental (24 guns) or divisional targets (72 guns) (with our 25-pounder guns). To add to the pressure on the gun crews many of the battery were plagued with a dodgy tummy from the flies and wasps feeding on rotting carcasses near us. The RASC gave a terrific service. During the afternoon their 3-tonners reversed up to each gun pit. The drivers and mates were unloading then breaking out the shells and cartridges. At times there were only three gunners available, the others were dashing to and from the latrines. As a reward the RASC took it in turns in pulling the firing lever. 'That's one from us,' they said.

At about 0100 hrs No. 6 Platoon (8th Middlesex) advanced to a position on the slopes of Hill 112 (wrote Eric Levy). The platoon commander and his batman went forward. He then gave the infantry 'close on me' signal (hand on head) with the exception of Jim Stickley the platoon sergeant, who was to the rear with the ammo, cooks and stores, all the NCOs left their carriers and formed an 'O' group. At the same time a Moaning Minnie opened up and the one you never hear landed in the middle of the group, wounding all the gun-line NCOs and the batman, who got the worst of it in both feet. The platoon commander did not get a scratch but he was now minus two section commanders, four number ones and his batman.

Cpl. Eric Levy and Don Linney were the only two casualties who eventually returned to the platoon. Eric was sent back to base hospital, 'so many wounded that the stretchers were packed like sardines – not an inch of space between. The engineer next to me, aged eighteen, had his foot blown off when he stepped on a mine. The Normandy casualties must have been tremendous, they could not get us back to England quick enough.'

All the front line signallers had a difficult and dangerous job. Telephone lines had to be laid between gun positions and OPs. These were frequently broken by shell fire or tank tracks and laboriously, often under fire, the signallers had to trace the break and repair it. Bombadier Tarrier, 94th Field, said:

We joined 4 Wiltshires just before dusk and Capt. Fletcher told me to get out my schmeisser as we were going on an OP recce. (Later) We crawled back again and at 0200 hrs he told me to lay him a line to be through by first light. When I had completed half the line it was cut in two places by Boche mortar fire. I continued towards Capt. Fletcher in the OP, cut off 20 yds spare from the end, crawled back, mended the breaks. I placed the line in old German trenches with dead, weeks old. The stench was unbelievable. The situation was very bad, radio sets went off the air, their carriers and jeeps having been knocked out. One crew took over the 19 set in a Churchill tank of 44 RTR until that too was 'brewed up'. Maj. Steele Perkins, our CO, although wounded received permission to fire all available artillery. He was later awarded the MC. We could hear the continuous whine of the Nebelwerfers so we knew the counter-attacks were still going in. Later in the evening the survivors of our OPs came straggling in, tired, dazed and dishevelled and we counted our losses.

Another diary was kept by Eric Codling, 8th Middlesex, 18 Platoon with 4.2-in mortars:

9 July. Recce party to orchard in wooded area south of R. Odon. The bodies of enemy soldiers lay where they had fallen, some in the river, a few inches deep, which was where our water supply was drawn from. 1,200 mortar bombs carried and stored for next barrage. After four weeks of hard biscuits, white bread, first for four years, appeared. Firing all day, mortar barrels became hot enough to toast the delicious white bread on. After a while the battering on our eardrums caused us to reel about like drunks such was the deafening noise. Mortar barrels had to be taken down and rolled in the lush grass to cool them because of licks of flame coming from the barrel mouths after a bomb had been fired threatened the next bomb about to be dropped in. . . . One of a group of German POWs sheltering from a bout of shelling picked up a copy of the *Daily Mirror* left lying by a trench. The headlines were about the Beveridge report about a health care scheme for post-war Britain. One German who could read English said Hitler had introduced a similar service ten years before!

21

OPERATION JUPITER

'Utmost Ferocity and Without Mercy'

The traumatic defence of Cornwall Wood lasted until mid-afternoon on 11 July, but immense German pressure and constant attacks by infantry and tanks continued throughout the night of the 10th and during Day Two of Operation Jupiter. During the darkness the enemy penetrated Etterville, then held by the Cameronians of 46th Brigade (15th Scottish Division) under command. Hand to hand fighting went on most of the night until 0800 hrs when the enemy withdrew, leaving over a hundred dead. All day Tiger tanks lying back from the crest of Hill 112 probed the Wyverns' forward defences and our Churchill infantry-support tanks were hopelessly outgunned. As Brig. Essame wrote: 'The least movement brought down intense automatic fire and the mortaring went on without respite. The crest of the hill was littered with evidence (of destroyed Churchills and other equipment). Meanwhile the constant stream of casualties continued to flow. It was only too clear that we had been forced on to the defensive.' 130th Brigade being temporarily non-effective, 214th Brigade extended its front from Chateau de Fontaine to the eastern slopes of Hill 112 with 1st Worcesters relieving the 4th Wiltshires.

Essame continued: 'The brutal fact had to be faced that so long as the enemy's machine guns (and mortars) perfectly sited on the reverse slopes of Hill 112 could continue to rake the flank of an attack, further progress was impossible. The SS troops of both 9 and 10 Panzer Divisions continued to fight with the utmost ferocity and without mercy.'

On 10 July the division very nearly bled to death. The well-trained green infantry from the West Country suffered 2,000 casualties in thirty-six hours. Maj.-Gen. Thomas must have grieved at these terrible losses. Reinforcements – equally green – poured in from the Reinforcement Holding Units already established in the beachhead. The 4th Somersets needed nineteen officers and 479 ORs to bring them up again to fighting strength.

The Cornwalls had a new CO, Lt.-Col. George Taylor, and Maj. R.A. St G. Martin, the new 2 i/c from the Oxfordshire and Buckinghamshire LI, plus reinforcements from the 4th Battalion DCLI, the Lancashire Fusiliers, the Royal Fusiliers, the Durham Light Infantry and the Bedfordshire and Hertfordshire Regiment.

> I was summoned by the Brigadier (wrote Col. George Taylor), and walked down the road, shell fire had splattered it with leaves and branches from the tall trees. I felt as if I was dreaming, it seemed so unreal. Essame was obviously a worried man. 'Go, George, and take them over and kick them up the backside.' This was out of character as Peter Essame was a man of generous spirit. I had no intention of doing this as I knew what a gallant fight they had put up. I found the officers and men who had survived one of the most terrible battles of the war, shocked, but unbroken in spirit. Some 300 reinforcements joined the Cornwalls. They were tired, dusty and hungry and the first thing we did was to give them a good meal. I shook hands with each one and said a few words of welcome.

Gordon Reinhold, Brigade Major (later Brigadier) wrote after Jupiter was over:

> We were all taken aback and sobered by the amazing, even fanatical way in which the Germans opposed to us defended their ground. We were very quickly and firmly disabused of any idea that the battle for Normandy would be a 'piece of cake'. It was one hell of a slogging match with huge amounts of fire power deployed on our side, plus the metropolitan bombers from the UK. The amazing tenacity of the German troops and the very high quality of their equipment – tanks, SP guns, machine guns, 'nebelwerfers' – the last being pretty terrifying – all came as rather a surprise. Thank God that the Germans were prevented from deploying their aircraft. In the congestion of the early bridgehead they would have wrought havoc!

Brig. Essame again: 'In these conditions comparable to the bombardment at Passchendaele, the Division remained in action for fourteen days. There were countless acts of unrecorded heroism.'

In the violent outside world few people heard about Field Marshal Rommel's near fatal wounding on 15 July and the succession to Army Group B by Gen. von Kluge, that on the 20th the Fuhrer had nearly been assassinated in his Berlin bunker, or that the Americans had taken St Lo. Or even that in Operation Goodwood on 18 July, Britain's finest armoured divisions had taken a terrible beating south-west of Caen in the killing grounds in front of Bourguébus ridge.

Capt. R.F. Hall, 4th Dorsets, had an adventurous week:

One evening Tony Cottle and I found a knocked-out German tank; it would not go but the gun was still in working order so we had a bit of fun firing the remaining rounds at the enemy. The Padre and the MO were wounded by the same shell (on 21 July) because they were squatting on the ground having a 'poo' instead of doing it in their slit trenches. A lesson for our children! Peter Steele Perkins (Artillery FOO) allowed me to control a 5.5-in gun about 6–8 miles back and I was lucky enough to hit several tanks. (Hall captured a German Pay Corps NCO loaded with currency, 23,900 francs). Silly me; I thought he had important papers in his bag and sent him back to Bn HQ!

Wally Caines, 4th Dorsets, wrote in his journal:

At noon (on the 11th) the IO Lt. Andrews saw Jerries forming up in a cornfield 800 yds away, behind them a few tanks. He stood on top of the Battery Commander's scout car directing the gunner officer on the position of the enemy. We thanked God for this, as within a few minutes down came our murderous artillery barrage crashing amongst the Jerries in the cornfield. Two enemy tanks went up in smoke and flames. The artillery came to the rescue again. Relieved by 5 Dorsets at 1800 hrs we had to march back 7 miles to Colleville rest area. It was a pitiful sight to see the thin column of marching troops, none of us were dressed alike. Several Padres met us with cheery smiles, giving us cigarettes, chocolate and sweets. I shared a trench with Cpl. Joe Penny, a cheery type. 12 July. Hot meal, went to sleep, all had a good wash down. Kits of deceased personnel had to be unloaded from the rear echelon vehicles. Tears came to my eyes as I looked through photographs of wives and sweethearts belonging to the boys I had known so well. 14 July. Some 300 reinforcements arrived. Bn formed into strong companies making the total strength about 400, remaining 200 newly joined fighting troops were told to remain in a field for the day. Col. Cowie was to leave us to join another part of the Army for duty.

Eric Codling wrote of the Middlesex part of the six-day battle for Hill 112: 'It was impossible to get out of the mortar pits such was the punishment received. One of the most bitter slogging matches of the Second World War. We ate, slept and even natural body functions had to be carried out below ground.' One of Eric's mates' pit received a direct hit wrecking the mortar. In panic he rushed to Sgt. McLeod's slit trench. He asked the sergeant to move up a bit – no reply. By the light of shell flashes he saw the sergeant's head was missing. German propaganda leaflets were spotted: 'these told us we were caught like foxes in a trap, better give ourselves up. Self-inflicted wounds were not unknown: one individual shot himself through the forearm.' Eric Levy noted: 'by now our officers were cutting off their pips and NCOs were putting mud on their stripes. The snipers were that accurate.' The 5th Wiltshires were relieved on 12 July. Harry Peace, the adjutant, remembers: 'We had been in continuous contact with the enemy and had suffered grievous casualties but we had stood up to the cream of the German Army and morale was high. Two days out of the line – but not so far as not to suffer inconvenience from high velocity overthrows and aerial attack at night with butterfly bombs.' But Ron Garner wrote: 'We stayed two days in Mouen. By now there were quite a large number of men causing self inflicted wounds – shooting themselves in the feet to stop from going back into action – such was the state of mind some men were being driven to.'

Maj. L.J. Wood was promoted to command 4th Dorsets on 14 July and on the 18th was wounded in the head by a mortar bomb, and Maj. G. Tilley from 5th Dorsets was promoted to command them. 'Rather a blow leaving my lads,' he wrote to his wife, 'but as I have lost practically all my officers and a lot of men it wasn't such a wrench. They were really grand, full of guts. In one very sticky spot they really backed me up to the limit. First class lads.'

Sydney Jary joined 18 Platoon 4th SLI as a young reinforcement officer. In his RHU in Bayeux a florid, moustached major said to him:

'Your life expectancy from the day you join the Bn will be precisely three weeks.' Ramblings of an old fool of forty! 18 platoon had been in battle for nearly three weeks and had lost two platoon commanders and three-quarters of their strength and had had enough. There was an unconscious resolve throughout the remnants of the platoon that things had got to change. Fortunately their ideas did not include a reluctance to fight. They wanted success but without the crippling casualties.

Infantrymen have always had a tendency to be rather rude about gunners – perhaps we were jealous of them. They used to ride everywhere whereas we had to march (wrote John Majendie, 4th SLI), but when we finally came back off Hill 112 down through Death Valley and were on our way back to a rest area, we marched through our own Gunners' 25-pdr lines (94th Field Regiment RA). The guns had got no paint left on their barrels at all. It had all been burnt off, they'd been firing at such a quick rate. I remember their Battery Commander walking over to us and shouting 'What price the bloody Gunners now!' . . . 'Col. Ted Luce (4th Wilts) offered to send an escort of snipers and a Bren crew as local protection for our OP on Hill 112 as it would be in full view,' Maj. Irish said. John Fletcher volunteered to do it alone as it offered a better chance of not being spotted. From 0330 hrs next morning he was able to carry out observed shooting on Esquay and Evrecy. He stayed out there *beyond* the infantry, quite alone, all day until after dark. Around him in the hot sun lay the unburied dead of ten days' slaughter. Next to him was a dead FOO from 11th Armoured Div. looking out unseeing at the German lines, his wireless set still switched on.

The MO of 7th SLI wrote:

After three days Padre I.F. Richards and I were the only original officers left in Bn HQ. We never had a period of more than two hours, day or night, without a casualty. Two RAMC men who were working with me were killed, my truck and ambulance were put out of action. During all the fighting Padre Richards visited the companies calmly and coolly. A great strain on him because he knew the men intimately, many of the casualties were his friends. Many burials to perform, many graves to dig. A shell hit the roof of a farm building near the chateau, killed the acting CO, Maj. Bruford, and the CO, 2 i/c of the Hampshires (Majors Mallock and McPhillips) with him in conference, plus

Sgt. Barnes the Provo Sergeant, and the IO and whole IO section wounded. Our mortars gave bomb for bomb and added a few for luck, gunners answered every salvo with four of their own.

Lt.-Col. J.W. Nicol was the new CO and back at Miebord, a mile behind the ridge, small bathing parties of Somersets were able to slip down into the valley and refresh themselves in the soothing waters of the pebble-bottomed stream. A large batch of reinforcements from the 9th Battalion Somersets arrived under Capt. Durie and Lt. Harvey and made up one new complete company. Pte. D. O'Connell wrote: 'Groans, moans and cries for Mother went up when we were informed that instead of breakfast in bed – our due – we had to go on a PT run first thing in the morning before breakfast.' Still, he ate steak and onions in the local café in Miebord.

On the 17th the 7th SLI were back on the slopes of Hill 112. They saw, according to Capt. John Meredith, 'a queer little undersized, half starved black goat. It led among the the shell-scarred fields a charmed life, trotted contentedly around slit trenches uttering idiotic little bleats. It survived the whole battle, welcomed visitors and was fed small pieces of tinned plum pudding.'

'Saturday 15 July was just another perfectly bloody day. We had been in action for twenty-one days without a breather,' recalls Maj. Anthony Jeans, 4th Wiltshires. 'We were beginning to get tired and irritable', but an issue (on payment) came up of a pint of beer per man. 'I shall never forget the taste of that beer as long as I live . . . a bottle of "Tolleys", the finest bottle of beer they have ever made or are ever likely to.'

The regimental history of the 4th Wilts records:

On the 13th relieved 4 Somersets on Hill 112, a grim place where three or four battles had been fought, the corn was flattened, littered with burned-out tanks, vehicles abandoned, broken equipment and blackened, mangled bodies. Northwards there was a wonderful view over the broad sweep of the Odon valley with Carpiquet beyond. Obviously the enemy positions had been prepared some time before the allied invasion of Normandy. Night 15/16 July. The 15th Scottish attacked Esquay but for 4 Wiltshires the most hellish night of the whole campaign (the three joint authors of *The Maroon Square* were

Maj. A.D. Parsons MC, Maj. D.I.M. Robbins MC and Maj. D.C. Gibson MC – all there at the time); continual rain of every type of missile including oil bombs to set corn on fire. The Bn CP had a direct hit and only the CO and a signaller unscathed. Capt. P.A. Boyd was killed and the adjutant, Capt. Prideaux and Mortar Officer Capt. Chappell both wounded. On the night of 17th/18th relieved by 7 Somersets and back to Mouen. A large draft of reinforcements arrived many from 7th Bn Wiltshires.

Stan Procter had a stand-up bath, washed his underwear and socks on the 15th and had a new job on the 17th when he joined 1st Worcesters as radio link in a white scout car whose canvas roof let in the rain and shrapnel. Signalman William Gould, Battalion HQ with the Worcesters at Chateau de Fontaine, recalls: 'Grabbing a jerrican I went to replace our water supply from a well near the stables. In the process of pumping a hail of mortar bombs descended and three senior officers (in O Group) were all killed. With the help of a colleague I dragged the bodies into one of the stables. As our historian Maj. D.Y. Watson observed: "Death stalks the rider who mounts its broad saddle."'

One young dispatch rider collapsed near his machine – he had been sampling the local deadly brew of Calvados. Another signaller went missing. 'He had discarded his drum of cable and was obviously beating a retreat to the river. His nerves had gone in less than a fortnight' wrote Stan Procter.

BSM Fred Fowler's diary: 'We see a film just in rear of position in an old German Luftwaffe HQ. We move out of line for a rest after six weeks' continuous action. Guns etc. overhauled, kits made up, cinemas and Ensa visits to Bayeux. Not much there, how quiet everything seems (after Hill 112).'

22

OPERATION EXPRESS

'Bloody Maltot – Again'

On the day after the great tank battles of Goodwood, 19 July, 129th Brigade were moved in torrential rain to the village of Rocrenil south of Bretteville-sur-Odon, 2 miles north of Maltot. Operation Express was planned to retake Maltot by 4th and 5th Wiltshires with the Churchill tanks of 7th RTR and strong artillery support. Air photographs were taken this time – they might have identified the dug-in Tiger tanks in Maltot in that terrifying disastrous attack on the 10th – and thereby saved a lot of nineteen-year-old lives. Brig. Mole, Lt.-Col. Ted Luce and Lt.-Col. 'Pop' Pearson plus 7th RTR and the gunners, studied the plan of attack on sand models, maps and, where possible, visually. 4th Wiltshires were to be on the left flank with the objectives of capturing the spur and woods to the east of the village. 5th Wiltshires were to attack on the right flank with Maltot village as their objective. 4th SLI were in reserve and 8th Middlesex mortars were to be backed by the power and fury of two AGRAs. The weather was dreadful and Express was postponed by one day, then by another.

At 1730 hrs on the 22nd the two battalions, each on a two-company front, set off from the start line, the Maltot–Caen road. Widely deployed, the men's faces were daubed with green camouflage cream and there was foliage in their helmets. The sun was shining but almost immediately enemy shells and mortar bombs were falling amid the Wiltshires in the open rolling cornfields. Soon they had to winkle enemy out of caves and quarries between the River Orne and the escarpment. 4th Wiltshires met bitter resistance in the woods by the River Orne. Lt. Donald Pope of 'C' Company was wounded four times, but continued to fire his Sten as he lay on the ground and shouted encouragement. Anthony Jeans described the scene:

> Donald decided to go in with the bayonet under cover of his Brens and 2-in mortar and shouting to his chaps to follow he

ran forward firing his Sten from the hip. He had not gone far across this 50 yds of hell before he was hit again. He fell, but scrambled up and ran on, only to be hit again, this time in the other leg. He decided that it was too big a job for him as only two men had followed him so he started to come back but was hit a fourth time. This time he went down for the count right in the middle of No Man's Land.

Donald survived and was awarded the MC: 'I took charge blowing my hunting horn for all it was worth, beckoned the chaps on. We made the edge of the wood in one long dash and everyone followed me but unfortunately a number of others were hit during the assault. (Later) The whole of this assault into the wood took about five minutes. It seemed an eternity. We were not too disorganised and the wood clearing went on more or less smoothly.' On their right 'A' Company was in difficulties and Maj. R. Joscelyn, CO 'A' Squadron 7th RTR, brought up his Churchills to help the Wiltshires continue the advance. Maj. T.R.M. Ottowell, OC 'B' Company, made for the spur east of Maltot but his advance was halted by heavy fire from the Chateau de Maltot. So 18 platoon led by Lt. J.H. Rutherford and Sgt. F. A. Eyer, supported by 7th RTR point-blank shell fire entered the chateau. Desperate fighting went on in the chateau in pitch darkness. Its thick walls seemed impervious to shell fire, its deep cellars and commanding battlements made it a near impregnable fortress. Finally after several attacks had been beaten off the defenders surrendered at dawn. This former Panzer HQ contained valuable documents. 'B' Company had taken heavy casualties and the platoon strength of 'C' Company was reduced to twenty, twelve and fourteen.

On their final objective 4th Wilts led by their CO with his Sten and RTR Squadron leader Maj. R. Joscelyn with his pistol joined a platoon assault for close quarter fighting. It was stirring stuff but casualties were very heavy, sixteen KIA and seventy-two wounded including five officers that day.

On the right 5th Wiltshires soon reached the outskirts of Maltot despite being sniped by seven Tiger tanks dug in on Hill 112, 2 miles to the west. Both Maj. F.S. Rimmington and Capt. F.I.C. Herridge were wounded as the main crossroads were heavily shelled. Strong fire came from a German RAP and as rifle ammo was now short, bayonets were used. Capt. 'Abe'

Lincoln with 'B' Company now burst into the village and close quarter fighting ensued amongst the houses and orchards as Pte. Long recounts: 'They would come rushing at you like wild bulls with bayonets raised above their heads. All we had to do was wait for them, parry their bayonet to one side, up with our butt to smash their jaws and then as they fell just stick 'em.' One man, Cpl. Wiltshire, flung a tin of bully beef at a German. His riflemen said of their company commander, 'Abe's in front, everything's OK.' 'Abe' could speak fluent German. He advanced on three German tanks, one hand imperiously raised, demanded to speak to their tank commander, who, quite amazed, thrust his head out of the turret to hear Abe demand his surrender. Each was trying to persuade the other to give in. The discussion or parley was rudely interrupted by British medium guns ranging on the German tanks.

John McMath, the signals officer, in his regimental history recounts:

> Maltot proved to be a dreadful spectacle, the streets and fields were still strewn with the dead (Dorsets and Hampshires who had fallen on 10 July) and lay in heaps around slit trenches with hardly more than the turf removed. The houses were shattered, roads cratered and full of debris; everywhere the sickly smell of death and destruction hung heavily upon the ruins. Enemy Tiger tanks overlooking the village were still dropping shells with deadly accuracy on our positions. Direct hits on two slit trenches killed two company commanders – Maj. Hankey of 'C' and Capt. Maskell-Dicker of 'D' and the Battalion 2 i/c Maj. Tanner, was hit and died of wounds. A squadron of tanks came up to reinforce the position. They met disaster in a few seconds, seven of them were set on fire from direct hits (Churchill infantry tanks were sitting ducks for Tigers). Pte. Cooling in Signal platoon dressed the tank crew wounds as they lay on the road amid bursting shells. One by one he lifted six badly wounded men on to a jeep and drove through rubble back to the RAP. Eventually RAF Typhoons rocketed three Tigers. But thirty-six hours after the Bn first reached the village, hungry, bomb-happy German soldiers emerged from various hiding places – trenches, cellars, cupboards, stables. Eventually the tally came to over 400 from a well-armed fresh enemy division, plus 600 British rifles captured from the previous battle on 10 July.

Sgt. Reg Romain with the A/Tank platoon 5th Wilts recalled:

We were in support of 'C' Coy and followed them and their Churchill tanks into the attack. (Later) We had lost a lot of men but had won Maltot and our Section Sgt. Short was badly wounded and two of our corporals – Sid Keen and Jack Taylor – were killed. In the morning we had orders to take up position in the front of Maltot in 'D' Coy area facing the German side of Hill 112. This was open for tank warfare in places. Six Churchill tanks coming up through Maltot set off across country to a wood. They were all knocked out like skittles by a Jerry 88mm gun which was in the copse under cover. It could have been tanks or anti-tank guns but they really massacred our tanks. The German 88mm easily outgunned our 6-pounder A/Tk guns starting off at about 1,000 yds. Our effective range was only 400 yds and our 17-pounder never seemed far enough forward to engage them.

Capt. Harry Peace, Adjutant of 5th Wiltshires remembers:

Pop Pearson our CO was well to the fore in the attack. He preferred to direct in person rather than stay behind and rely on uncertain wireless. The Padre the Revd Jimmy Douglas was always well forward with the RAP. He saw that all those killed had a decent burial with a short service and their graves marked with a wooden cross often with flowers. He took care of removing personal belongings, not a pleasant task from often mangled bodies and saw they were sent home. A truly splendid chaplain.

Ron Garner with the Intelligence section recalled:

Maltot village was a nasty sight with many unburied dead. In the main street was a German who had been killed. A tank had run over his head. Another opposite, hit by an infantry gun, had been dead for a week or more from the state of him. (Later) Col. Pearson and I were crossing a field next day when a couple of Czechs popped their heads up from a trench a few feet away. They were frightened and surrendered to us. They had been fighting for the Germans and were firmly convinced we were going to shoot them. Currier, one of the batmen, went into a house by Bn HQ to find some plates and cutlery, opened a cupboard; out tumbled three Germans who immediately surrendered to him. Currier in his shirt sleeves, weaponless, was more surprised than they!

Ron was promoted to Lance-Corporal, 'I' Section, on Sunday 23rd. Sgt. C.G. Cleal, 4th Dorsets, with Canloan officer Lt. Andrews 'went back into Maltot. We witnessed the appalling spectacle. The place was eerie in its horror and silence. It was uncanny to see enemy dead still crouched behind their machine and anti-tank guns. The smell was atrocious. . . . I felt revulsion, bewilderment and anger.' On the 25th the Wiltshires were relieved by the Royal Welch Fusiliers. 'With dragging steps we marched back a couple of miles behind the line between Verson and Bas de Mouen. We had had no sleep for three nights and were very, very weary,' wrote Ron Garner. Then next day they marched 15 miles back to Condé-sur-Seulles.

23

THE WORCESTERS' NIGHT ATTACK

A diversionary attack involving the 1st Worcesters and 5th DCLI was less successful. On the 22nd they were ordered to make a night attack to gain a triangular field on the far side of the crest of Hill 112.

Before the attack the Bn had taken up positions in Baron and during our short stay Bn HQ was settled in a house. When the signal office was demolished two or three of us were slightly wounded (recalls William Gould). The night attack finally went in and two companies 'A' and 'D' were formed up on the start line by their commander, Maj. Weston. The copse, our objective on Hill 112, would afford an excellent view of the German positions if captured. Everything went like clockwork for the first 500 yds and we had high hopes of an easy task. (Later) 'A' Company by this time had run into an ambush and received many casualties. The German forward positions had been (placed) well ahead of the main body in order to forestall any night attack. Our men had run into heavy trouble. They made a disorganised retreat. Maj. Weston, perhaps the best loved officer in the whole Bn, was killed at the head of the attack.

Heavy counter-attacks forced the Worcesters back. Peter Weston and his CSM Southwood were killed by MG fire. Lt. Revnell was missing and Lt. Fiset and Sgt. Dalloway were wounded. The padre, Capt. Spiers, acted as a second MO in the RAP on the crest of the hill.

Lt.-Col. George Taylor, now commanding 5th DCLI, wrote:

Zero hour. As the Worcesters went in we launched our diversionary attack. Very lights and star shells illuminated the dark night and we could hear the staccato bark of the enemy tank machine guns. Tracer bullets criss-crossed the night sky and our positions came under mortar fire. Our new Scout Platoon would be supported by 'A' Coy and backed up by our 3-in mortars. Dawn brought the depressing news that the attack had failed. I ordered Maj. Colwell to move his company forward to contact the Worcesters. He had just joined, made his recce, stood up and was shot through the head. On the 25th a mortar concentration on the CP killed Capt. Marrian (newly out from Camberley Staff College) and wounded four other ranks. But a misty dawn brought a surprise 'bag' for our lookouts in the forward positions. There just a couple of hundred yards ahead were three dozen Germans on drill parade. (Via Capt. Gorman, the adjutant, and Maj. Tom Brewis, commander of 173rd Battery, 179th Field Regiment RA) the German parade was dismissed in a very disorderly way by command of the Royal Artillery. (Later) A Pioneer party crept out into No Man's Land during darkness and erected a small sign inscribed 'Cornwall Hill, 1944'. The battalion had indeed left its mark.

24

A SHORT INTERLUDE

'Carefree Days of Rest'

For five days the battered Wyverns were out of action. The 53rd Welsh Division took over the battle-scarred slopes of Hill 112 and the sad, desolate ruins of Maltot. Maj.-Gen. Thomas watched his infantry marching rather slowly back to the designated rest area around Ducy-Ste-Marguerite, 4 miles south-east of Bayeux. One wonders what he must have thought of his superbly trained division who had landed a month before. More than two thousand were no longer with the colours. Many of them were buried in Norman fields. Around the Chateau de Fontaine there was a large new cemetery. Nine regimental COs were already dead or wounded. Casualties among the young leaders – the eighteen- and nineteen-year-old section leaders, the twenty- and twenty-one-year-old platoon commanders – were immense. Of Corporal Doug Proctor's 18 Platoon, 4th Somersets, 'out of thirty-six men who so bravely went into battle on Hill 112, only nine remained. Waiting for us in the village were more reinforcements. We were joined by a new officer (Sydney Jary) and a new sergeant.'

During the rest period Stan Procter received mail from his girlfriend Audrey, tucked in at the mobile NAAFI, went to see George Formby in an ENSA open-air concert, and listened on the Forces' radio network to Bing Crosby singing 'White Christmas', 'I'll be seeing you' and Alice Faye singing 'Long Ago and Far Away'. Brig. Essame wrote:

> It was pleasant to bivouac in the shade of the apple trees away from the din of the battlefield and the all-pervading dust and traffic of the bridgehead, or to visit the mobile bath unit established by the RAOC on the River Seulles and to enjoy the luxury of a bath and clean underwear. Bayeux, choked with the necessary but glamourless military population, the tail of an army, offered few attractions. The mobile cinema gave continuous performances of *Four Jills in a Jeep*. Many

members of the division were to see it at least four times during the coming months.

But Col. George Taylor noted: 'before us stretched three glorious carefree days of rest. The sheer bliss of a bath, the luxury of clean underwear. Parties of all ranks went to Bayeux. With two of my officers we dined with a French family there. There were ENSA and cinema shows. A small party of nurses visited the battalion and were entertained in the HQ mess. The war could have been a million miles away.'

Gerald Tilley, now commanding 5th Dorsets, wrote to his wife:

24 July. All quiet on the western front and the sun is shining . . . poor old Johnny Hiscocks got his eyes damaged by the blast of a shell from a Tiger tank, Paul Gornich, the little major with glasses, went mad, John Tilley just got a Blighty in the shoulder. I did not lose too many men compared to some. 26 July. Bn coming out of line to refit after five weeks on the go, the whole time. The French civilians do not seem very interested either way. Poor devils, I expect they are tired of being occupied. 28 July. I have been able to buy over 300 cigarettes, two bottles of Scotch, one of gin, so life looks brighter. . . . I spent an hour in the (Bayeux) cathedral with my old CO – Tim Wood – glorious building reminiscent of Notre Dame. I have come back from a Communion Service. I feel better for it, does me a lot of good.

Harry Peace, Adjutant 5th Wiltshires, remembers: 'Rest and Recuperation – a bath, clean clothes, being able to take one's boots off at night. What bliss! There was plenty of work to be done, fitting replacements, arranging promotions of the four officers commanding rifle companies, all were casualties – in many cases their replacements had become casualties also.'

L/Cpl. Garner, 5th Wiltshires, wrote: 'There was a cinema show – George Formby in *Bell Bottom George* at Cancagney, the Brigade HQ. This show was in an old French barn, not very large, but it was much appreciated. The whole bn was re-equipped. The Quartermaster was very busy fitting everyone up with a new battledress. We had baths and got our first pay in francs. The Padre, the Revd Douglas, later held a memorial service during those days of rest in remembrance of the men who were no longer with us.'

I went in to Bayeux with some of our new invasion money but found there wasn't much to buy only cheese and butter and you couldn't carry much of that far in the hot July weather, especially Camembert. We did manage to see the Cathedral but were soon heading back from our rest area where I can remember we bathed nude in a stream with a waterfall or a mill wheel in it, only to be scared off by the farmer's daughters laughing and giggling. Funny how such battle hardened soldiers could be shy.

These were Sgt. Reg Romain's recollections of 'out of the line'. The 4th Wiltshires were resting nearby at Ducy-Ste-Marguerite, 7 miles north-west of Cheux, and in the sunny weather, Staff Sgt. Instructor Hagen APTC, a footballer of renown with Sheffield United, had a smile and a joke for everybody and soon footballs were being kicked about in a large field.

Maj. John Fry drew the sum of 281,000 francs for the pay of the 5th DCLI and was puzzled as to how it was going to be spent, the only purchasable commodity seeming to be Camembert cheese. Pte. Robert Thornburrow, Defence Platoon 129th Brigade, remembers that there was an alternative. Calvados diluted with red wine or rough cider produced a lethal drink nicknamed 'Stuporjuice'.

25

OPERATION BLUECOAT

Gen. Montgomery on 27 July ordered the British Second Army to strike south from Caumont, and on the 30th to capture Mt Pinçon (as vital a hill as 112) and to get astride the road that runs from Vire through Vassy to Condé-sur-Noireau. 8 Corps was on the right and XXX Corps on the left. The Wyverns were to be part of XXX Corps which included 50th Tyne and Tees Infantry Division, 7th Armoured, 56th Infantry Brigade and 8th Armoured Brigade. Brig. Essame wrote:

> The battle was to open with an assault at first light on 29 July with 15th Scottish on the right, 43rd Wyverns in the centre and the 50th on the left. The division's task was to punch a hole in the enemy position at Bricquessard and north of Cahagnes. It was then to advance via the important crossroads at St Pierre du Fresne to seize the high ground south and south-west of Jurques. Another responsibility was to protect the left (eastern) flank of the Corps by seizing and holding the Robin feature. Finally it was to swing east and capture the high ground at Ondefontaine.

A new alliance was to be formed with 8th Armoured Fox's Head Brigade, which was to last for the rest of the campaign. Brig. G.E. Prior-Palmer commanded three armoured regiments – the 4/7th Dragoon Guards, 13/18th Hussars and the Sherwood Rangers, all equipped with Sherman tanks. They were not much of a match for Tigers, Panthers and Ferdinands – but a more solid proposition than the Churchill infantry tanks. They were supported by 12/60th KRRC motorised infantry in carriers and halftracks and 147th Field Regiment (Essex Yeomanry) with 25-pounders on Sexton-Ram SP chassis.

For the first time the Wyverns were venturing into genuine 'bocage' country – 'la Suisse Normande' – heavily wooded with hills, valleys, small rivers, minor winding roads and deep narrow lanes. Fields would be small with thick hedgerows on top of 3-, 4-, even 5-ft earth banks. Ideal defensive country, for the artillery and the RAF could not pinpoint targets easily and every road corner was a hazard for tanks and infantry. The Germans had had plenty of time to prepare their defences and to lay minefields. 'Potato-picking' was the term used for the difficult and dangerous technique of clearing minefields. Teller (plate) mines would wreck any vehicle and 'pepperpots' and Schu mines would cripple any soldier who trod on them.

The distance from Caumont to the commanding slopes of Mt Pinçon (365 m) was only 15 miles – but it was good ambush country and the Wyverns were going to have a number of very nasty little battles before they got there. In the bocage countryside the battle broke down into a series of ferocious individual actions, impossible to co-ordinate or control.

Initially 130th Brigade plus 4th Somerset LI was to pierce the enemy's defences between Bricquessard and Caumont. Then 214th Brigade would pass through and advance 4 miles to St Pierre du Fresne. Finally 129th Brigade would continue the advance. It was known that 216th German Infantry Division was holding a 9-mile front south-east of Caen with two of its three infantry regiments fully committed. British, American and German divisions had laid minefields almost indiscriminately and Corps HQ could not provide a minefield trace.

130th Brigade started Bluecoat at 0800 hrs on 30 July from Livry, 2 miles north-east of Caumont and the village of Cahagnes, their first objective, was a mile due south. 4th Somerset LI were on the left flank and 5th Dorsets on the right, with 7th Hampshires in reserve. The whole division watched 500 Lancasters wreaking havoc with their carpet-bombing tactics. Cpl. Doug Proctor related in *Section Commander*:

> Our immediate task was to take the village of Bricquessard and secure a bridge 200 yds to the far side of the village. We were one of the forward platoons (No. 18) being on the left flank immediately to the right of the road. I led the left section, Cpl. Douglas the right one and Cpl. Jim Kingston (a West countryman with a softly spoken Somerset burr) was in reserve. . . . It was impossible to observe anything beyond the nearest hedgerow. It was a hopeless situation.

The Sherwood Ranger Shermans quickly discovered that the road was mined and the two leading companies soon suffered numerous casualties from Schu mines scattered in the fields. Doug Proctor again: 'The barrage started and all hell was let loose. Scrambling out of our slits we began to advance and immediately ran into a hail of small arms fire. Flinging ourselves to the ground we tried to locate the Spandaus. The field was strewn with anti-personnel mines. It was a lottery where one trod.' Pte. Vic Caldwell with 7th Platoon 'A' Company advanced through a minefield: 'Schu mines could blow your feet off or you could lose your manhood; they were deadly.' Vic was No. 2 on a Bren gun, carrying spare Bren gun magazines. 'As I crawled through a gap in the hedgerow I felt a thump in my chest.' Vic was lucky – the bullet was deflected off a magazine, ricocheted down and hit his left leg. He was patched up at the RAP, then sent to ADS. Later he rejoined his battalion. Majors Mallalieu, OC 'C' Company, and Braithwaite, OC 'D' Company (although wounded by a Schu mine), pushed their companies forward. Meanwhile Sgt. Hayman and his Pioneers lifted fifty Teller mines under small arms fire and enabled the Sherwood Rangers to keep going. At midday Maj. Thomas took 'B' Company through and seized the bridge across the stream and Col. 'Lippy' consolidated his battalion into a 1,000-yd salient.

Cpl. Doug Proctor recalls: 'One German soldier ran towards us from the left flank. His hands were raised as if surrendering but I could see he was still armed with a few stick grenades that were in his belt. His arm dropped and grasped a grenade; without the slightest hesitation or compunction, I shot him.' Other units were following up and mopping up behind. 5th Wiltshires lost their gallant company commander 'Abe' Lincoln, killed in a short sharp battle on the 30th at Livry. Pte. Bigwood, stretcher-bearer, went forward alone 400 yds under fire to bring him back to the RAP – alas too late.

Capt. Maurice Edwards, adjutant of 5th Dorsets, wrote in the battalion history:

Our task was to form a tight bridgehead over the stream running through the village of Le Mesnil Leveau and to take the village of Le Quesnay (a mile south of Bricquessard). 'B' Coy under Maj. K. Mead on the left moved forward but were halted at the main road (Caumont–Villers-Bocage) by heavy MG fire and were unable to advance. Intense enemy shelling caused severe casualties and one salvo knocked out the Coy HQ. Capt. P. Aspinal CO 'A' Coy in the centre made some progress with Lt. Champion's platoon but the rest of the company suffered considerable casualties from mines and were held up. On the right 'C' Coy suffered a similar fate, found themselves in the centre of a dense minefield 300 yds from the start line and were unable to move. Maj. Favell and Lt. Wetherbee were both wounded on mines. 'D' Coy under Maj. G.R. Hartwell were still waiting to pass through to Le Quesnay. It was decided that the clearing of the minefields should be done that night. The next morning a further unsuccessful attempt was made to reach the villages and it was decided to wait for the tanks to come through. But 'D' Company worked round the left flank and cleared the orchards down to the river. In the afternoon tank support arrived, 'A' and 'C' companies were successful and 'B' reported their area clear at 2200 hrs.

The evening of the 30th, Brig. Leslie moved 7th Hampshires round the right flank of the Dorsets towards the spur north of Cahagnes. By midnight all four Hampshire companies were three-quarters of the way up the hill slopes despite counter-attacks. Cahagnes was badly damaged by the RAF and was still burning. L/Cpl. Bryant distinguished himself in a grenade melée and eventually 180 prisoners were taken. Over a hundred German dead lay in the well-concealed defences in front of Cahagnes. It was known that 15th Scottish attacking on the right had made a spectacular advance of 6 miles, but on the east flank 50th Division was also held up by deep minefields. And on the 31st 4th Dorsets put in an attack on Montmirel near La Lande (taken by 7th Hampshires) 1 mile east of Caumont. A set-piece attack took eighty-seven POW with only half a dozen casualties. The Pioneers under Sgt. Blandemer cleared anti-personnel minefields with diligence and bravery.

26

CAHAGNES AND
ST PIERRE-DU-FRESNE

50th Tyne and Tees Division was still held up at Amaye-sur-Seulles, a large village halfway between Caumont and Villers-Bocage, so the divisional gunners and Middlesex 4.2-in mortars joined in a Corps bombardment. At 1730 hrs on 31 July Brig. Essame directed 1st Worcesters riding on the Shermans of 'B' Squadron 4/7th Dragoon Guards on to the main Caumont–Aunay road. They quickly took the smoking remains of Cahagnes. 'A' Company under Capt. Marshall and 'B' Company under Maj. Algy Grubb pushed ahead to their objective a mile south of Cahagnes. At dusk the battalion sent out patrols and consolidated for the night.

Now 7th Somerset LI with their new 'big friends' 4/7th Dragoon Guards passed through flaming Cahagnes. A thick coating of fine white dust smothered vehicles, tanks and the riding troops. A night advance with a half moon was planned, to take St Pierre-du-Fresne 2 miles ahead. 'B' Company led boldly ahead and duly reached it. The small stone church and immensely strong farm buildings had to be searched carefully. Pte. Len Stokes wrote:

> In the dark on the road two enemy halftracks drove right into our midst firing their machine guns like mad. This was nothing like 43rd Division battleschool. Most of us were scurrying around looking for non-existent cover in the dark. Maj. Whitehead took immediate action. He snatched the loaded PIAT gun out of my hands, thrust his rifle at me. He then fired one shot at the first halftrack which exploded and burst into flames. He then took up his rifle and fired at a German. The man fell back into the flames with his arms outspread. No. 10 Platoon had not got their PIAT ready to fire so the second halftrack escaped.

By 0200 hrs on 1 August 'B' Company was in position around St Pierre, and Company HQ spent the night in a large stone farmhouse with a vast courtyard – the three platoons had to dig trenches. Patrols had been sent out and soon after dawn one of them reported a Tiger tank about 300 yds away towards the stream. Suddenly in the lifting mist enemy infantry in great strength were seen. Leaving Lt. Pizzey to deal with the tank Maj. Whitehead called down the defensive fire of the divisional artillery. When Len Stokes came to the road, 'I cautiously looked left and found myself looking down the barrel of the biggest gun I had ever seen, on the biggest tank I had ever seen, which was encased in a layer of concrete and slowly moving towards me.'

'Early in the day', wrote Capt. R.K. Kerr, 94th Field Regiment, 'I was going in a RE carrier to meet the CO of 5 Wilts near the church of St Pierre-du-Fresne. A hundred yards short of the crest on which the village stands, the infantry by the roadside warned us not to go any further. We turned the carrier in the road when a Ferdinand (much the same as a Tiger and equally nasty) appeared over the rise, put a shell through the carrier from back to front.' The tanks were monster Ferdinand SP Guns. The indomitable Pte. Jones, 11 Platoon, stalked one of them and put two PIAT bombs into its rear from close range, and Pte. Johnson from 12 Platoon put a further four PIAT bombs into it. The crew rather quickly abandoned it, leaving it grinding forward in gear. Cpl. McLernon threw phosphorous grenades at the second Ferdinand which withdrew. 'The mist had cleared by now and several hundred enemy soldiers were seen to be coming down the hill towards our position. It seemed that "B" Coy was to receive the main weight of the attack and by this time they had already over-run our forward post. The German attack was smashed to smithereens,' noted Pte. Stokes. The company had by now exhausted their whole stock of grenades and smoke bombs and close-quarter fighting took place in which the whole company including HQ joined except for Pte. Catt, who had better things to do. As Maj. Whitehead's batman he was cooking his breakfast. Eventually the enemy scarpered leaving twenty bodies behind and forty prisoners. Incredibly 'B' Company had only four killed and seven wounded. 'Maj. Whitehead was a really first-class officer; he received the Military Cross for gallantry in this action,' wrote Len Stokes. Cpl. McLernon received the MM and Pte. Johnson was MID.

But that was not all. 21st Panzer Division had sent three

companies and seven tanks against the Somersets. The OC 'D' Company in the left rear of the village noted:

> About 0930 hrs on 1 August information came over the air that a strong enemy force was attacking 'B' Coy, some infiltration had taken place. I ordered my company to stand to, went myself to the left flank where one of my platoons was still digging in. A Bren gun gave the alarm that enemy were advancing across the fields on the opposite side of the valley. We waited until they were in open territory, order to fire was given. Our troop of tanks opened up with BESAs. The tank men saw thirty enemy further down the valley engaged and scattered them. They fired Very lights and put down smoke so I called up our own 3-in mortars on the retreating Hun. Our artillery joined in. The field was covered by dead Boche. I ordered a patrol led by Lt. Tharp to investigate some houses and orchards. When the patrol reached them I was amazed to see five Germans stand up – three from a large shell hole and two supposedly 'dead'.

The Somersets spent the next two days in St Pierre.

During 1 August 5th DCLI were mopping up pockets of resistance left behind south of Cahagnes and, rather surprisingly, 1st Worcesters had some unexpected guests. At about lunchtime Col. Taistler, the German regimental commander, with his adjutant and fifty-eight ORs marched in to surrender. The Wyverns had so savaged his three battalions that he thought future resistance was futile!

BOIS DU HOMME AND HILL 361

Three miles south of St Pierre-du-Fresne is a long, thickly wooded ridge with steep approaches, about 2 miles west to east at a height of 273 m to the peak of 361 m. This task was now given to the 5th Wiltshires. Harry Peace, their adjutant, wrote: 'We moved forward at 8 p.m. on 1 August and duly reached the foot of the hill. We had previously caught the enemy by surprise and Typhoons had disrupted them to some extent.' John McMath, signals officer, reported:

> We captured a German ambulance (laden with bread and loot). A Ferdinand came rumbling down the road and had a track

blown off by a PIAT (from 'B' Company) but our gallant FOO (known as the General) who had given us such magnificent support was badly wounded. The crew of the Red Cross ambulance had no wounded aboard, no medical supplies and were armed to the teeth. A Scout car owned by 9th SS Panzer div went into the bag. 'D' Company moved into Le Parquet, found another Ferdinand which was knocked out by artillery fire. The attack on the steep ridge of Bois du Homme found 'D' Coy on the summit. Maj. R.M.C. Thomas sent out patrols, after digging in and 'C' followed on their left, 'A' on their right. Suddenly a German armoured car and three more Ferdinand SPs drove straight in amongst them swinging right across the open ground in front of 'D' Coy. One was soon bogged down and immediately destroyed. The remaining two smashed their way through 'C' Coy causing casualties to the men in slit trenches. A second Ferdinand was bogged and destroyed. The remaining SP swung back, after running over some of 'A' Coy's men, KO'd by a direct hit from 235 A/Tank battery M 10 emerging into the clearing below the escarpment. All over in a few minutes. As a result A/Tank guns had to be hauled up hillside, 200 ft up half a mile distance in a thunderstorm! Forty men required to haul each gun. The battalion had a good breakfast in the morning. The 2 i/c Maj. Metcalf's truck had run into enemy lines during the night and was captured with the Battalion's mail. The driver, Pte. White, escaped, truck later recovered by 4 Wiltshires with most of the mail, but all the fags had gone.

Reg Romain, with A/Tank Platoon: 'The Germans seemed to be pulling out of action on our front so we had to carry our infantrymen on our carriers. The crew were gun commander Cpl. Len Wrintmore, driver L/Cpl. Jenkins, and gun layer Cpl. Holborn.' Ron Garner took part in an unusual expedition:

We captured the German Medical Officer and at 0100 hrs Capt. Ambrose Dobby, the Padre Mr Douglas, the German MO and half a dozen men set off to find the German RAP in no-man's-land to evacuate their wounded. A ticklish business in case of treachery. The RAF had blasted the roads and craters caused detours. Eventually their RAP was reached. Three ambulances were crammed full of clothes, cutlery, silver, silks – loot collected during the German retreat.

Harry Peace summed up the Bois du Homme battle: 'Pop Pearson's leadership and inspired thrust had won us a famous victory. Congratulations came in from all sides and people came up, from as far back as Corps, to survey the loot and the three captured Ferdinand SP monsters.'

Torrential rain now stopped 'play'. Trenches became full of water, fallen trees and branches blocked tracks, and the lanes became a sea of mud. Temporarily the Wilts were part of mountain, even jungle warfare.

JURQUES AND LA BIGNE

At long last the Recce Regiment – Fifth Glosters – was in action. Gen. Thomas gave them orders to pass through the infantry holding the general line Jurques-Point 309 and advance on two axes: south-east to Jurques–La Bigne–Ondefontaine and south to Jurques–Le Mesnil Auzouf–La Tautainerie. Now it was 130th Brigade's turn to lead, with 4th Dorsets in the van.

Brig. Essame takes up the story:

The enemy were holding the commanding ridge about $^3\!/\!_4$ mile to the south in strength and had excellent observation over the road the brigade was now to take to La Bigne and l'Oisonnière. It proved to be a day of slow progress in the face of heavy mortar and MG fire. But La Bigne was captured in the afternoon. Patrols reported the dense wood between these villages and Ondefontaine (5 miles south-east) was strongly held. It was now up to 5 Dorsets to continue the advance.

The diary of Sgt. Wally Caines, Signals Sgt. 4th Dorsets reads:

1 August still blistering hot, shirt sleeve order. At 2100 hrs Lt. Col. G. Tilley succeeded the unfortunate Lt. Col. Woods. 2 August on the way to Jurques, terrible night, troops were lifted on tanks continuously dropping off to sleep. Signals scout car travelling behind the leading company went off course, blown up on a mine, killing the Adjutant Capt. Goddard and the control operator Cpl. Penny. Battalion passed through Jurques fairly easily, battered town but then faced hell of a resistance. Jerry SPs opened up with all he had. SP guns fired like hell let loose, Spandaus rattled the whole area. Brigade and Bn control sets were knocked out. Several tanks were knocked out by

carefully concealed A/Tank guns. Maj. Letson 'D' Coy badly wounded, also several sergeants and other NCOs. La Bigne 2 miles south of Jurques captured but Bn suffered numerous casualties again and were feeling the worse for wear.

Maj. M. Whittle, 4th Dorsets, wrote:

On approaching Cahagnes at 0115 hrs 2 August we found a divisional MP on the crossroads. He thought he was in Caumont (5 miles north-west). We came upon two Tiger tanks on the road. A lot of excitement caused, but they had been abandoned. By 0915 hrs we were half a mile from Jurques, minefields everywhere. The road was heavily cratered (by the RAF), we searched for mines and MGs opened up. A few fanatics were holding the village itself. These fools were dealt with.

Capt. R.F. Hall with 'A' Company 4th Dorsets recalls:

After Maltot we had many reinforcements from the Essex Regiment. My new company commander was Jimmy Grafton. He was an impresario and produced many theatrical productions. In his pub 'Graftons' off Victoria Street the Goons were formed with Harry Secombe and Michael Bentine. 'Rommel' Crawford our new CSM came with Jimmy who officially dubbed me 'mad' as I used to walk around organising things when everyone else was cowered on the ground. I saw Jimmy Bogan (after he was blown up in the scout car) coming towards us on a m/cycle tied to the back of a signals DR. He virtually had no face. Later his face was completely rebuilt. The only scars you could see were behind his ear which showed up when he was drunk.

Eric Codling and his mates of 8th Middlesex came to a farm on the outskirts of Jurques:

it had been occupied by a German infantry unit with cycles, now abandoned, with tyres let down but pumps left behind. We careered at high speed round the farm enjoying the distraction! Dave Denyer and myself went into the village of Jurques, saw the abandoned cafés, outside was an abandoned Sherman tank. The flies were clustered in the open turret. Inside the tank was the commander and gunner slumped forward in their seats very dead. A small hole in the turret by an AP shell caused their death.

Brig. Essame takes up the story: '7 Royal Hampshire took over Jurques later in the morning (2 August), spent a very unpleasant day under heavy shellfire from 88s to their immediate front. Tiger tanks were clearly visible on the high ground which dominated the road running uphill due south of the village. Typhoons had no success.' A night advance was now planned by 'C' Company (Maj. L.S. Nayler) and 'D' Company (Maj. J.L. Braithwaite) to try to seize Point 321. They were halted by dug-in tank and heavy MMG fire. At dawn Maj. Gordon Viner with 'A' Company made two attempts to work round the right flank but was repulsed by heavy fire. The thick mist meant that observation was difficult and little artillery support could be brought down.

On their way to La Bigne the 'O' group of 5th Dorsets was shelled before dawn on 3 August. The padre, the Revd W.R. Musgrave, was killed and the 2 i/c, Maj. N.J. Newton, wounded. 'La Bigne was a very confused battle,' Maurice Edwards, the adjutant, recalls. 'Bn HQ established itself close to a crossroads in a comfortable farm house – perhaps an unwise location. I remember Aubrey Coad our CO giving out orders in the kitchen when there was the most terrific and lengthy stonk. Some vehicles including my Scout car and a number of jeeps in the yard received direct hits.' The road from La Bigne to Ondefontaine ran through woods. 'C' Company (Capt. Lawrence) and 'D' Company (Maj. Hartwell) led the advance, and came under heavy fixed line fire from tanks and MG. Against this heavy opposition 'D' Company were sent northwards to outflank the enemy but failed to turn up at an agreed crosstracks. They were completely lost so Maurice Edwards set out to find them. They said over the wireless that they were near a farm guarded by a fierce barking dog! Maurice found a farm with a barking dog but no 'D' Company. Eventually the problem was solved over the air. 'D's dog was a terrier, Maurice's was a spaniel! 'D' Company remained lost and unlocated until the morning.

The battalion took up an all round defensive position west of La Roserie. 4th Dorsets had a more torrid time as Sgt. Wally Caines wrote in his diary:

3 August. 'O' group to attack Ondefontaine 2½ miles ahead. 1330 hrs attack commenced. Forward troops left their trenches

only to meet stiff enemy resistance. They were cut down like flies – every man pinned to the ground as all round Spandaus fired murderously. There was no hope of advancing. Our artillery plastered the Jerries. The attack kept for about an hour then it was decided to withdraw to the original position. Our casualties were very heavy (fifteen KIA on 2 and 3 August) and many men still laid wounded amongst the dead in the cornfield. Some managed to crawl back to safety, others laid up until dark whilst a few remained to die of their wounds and where they fell. (The next day – the 4th – another attack on Ondefontaine was held up by desperate resistance.) Final assault at first dawn (4th Dorsets). Very few officers left to attend the 'O' group as no reinforcements had yet reached us but casualties suffered in the last few days were terrific. The unit certainly has taken a knocking. Attack opened at 0530 hrs with two companies up, bayonets fixed: village of Ondefontaine taken by surprise. The enemy had moved out a few hours earlier many killed and bodies were littering the area.

The enemy held Ondefontaine determinedly and part of the Wyverns' success was due to 5th Dorsets who in the mist very early on the 4th had entirely outflanked and unhinged the enemy's defence. Maj. K. Mead, 'B' Company, encountered two MGs on the ridge and killed or captured their crews. Battalion HQ and their FOO were in the unusual position of watching the battle go on *behind* them!

TIGER HILL

Still on 3 August 214th Brigade were called forward into battle again since the Hampshires were making little progress south of Jurques and 4th and 5th Dorsets were fighting hard for the villages of L'Oisonnière and Ondefontaine, 2 miles to the south-east. The 5th Cornwalls were ordered to clear the opposition confronting the Hampshires around Jurques to enable the main advance to continue towards the key objective of Mt Pinçon. For three or four days 214th Brigade had had a relatively peaceful rest period around Canteloup south of Cahagnes.

Lt.-Col. George Taylor and the Cornwalls were given the task of advance guard down the main road south from Jurques. He sent the carrier platoon under debonair Capt. G.L. Holland off at midnight. Up the long hill they climbed noisily in low gear. At the top they were ambushed by 88-mm, Spandau and hand grenades. At dawn a squadron of Shermans of 4/7th Dragoon Guards appeared. So did Brig. Essame who instructed the Cornwalls to clear the ridge ahead. The attack went in at 0815 hrs. Lt. F.W. Durden relates: 'we were moving close to our bursting shells. Suddenly we saw the enemy in their slit trenches. We charged forward firing from the hip. We killed several of them. The rest got up and ran away. We hit a number of them.' Capt. Ruck-Keene, 'C' Company CO, using fire and movement skilfully worked round the right flank, and they found themselves amongst cleverly concealed tanks, 'but we could not get close enough to engage them with our PIATs'. So Durden's men, much reduced by casualties, retreated into cover. 'This position was no better than the open, gorse-covered hill as the 88 shells and mortar bombs burst in the trees. Casualties began to mount. With the wireless set out of order, Maj. John Fry, 'D' Coy, sent me (Durden) back to the command post to report the situation.' Two Shermans were knocked out. 'The enemy mortar fire was a terrible and frightening sight as it crept its sinister way forward like some evil, gigantic black beast from the bottom of the lovely green valley upwards towards our command post until the bombs were exploding around us,' were Col. George Taylor's words. The Cornwalls were withdrawn 500 yds to allow the medium guns to try and knock out the dug-in Tiger tanks. Fighting went on all day with the two leading companies taking heavy casualties. 'We had come up against a brick wall. After the losses on Hill 112 we could not afford another disaster. We had to approach the problem by more devious means,' continued Col. Taylor. He sent out a sniping team, Sgt. Long, Ptes Chapman and Nichols, who crawled for a mile through hedgerows and ditches to harass the enemy from a flank.

The Cornwalls had been opposed by eight to ten tanks – Tigers and Panthers of 10th SS Panzer Division, who had retreated from the Esquay area near Hill 112. They were firmly dug in on 'Tiger Hill' and 5th DCLI had suffered another blooding, twenty dead, sixty-nine wounded and ten missing in one day. 'We counted thirty dead Panzer Grenadiers and many wounded were taken away,' wrote the Colonel, 'but the Brigadier should have told us to *contain* the enemy only whilst he put in a hook with the Worcestershires.' RAF Typhoons were not much help that day. They failed to destroy any German tanks on their hill. They bombed the Cornwalls, wounding two men, attacked 'B' Squadron 43rd Recce Regiment and strafed most of 94th Field Regiment in their gun positions near Jurques. Not the RAF's best effort! Brig. Essame now ordered 1st Worcesters to outflank the enemy through the thickly wooded country on the right flank. Eventually Maj. Algy Grubb led 'B' Company through the forest to the summit of Tiger Hill. At dawn RSM Hurd led a patrol into Bremoy in the valley below and the nasty battle of Tiger Hill was over.

27

ADVANCE ON MT PINÇON

214th Brigade was now established around Le Mesnil Auzouf, 7 miles due west of the key objective of the 1,200 ft high Mt Pinçon. It was the turn of Brig. Mole's 130th Brigade to attack the rather desperate enemy. Desperate because the line between Vire and Mt Pinçon was under immense pressure from 11th and Guards Armoured Divisions and 15th Scottish on the immediate right. By the evening of 4 August the Americans had made a key breakout at Avranches and Gen. Patton's Shermans were streaming into Brittany. The brigade objectives were Le Plessis Grimault, a village on the south-east flank of Mt Pinçon itself, and St Jean-le-Blanc, a village 4 miles to the south-west. Later it was discovered that St Jean was a key position in Panzer Group West's new defence line and no less than eight infantry battalions were concentrated on a 4-mile front. The 4th Wiltshires would be on the right axis (southern) and 5th Wiltshires on the left (northern) axis. 4th Somerset LI were to follow up. All three battalions were mounted on top of Sherman tanks to put into practice the 'quick lift' technique of close infantry-armour support. By nightfall on 4 August after a move forward of 14 miles, the leading column reached Montchauvet. For the first time in the campaign the Recce Regiment was in action all day. They had encountered German Panther and Mark IV tanks, snipers, mortar stonks and Spandau fire, almost ambushed the Cornwalls and in Le Mesnil Auzouf were involved with celebrations of the liberated villagers. A number of brisk skirmishes were fought around La Tautainerie.

Maj. A.D. Parsons described the 4th Wiltshires' advance:

4 August. An uncomfortable feeling as we rode along closely packed on top of the Sherman tanks of B Sqn. 13/18th Hussars and our already overloaded wheeled and tracked vehicles. On the way to Mt Pinçon the countryside resembled Devon, steep and wooded hills, lanes with high banks, large undulating cornfields. Weather was very hot and sunny, the roads lay thick with white dust and dead horses. There was a new threat of roadside mines. 5 August. At Ecures a large

chateau was burning, the bridge was blown and both banks were mined. On the way to St Jean le Blanc up the steep slopes it was slow, costly bitter work by 'C' Company, eight hours of desperate fighting under a burning sun. Our FOO Capt. J. Fletcher was tireless, invaluable. L/Cpl. Jenkins ('A' Coy) commanded a platoon reduced to seven men, and for his daring later received the MM. All three NCOs had been hit. That night 'C' Coy dug in, hungry and exhausted with the sad task of burying their dead. As night fell the tanks withdrew. Our only friends the Gunners, Capt. Fletcher fed every man in the Company with biscuits, bullybeef and water from his carrier. Enemy tanks or SPs were defending St Jean-le-Blanc. A bitter and largely fruitless day's fighting in difficult country under the hot sun, little or no food. We lost twenty-two killed and thirty-nine wounded. A bitter day for the battalion.

Brig. Essame completed the story:

Maj. D.I.M. Robbins led his company across the stream (at St Jean le Blanc) and up the steep and wooded slope ahead. Almost immediately at close grips with a well-concealed and determined enemy. The pioneer platoon under heavy mortar and Nebelwerfer fire constructed a crossing over which a troop of tanks passed later in the day to aid the hard pressed company. 'A' Coy had advanced (into the outskirts) of St Jean le Blanc defended by well-entrenched infantry supported by tanks who fought to a finish amongst the orchards and cornfields. Although the Wiltshire battalion was across the stream it was clear the village was strongly held.

The GOC now ordered Brig. Mole to order Lt.-Col. Luce to disengage. The objective was Mt Pinçon, not the taking of St Jean-le-Blanc.

The 5th Wiltshires arrived from Montamy and Le Mesnil Auzouf with the objective on 6 August of securing the bridge over the stream half a mile short of the slopes of Hill 275. 'A' Company, which was leading, secured the crossroads near Duval. Next 'D' Company under Maj. R.A.C. Thomas passed through with orders to seize the bridge across the stream half a mile ahead.

'D' Coy succeeded in crossing the stream and forming a tight bridgehead but under intense fire. As Bn HQ took up a position in farm buildings, a salvo of shells arrived, killing our much loved chaplain, Revd 'Jimmy' Douglas, the cook 'Double' Davis and inflicting other casualties (remembers Harry Peace, the adjutant). Meanwhile two direct assaults on the bridge by 'C' Coy under Maj. E.R.B. Field failed with heavy losses. The CO returned at midnight from Brigade HQ with orders to attack and secure Mt Pinçon at 1430 hrs. On the following day reconnaissance patrols were sent out and discovered little in the dark except that enemy were still lurking in the Bn area.

'It was a bright moonlit night,' recalls Vic Coombs, 'A' Company, who was with the patrol, 'the enemy must have had this (road) corner under observation as they opened up with a machine gun and literally sprayed the area with bullets. Lt. Chittenden was killed instantly.' So Vic led the rest of the patrol back. 'During the night Maj. Thomas arrived at Bn HQ having run the gauntlet from 'D' Coy's bridgehead to report they were surrounded and their position was untenable. He was given permission to withdraw,' said Harry Peace. 'D' Company was extricated with great difficulty, with only thirty-eight survivors. The battalion casualties were now so high that 'A' and 'B' Companies were merged under Maj. Milne and 'C' and 'D' under Maj. Field. Maj. Thomas had been riddled with MG bullets during 'D' Company's withdrawal from the bridgehead.

THE TAKING OF MT PINÇON

In his memoirs Lt.-Gen. Brian Horrocks, GOC XXX Corps, wrote:

Every day we were closing up on Mt Pinçon. On 4, 5 and 6 August the 43rd Wessex Division slowly fought its way forward in very hot sultry weather against the most stubborn German resistance. Unfortunately their casualties particularly in officers were disastrously high. The 5th Wilts for instance were reduced to 500 men commanded by a comparatively junior officer. (When Lt.-Col. Pearson was killed, Harry Peace, the adjutant, took command.) By the evening of the 6th the 43rd had reached the foot of Mt Pinçon and it looked as though we were in for a tough fight before we got to the top as the whole feature was strongly held. . . . Seven weeks hard slogging in the thick bocage country had taken their toll and the gloss had gone from the magnificently trained army which had landed in Normandy . . . the cutting edge of a division becomes blunted. . . . This was obviously what had happened to the 43rd Wessex, one of the best trained divisions which has ever left our shores. . . . Yet the battle was going well. The weather was hot, the country damnable and the Germans in the Mt Pinçon area even more bloody minded than usual.

The crest is a plateau covered with heather and bracken interspersed with some birch trees. The higher slopes are well wooded and very steep on the southern and south-west sides. Small fields divided by thick hedges stretch down the lower slopes towards the stream at the foot. La Varinière and La Quesnée are two typical 'bocage' villages, strongly built of stone, surrounded by orchards and a labyrinth of sunken lanes and strong walls.

This was Brig. Essame's description of Mt Pinçon.

Rather optimistically Corps and Division expected the Wyverns to *complete* the capture of the summit by 1000 hrs on 6 August and then to advance 9 miles south on Condé-sur-Noireau!

Brig. Mole decided to attack on 6 August with 4th Somerset Light Infantry on the left on the line La Toque/La Roguerie and then to Point 365 and the road on the high ground on the eastern edge of the hill. On the right would be 5th Wiltshires continuing through La Varinière crossroads – a vital objective – and thence to the south-west of the mountain. 4th Wiltshire were in reserve near La Toque behind 4th Somerset LI.

Sydney Jary, a new platoon commander with 4th SLI, wrote in his book *18 Platoon*:

The approach march to our forming up place had been a nightmare of swirling abrasive dust, shelling and the stench of exhaust fumes from our tanks that transported us forward. We were due to attack at 1500 hrs with 'A' Coy leading on the right and 'B' Coy on the left. The ground before us descended to a small stream at the foot of Mt Pinçon then rose steeply through typical bocage fields with thick hedgerows to a thickly wooded area. The top of the hill was open and crowned with gorse. The forward platoons of 'B' Coy had barely crossed the stream when concentrated Spandau fire came from the front and from both flanks. There must have been about twelve machine guns firing at one time. This devastating firepower stopped the Bn dead in its tracks. There was no way forward or round it and no way to retire. Capt. Scammell commanding 'A' Coy was severely wounded and Maj. Thomas commanding 'B' Coy was killed in La Roguerie and their companies were badly cut up. As the afternoon turned to evening, shelling and mortaring increased. Shortly before dark a troop of tanks arrived . . . gave some brave close support.

Capt. Nicholls was a FOO with 94th Field Regiment supporting the Somersets:

The attack went well for the first few hundred yards and then very suddenly the leading company was pinned to the ground by at least eight well-sited machine guns. The company tried every way of locating and destroying the trouble but to no avail and lost many men in the process. The FOO there was Capt. Clarke with Bdr. Eveleigh, Bdr. Bell and gunner Jones. Clarke crept forward with Eveleigh and shouted fire orders back through him to the waiting carrier. Two Boche machine guns were shot up, but the enemy began to use heavy mortars and 105-mm guns against us. The situation was grim.

Cpl. Doug Proctor, 4th SLI, takes up the story:

As dusk fell a new plan was drawn up. The night air was chilly and misty and a smokescreen was laid across the entire valley at the foot of the mountain. This enabled 'C' and 'D'companies to regroup. The new plan was for each company to infiltrate the enemy positions advancing stealthily in single file. The night and darkness was our ally . . . the German soldier didn't relish night fighting. It seems incredible that a battalion of infantry having once been stopped for dead, could rise up like wraiths from the mist and slowly but inexorably advance to the top of the hill. Not one shot was fired against us. We slipped by their positions without being noticed. 'C' and 'D' companies were quickly followed up the hill by the remnants of 'A' and 'B'. On the summit we were cold, wet and thoroughly miserable being in shirtsleeve order. At about 7 a.m. a very welcome meal reached us brought up the hill via the 5th Wilts axis.

Around Point 365 they dug in. 'B' Squadron 13/18th Hussars soon joined them in thick fog.

The 5th Wiltshires started their attack west of La Varinière crossroads at 1430 hrs supported by 13/18th Hussars. Reduced to two companies by their losses of the previous day, once again they met with very heavy shell and mortar fire. Machine guns opened up from the orchards. The adjutant, Harry Peace, reported: 'Maj. Milner's company was to attack on the left and Maj. Field on the right. With the usual intense artillery bombardment some tanks succeeded in crossing the stream but the infantry were held up by well-sited MG and mortar fire. The CO immediately went forward to sort out the situation and encourage the men forward.' 'Pop' Pearson said to Harry, 'I have never been so frightened in my life.'

The CO walked into the farmyard and stopped to talk to me (wrote Sgt. Curly Coundwell, who had won the MM at Maltot). Noticing the rose in his helmet I said to him 'Why the red rose, Sir?' 'Ah,' he said, 'that is for Minden day.' (Col. Pearson was originally from the South Lancs.) So not to be outdone by a Lancastrian, being a Yorkshireman myself by birth, I picked a white rose from a nearby bush and stuck it on my helmet. He looked at me and laughed. I said 'We have our own little War of the Roses, Sir.' He said 'Not just yet, Sergeant. . . . Let's get this battle over first – my best wishes to you and your men – good luck.' Down the road the Colonel walked still twirling his walking stick.

He was followed by his Bren gun carrier with the IO, Lt. Keeling and the wireless scout car – the link with Battalion HQ in which were travelling Capt. Harry Peace and Capt. John McMath, the signals officer. 'Reaching the bridge, he saw his men taking cover in the stream and urged them on. They obeyed his command, up and over and then the CO fell, shot through the heart by a sniper. Cpl. Mackrell saw him fall, grabbed a Bren gun, fired a burst into a tree and the body of the sniper riddled with bullets came tumbling down.' This was John McMath's description.

Maj. J.F. Milne, CO of 'A/B' Company got too far ahead of his men and was taken prisoner. He feigned serious wounds, and later ran back and rejoined the battalion. Harry Peace took over command of the sadly diminished Wiltshires and together with Maj. E.R.B. Field, CO 'C/D' Company, inspired their men. Brig. Mole ordered them to take the crossroads at La Varinière at all costs.

L/Cpl. Ron Garner, HQ Company 5th Wilts:

With Norman at Forward HQ we dug furiously to make a suitable trench. Every few minutes a German MG would fire into the area, make us duck. After two feet down we struck water. Once a salvo of mortars landed. I dived into a sewer to find three other men in occupation – one reading his pocket Bible. (After Harry Peace the adjutant took command) our IO Lt. Keeling became adjutant. We had well over a hundred prisoners. A few of them were put to digging graves for our men who had fallen. They thought it was for themselves. 'Nobby' Clarke was mortally wounded, so was Nick Carter one of the snipers and George Harding was killed: he was a sniper, called up with me at Gloucester. We had a total of sixty-six men left from all the four rifle companies put together.

Sgt. 'Smudger' Smith had several adventures. 18 Platoon passed a bungalow house where the French lady owner asked, 'were we English soldiers? Yes, said the lads – proud as Punch – what we didn't realise the place had not been searched.' After dark the German soldiers hidden within came out behind 'D' Company and cut them off. Later he saw:

. . . an Airborne Major run the gauntlet on the bridge over the stream. The Germans were clever and cunning and let his carrier through. He brought with him – a dixie of rice pudding and the order 'Sorry, lads, you're cut off and it's every man for himself.' He didn't wait for the empty dixie – it was 'cheerio, lads, the best of luck.' Off he went to the bridge. He was shot but the lucky driver got through. (Later) One of our lads stepped on a string of seventy-seven A/Tank mines we had laid. He was like a burnt piece of toast, but still breathing, gurgling. We laid him in the hedge and said goodbye.

Another soldier wounded next to 'Smudger' at La Varinière crossroads the next day was Tommy Whittaker, who was the running 'pacer' to the famous miler, Sydney Wooderson. Poor Tommy had his hands blown off, but a Red Cross jeep took him back to the RAP. In a barn near the crossroads 'Smudger' found a German Opel car. The relieving battalion also found it – full of gold, watches, earrings and jewellery: 'We never had a smell of anything!'

Maj. Le Quesne, the battery commander supporting 5th Wilts, put down a large number of heavy defensive fire plans on all likely places including his ancestral village, La Quesnée. Harry Peace described him as 'playing the piano from one point to another. One German battalion of sixty men and four tanks had stopped at a crossroads to check their maps, forming up for a counter-attack. Only a few stragglers got through and they were seen off at hand grenade range.' The Middlesex played their part as Eric Codling notes: 'We rushed forward throwing caution to the winds to support the small band of 4 Wilts and 13/18th Hussars which had slipped through the enemy defences under cover of darkness up to the summit. OPs were on the heights to cause havoc to retreating Boche.'

The friendly artillery barrage had long outstripped the advance but the 13/18th Hussar tanks still there gave great help as the 5th Wiltshires forced their way into La Varinière and took a hundred prisoners between the bridge and the village. Despite enemy counter-attacks on the crossroads, the tanks and the infantry, now reduced to five officers and seventy men, held on grimly. But Harry Peace, who had inspired the grim defence, was badly wounded by heavy artillery fire.

Brig. Mole now ordered 5th Wiltshires to hold the crossroads and pass 4th Wiltshires through to capture Mt Pinçon. They were still 2 miles further back at Danvou, and Col. 'Ted' Luce had been told to 'take Mt Pinçon, *any way he liked!*' The 4th Wilts had had a very difficult start to their day. They had arrived back in reserve at dawn, dug in the stony red earth but their breakfast had been interrupted by heavy shelling causing many casualties to 'D' Company (ten KIA and twenty-nine wounded) and to the MMG Company of 8th Middlesex. Their concentration area was under full observation from enemy mortars a few hundred yards away.

Now occurred one of the most dramatic episodes of the Normandy battles. At 1800 hrs Lt.-Col. Dunkerley sent an armoured patrol of his 13/18th Hussar Shermans forward to scale the 'heights of Abraham'. From 'A' Squadron Capt. N.N.M. Denny, Lt. Elliott and Lt. Jennison's troops set off up a very narrow steep track. One tank overturned into a quarry, and another had its track blown off. Within half an hour under cover of a smokescreen, the 13/18th Hussars had seven tanks in an all-round defensive position on the summit. At 2000 hrs the CO arrived with the rest of the squadron – an audacious and brave adventure.

By about 2100 hrs 'B' Company of 4th Wiltshires led their assault on the mountain and Maj. A.D. Parsons recounts their trek:

Enemy resistance was slight and the chief difficulty was the physical effort of climbing, for the slope soon became very steep and covered with scrub. It was a strange feeling as we toiled up, heavily laden with weapons, ammunition, picks and shovels expecting to find ourselves surrounded at any moment. The sergeant (A.G. Jenkins) commanding the leading platoon very resourcefully told his men that they were not doing an *attack* but were going to relieve another unit already there! This materially helped the speed of the advance. As we neared the top a thick fog came down. We could see no landmarks but we found the (13/18th Hussar) tanks. They were relieved to see us! Germans could be heard shouting and digging close by. We were as tired as any troops could be and many of us fell asleep as we were digging positions in the rocky soil, falling headlong, pick in hand into the half dug trenches, dead to the world. (Col Ted Luce was first to reach the top at 2215 hrs, went back down again to cheer and encourage his men. The day's losses were thirteen KIA and forty-nine wounded.) For us the Mt Pinçon operation was bitter and fruitless. The day before St Jean-le-Blanc, the withdrawal following it and then an equally bitter battle to reach and hold the summit. Not a battle against the Germans, so much as against the burning sun, the choking dust, our parched throats and empty bellies, the craggy slopes and tangled thickets, the rocky earth and above all against our utterly weary bodies.

On their move from Danvou the good Samaritans were still around. Two FOOs of 224th Field Battery (Capts Townsend and Fletcher) fed two rifle companies and watered all four companies from their reserves in their OP carriers and handed out snacks to the tired, hungry, thirsty troops as they passed by.

Gen. Thomas had ordered 130th Brigade to make a diversionary move on the northern flank of Mt Pinçon to distract the attention of the enemy. As Brig. Essame pointed out: 'This contributed to the startling success of 129th Brigade.' Under their temporary CO, Maj. D.B. Rooke, 7th Royal Hampshire at 1100 hrs on 6 August started to make a frontal attack on the hamlets of Plecière, Roucamp and Pasty – 'C' Company on the right, 'D' on the left under Maj. Braithwaite. Against strong defences 'C' Company took very heavy casualties including all their officers. The battalion dug in around Plecière and battled against three enemy companies. Altogether in the last fortnight nine officers were casualties including three KIA.

In thick fog 7th Somersets relieved 4th Somersets on the crest of Mt Pinçon and by 1130 hrs 1st Worcesters had taken over from 4th Wiltshires. Lt.-Col. Harrison of the Worcesters was evacuated on the 6th suffering from battle exhaustion and the new CO was Lt.-Col. R.E. Osborne-Smith, late 2 i/c 4th Wiltshires. Each Worcester had been ordered to carry four unfilled sandbags to make two-men slit trenches easier and quicker to construct in rocky terrain, but were also warned not to make themselves too comfortable – as funk holes, instead of fighting 'compartments'. The top of Mt Pinçon was described as a moles' colony. The Worcesters and Wiltshires arrived in darkness and feverish digging went on. Albert Kings wrote:

> In the climb up Mt Pinçon I thought I had reached the limits of human endurance. I had five magazines for the Bren, plus a bandolier of fifty rounds and the utility pouches of four more magazines off my No. 2. He was much older than I, invariably got left behind, Percy Hopkins was his name. The sweat ran into my eyes. I could hardly see. I felt absolutely shattered. Digging in was impossible in chalky soil. We lost Lt. Booth that day killed by 88-mm shell.

> I was wounded on the top of Mt Pinçon (wrote Maj. K.J. Whitehead, OC 'C' Company 7th SLI), a shrapnel wound in the chest – from a shell which wounded other members of my company including Capt. Pinn and killed L/Cpl. Reilly and Pte. Oldfield of the mortars. I thought I was going to die. All wounded people, I am told, are the same. The shock stuns their senses and makes them silly. I wanted someone to be firm and kind with me. I went and sat on the edge of my slit trench. Soon our stretcher-bearers arrived, bound me up and at once I felt better. Comforting pair of men – methodical, efficient and stern. Shells were still raining down. (By jeep the wounded were taken a mile over bumpy heather to the foot of the hill where) three brewed-up Sherman tanks exploded violently on the main road. An exploding tank is a strange sight. As each shell explodes it leaves a 'smoker's ring' of quivering

smoke about it. It is frightening too. We wounded cared not a bit, wounded never do. The RAP was a haven of rest. MO cool but obviously upset by his casualties, settled inside a big barn. Tea was being made. Padre Richards moved around, kind, sympathetic, steadying us with just the right words. The night was spent with yelling Germans on either side. Our own wounded are so patient. The Germans yell with fear.

From the top of Mt Pinçon Pte. O'Connell recalls: 'If one braved the still falling mortars, bullets and occasional shells one could see a great view of France that was won, and the France still to be fought for. To the west big dust clouds where the Yanks advancing.' Pte. J.V. Webb had joined the Wiltshires from 5th Royal Berkshires 'just after the carnage of Mt Pinçon. We followed the line of a hedge until we found 'A' Coy dug in there. About twenty-five men were resting in their slit trenches, asked them if they were part of 'A' Coy. I still remember the look in the fellow's eyes as he answered "We *are* fucking 'A' Company."

Lt.-Gen. Horrocks, 'Jorrocks' to many, took over command of XXX Corps on 3 August and he wrote in his memoirs:

Mt Pinçon had assumed an almost impregnable and sinister character. It was the cornerstone of the enemy defences in Normandy. Its capture made all the difference to me. From now on we could overlook the Germans. On the top with my chief gunner (CCRA) Stewart Rawlins beside me with 300 guns at the end of our wireless mast, we could concentrate in a few minutes the fire down if any units were held up. It was a very hard time for the gunners who were never out of action day or night. They formed two teams for each gun rounding up cooks, drivers, orderlies all roped in to serve the guns.

Mt Pinçon will always be remembered as a major battle honour for the Wyverns.

28

LE PLESSIS GRIMAULT

Although the summit of Mt Pinçon had been taken there was one more battle to be fought on the lower slopes. Around La Varinière crossroads intense, continuous and accurate shelling still rained down. The new objective was the capture of the straggling village of Le Plessis Grimault. No less than seven roads feed in including the main road from Aunay (where 7th Armoured Division were still struggling) south to Condé-sur-Noireau.

Late on the afternoon of 7 August, Brig. Peter Essame arrived at 5th DCLI HQ and said to their CO: 'George (Taylor) I want you to capture Le Plessis Grimault, an important communication centre at the southern foot of Mt Pinçon.' Col. Taylor called it Operation Matador, which turned out to be one of the classic and successful operations in Normandy. First of all the Worcesters moved down Mt Pinçon to hold the crossroads at La Varinière. Then a noisy feint attack was made by 'B' Squadron of 4/7th Dragoons under Maj. Steve Jenkins and Lt. Welch's platoon of 'C' Company of the Cornwalls who would advance eastwards from La Varinière. Finally the bulk of the Cornwalls would make a silent night attack from the slopes of Mt Pinçon southwards into the northern sector of Le Plessis Grimault. Maj. Harry Parker, 'A' Company, after a forced march of 4 miles would be the main assault team followed by 'C' and 'B' Companies. A block barrage from the divisional artillery and a medium regiment plus mortars and machine guns were to cover the right flank. The barrage opened at 2130 hrs as light was fading, and the Shermans spitting BESA fire advanced on the village.

George Taylor recalls: 'It was now dark. Suddenly there was a deafening explosion as an enemy ammo store exploded in a fury of gold and red flame. This magnificent bonfire acted as a beacon for the attack. The night was alight with tracer bullets but heavy mortar fire was coming down on our tanks.' At 1010 hrs the silent Cornwalls entered from the north as the barrage stopped. Although their PIATs had been destroyed while forming up, Maj. Parker ordered his 2-in mortars to fire, plus every other weapon, at two enemy tanks in the centre of the village. A mortar shell landed on an ammunition lorry replenishing the tanks, and ten seconds later one of them was enveloped in flames and the second withdrew southwards.

It was close quarter work and a lot of grenades were used. George Taylor again: 'After an hour's fighting the defence collapsed. Harry described it as a "sweet battle"; he was a warrior. I will never forget the sight of enemy prisoners being marched down the village street by the glow of burning houses. German dead (thirty-one) and wounded lay scattered about. The village had been held by two rifle companies. We captured 125 of them and our losses were two men killed, one missing and five wounded. No tanks of ours were knocked out.'

Two counter-attacks in the morning were beaten off, but unfortunately Harry Parker was wounded in the jaw and shoulder by 88mm shell fragments. The 62 Royal Tiger tank captured was the first of its kind to be destroyed in Normandy. Lt.-Col. George Taylor was awarded the DSO for this fine action.

On the 8th and 9th the 1st Worcesters under Lt.-Col. Osborne-Smith had two nasty and costly little battles. The first was to clear the pocket between the 'Hell Fire' crossroads at La Varinière east towards Le Plessis Grimault. 204th Field Company RE under Maj. Evill were clearing the road with armoured bulldozers when they were caught by heavy machine gun fire and their five Brens were swamped by a dozen Spandaus. So the Worcesters took over, as Pte. Albert Kings relates:

The night before the attack at La Varinière was a bad one for the Bn, shelling was particularly severe and many casualties resulted. Jerry was getting desperate now. We had no sleep that night (7 August) but still next day with 'B' Coy (under the 'Mad Major' Algy Grubb and supported by 'C' Sqd 4/7 Dragoon Guards) forward, 12 platoon leading, we were to spearhead the breakout. 'B' Coy's strength after this attack dwindled to only twenty-eight. This was one of my better days, for some reason I was not afraid, any other time I was almost petrified with fear and I don't mind admitting it. My Platoon Commander was badly wounded, that upset me. (Albert's company took eighty prisoners.) My anger was very real. Afterward Hoppy (Percy Hopkins No. 2 on Albert's Bren gun team) said 'I thought you were going to kill those prisoners when you wanted them to run.' But for his calming influence I may have done just that: I was in no mood for messing about. Capt. Newman was also badly wounded (as were Lts Everitt and Henry; Lt. Brath, the carrier platoon CO, was missing). Cpl. Holbourne had a near miss, a bullet went through one of his ears, they don't come much closer.

Pte. T.C. Dutton, 17 Platoon 'C' Company recalls: 'The crossroads was a hotspot. We were dug in in a small orchard facing La Quesnée, shelled and mortared constantly. Enemy dead and burning tanks nearby. I placed a gas cape over three dead Wiltshires – two stretcher-bearers and a casualty on a stretcher.'

The second attack for the Worcesters came on the 9th when they were ordered to clear 'the ulcer of La Quesnée by La Varinière' as Brig. Essame wrote:

The place was strewn with dead cattle bloated and stinking. In the orchard before the village stood a burnt-out German SP gun with the charred and decaying bodies of the crew still inside. All around chickens, ducks and geese roamed, tame and unconcerned. Close quarter fighting between 'A' Coy under Maj. D.Y. Watson and an exceptionally truculent German garrison continued until a late hour. The strong point was a maze of cunningly concealed earthworks, sited under piles of brushwood, cornstacks and concealed banks.

William Gould, signaller, wrote:

'C' Coy had been given the job of left flank protection. We ran into most severe opposition. An NCO from 'C' Coy directed us into a copse. There we found a rather wild-looking Maj. Matthews who was in a desperate mood. He had lost a considerable number of his men and things were very serious. He roundly cursed me for taking so long to catch up with our field telephones. At last he could inform Bn HQ of his plight and ask for immediate aid.

A group of twenty to thirty Germans made signs of surrender so Capt. K.R.H. James with a handful of Worcesters, walked out into no man's land to receive them. When they were well out in the open, to his surprise and horror a German officer in field boots and stiff cap appeared with two belligerent soldiers armed with sub-machine guns. Capt. James said in German: 'You are my prisoner.' German officer: 'No, you are my prisoner.' James: 'Your men wish to surrender to me and I demand that you do so also.' German officer: 'Your men wish to surrender to me.' Pause, then everybody scuttled back to their positions like rabbits. RSM Hurd (over fifty) a great egg hunter, often arrived back at Battalion HQ with snipers he had caught. The captured prisoners now included French, Polish, Czech, even Chinese. In the two-day fighting the Worcesters had 230 casualties.

To protect the right flank of 50th Tyne and Tees Division, who were to advance towards Condé-sur-Noireau from Le Plessis Grimault, on 9 August 7th Somersets were ordered to capture four hamlets 1 mile south of Mt Pinçon – Les Hameaux, Le Haussay, Hameau au Roi and Le Saussay. 'D' Company (Maj. Young) was directed on Le Haussay on the right, 'A' Company towards Les Hameaux on the left with 'A' Squadron 4/7th Royal Dragoon Guards in support. Eventually the attack started under the usual friendly barrage and unfriendly retaliating mortars and 88s. All the tracks were mined, the hedgerows and trees made for tank obstacles, but the Pioneers cleared a safe lane.

A six-hour battle ended in total success. By 1530 hrs 'D' Company had advanced 1,200 yds and taken Les Hameaux and Le Haussay, but 'A' Company under Maj. Baker had defended bocage hedgerows in front of them. Capt. Baden with the carrier platoon on the right flank fought his way through and then 'C' Company under Capt. Bailey pushed ahead to capture Hameau au Roi. Finally 'B' Company burst through the tangle of orchards, hedgerows and farms to advance 900 yds and seize Le Saussay.

And Pte. O'Connell with 13th Platoon recalls: 'we had a task with our carriers of collecting the dead of that advance and bringing them back to a point for burial by our Padre. We were offered a reward if we ever found and delivered the sights of a German mortar. There was no success. We flew a Wyvern flag, or Pregnant Prawn as we lovingly described our Divisional sign, from our carrier.'

By 1830 hrs the Somersets had taken all their objectives, taking 242 prisoners but suffering 79 casualties. John Meredith wrote: 'As Capt. U.S. Bailey, Lt. E.F. Larret (Canloan) both wounded were brought back to the RAP at Bn HQ, the CO, Lt.-Col. Nichol smiled at them, "What, you too Larret?" "Yes, sir, I'm sorry, sir." I remember Bailey and Larret apologising for being wounded as though it was their fault. As ever the CO's conduct of the battalion was superb.' On the 10th they captured Crépigny and advanced 1,000 yds to the south. Even when units were not fighting a pitched battle they still remained 'in action'. On the 9th Sgt. Wally Caines, 4th Dorsets, wrote in his diary:

Weather still blistering hot. Maj. Jimmy Grafton, 'A' Coy CO, Capt. Andrews (Canloan) went out on a patrol but suffered several casualties. On their return Andrews, the RMO and a NCO went back to try to rescue a missing man. The Jerries had paid a visit to his corpse for they had removed his socks and boots. A Spandau opened up. Andrews received a burst straight through the head and was as dead as a door nail. A great character who feared nothing, gave up his job as IO to fight with the boys of a gallant company.

He was awarded the MC posthumously.

The Recce Regiment (Fifth Glosters) had now had their first non-stop week in action and in a score of villages – La Tautainerie, Duval, Danvou, St Jean-le-Blanc, St Pierre-la-Vieille – had fought brisk armoured car actions and had had a dozen officers and men killed in action, including Lts Banks, Vache and Withers. Several MCs had been earned and Sgt. Carleton and Sgt. Darvel were awarded MMs. Lt. D.E.R. Scarr recorded their routine:

The days were long and the nights were short. A troop was in reserve one day out of four. It was usually dark – past ten o'clock when the troop reached harbour. Each individual was tired, very tired and faced with the prospect of a 4 a.m. reveillé and another strenuous day ahead, his only wish was to crawl in between blankets and get some sleep. The Troop Sergeant, the busiest man of all, collected fresh rations and then split them down to vehicles. The guard for the night was detailed and several weary troopers would curse their fate. Maintenance consisted of drivers groping in the dark to check their petrol tanks, pour in one or more jerricans. For a mechanical defect the fitters would be called in, sometimes working through the night, masking their light with a tarpaulin. The Troop Leader would wait outside the CV (Command Vehicle) waiting to receive his orders for the next day . . . four hours of sleep was good going especially if one could take one's boots off. The month of August seemed a life-time to most people.

The Recce Regiment carried out a dozen different, dangerous tasks. First into a village which might draw fire from a tank or

88-mm and inevitably be one-sided, first to go up untrodden lanes risking mines and ambush, lifting mines around crossroads or at bridges, over culverts or rivers, frequently under mortar fire. With their BESAs they could destroy enemy infantry but often they had to leave the comparative safety of their armoured car to carry out a recce on foot armed with a Bren, and they were always on the blower to squadron, to regiment, sometimes to brigade and division, pinpointing their positions and sending back information.

29

OPERATION BLACKWATER

This was the codename for the final phase of the Wyvern's advance southwards from Mt Pinçon towards the River Noireau, there to form a bridgehead.

There were signs that the enemy was withdrawing, slowly but inevitably against the enormous Allied pressure. By the morning of 11 August the high ground overlooking the River Druance, 5 miles south of Mt Pinçon, was secured by 214th Brigade. On the left 50th Tyne and Tees Division too was pushing south from Cauville toward St Pierre-la-Vieille and the high ground beyond. 129th Brigade had entered Cauville and pushed another mile south-east, although 5th Wiltshire had a tough night action against La Vardière. It needed two attacks backed by divisional artillery to close this pocket, taking numerous prisoners. The next day it was the turn of 7th Somersets to take neighbouring Mt Gaultier and the Cornwalls to occupy La Trulandière village near Culey-le-Patry.

Maj. Harvey, OC 'B' Company, and Maj. Young, 'D' Company 7th Somersets, both distinguished themselves in the task of dealing with Mt Gaultier under machine gun and mortar fire. The former played football rather successfully with his own hand grenade, kicking it into a German slit trench. Lt. D.F. Bean, OC the Pioneer Platoon, helped clear minefields under fire but died of wounds received gallantly shielding a wounded man from mortar fire.

The first objective was the village of La Trulandière, then to the bigger settlement of Culey-le-Patry (recalled George Taylor, the CO). H-hour was 2000 hrs. Rucke-Keene's 'C' Coy kept the attention of the enemy holding a long ridge protecting Culey, and 'D' Coy under Maj. John Fry skilfully outflanked by a covered approach round the left flank. Lt. R. Prowse quickly eliminated MG posts, drove the enemy back across the River Orne taking twenty prisoners, leaving ten enemy dead. Lt. Prowse suffered the personal trauma of having an anti-tank missile pass between his legs. The only wound he suffered was to his dignity.

That same evening 4th Wiltshire under Maj. J.E.L. Corbyn and 4th Somersets were in action clearing the spurs and ridges south-east of St Pierre-la-Vieille in rather confusing conditions. As Brig. Essame pointed out: 'The country was close and undulating, the maps conveyed little information of any value. Nothing was known of the enemy.' Dawn came on the 13th with heavy mist and from west of Les Forges 4th Wiltshire advanced eastwards for 4,000 yds to capture a spur of high ground south-east of Cauville. On the way Maj. A.D. Parsons, OC 'A' Company, lost touch with the supporting tanks in the woods and fields, and found himself on a hill – his objective. In the valley below was an obvious target. The 5.5-in medium shells which he called down fell – due to the inaccurate maps – on 'A' Company. Moreover 'B' Company 600 yds to the east were efficiently attacked by RAF Typhoons. And enemy SP guns, now that the mist had cleared, opened up at close range on the unfortunate 'C' Company Wiltshires. Heavy casualties included the MO, Capt. Binnington, Lt. C.J. Mills and CSM Webb, who had served eighteen years with the regiment. By 1700 hrs most of the key ridge was taken. Since 9 August the battalion had had forty-nine casualties including four officers.

Ron Garner, Intelligence Section 5th Wiltshires, remembers:

During the afternoon (of the 13th) our signals intercepted a message from Monty saying 'the end was in sight'. Naturally we could not see this but later realised this was the beginning of the Falaise pocket. News came through that 3,000 enemy vehicles had been shot up during the day by the RAF (including some of the Wyverns). On the 14th the Bn moved to La Rue in a valley near Condé. Hundreds of French refugees came to greet us and to beg for food. They were a pitiful sight and we couldn't very well refuse: out came our tins of sardines and corned beef. What they wanted most of all was bread. They were given army dog biscuits and seemed to enjoy them quite a lot.

Ron also met the underground Maquis equipped with captured German rifles or British Sten guns dropped by the RAF. In a 2-mile long tunnel near battalion HQ were 2,000 French refugees from Condé.

Proussy was a long straggling village on the main road south from Aunay only 3 miles north of Condé, and it was strongly held. 5th Dorsets were given the task of clearing it after a fighting patrol had, on the night of the 13th, reported the village still occupied. The battalion attack went in on the morning of the 14th under a rolling barrage from divisional artillery and Middlesex mortars under Maj. Kaines. All went well with 165 prisoners taken, but Lt. Channell was killed, Capt. J.L. Betts and 2nd Lt. Champion were wounded. Maj. Mead then seized the hamlet of Les Haies half a mile ahead. The RMO, Capt. J.N. Blair, had been losing articles of food and a bottle of wine, and finally discovered the thief to be a German soldier hiding in the RAP during the battle!

Lt.-Col. B.A. Coad was now temporarily brigadier of 130th Brigade and directed 7th Hampshires supported by 'B' Squadron Sherwood Rangers to seize another large, straggling village – St Denis-de-Mère, a mile south-east of Proussy and 2 miles north-east of Condé. Under a massive barrage of six field regiments and three medium regiments the attack started at 1400 hrs. Despite the opposition of four SP guns which destroyed four Shermans, the village was cleared by 1900 hrs and seventy-four prisoners of 752nd Grenadier Regiment were captured, although the Hampshires took twenty-nine casualties.

Gen. Thomas planned to cross the River Noireau near Cahan where there were road and rail bridges. A long plateau dominates the north bank of the river with a network of parallel roads running east–west. 4th Dorsets were now directed on Point 201 which, on the north bank, overlooks the Cahan crossings. By nightfall after a difficult advance of 1 /2 miles through typical bocage hamlets, Point 201 was reached, though many enemy pockets were bypassed. Wally Caines reported: 'Many prisoners a pitiable sight to see, unshaven, hungry, and every one badly clothed.'

The RAF, and perhaps the Germans too, had done a thorough job of destroying both rail and road bridges. Minefields were likely to hamper the forming up before the crossing. The Noireau is a small tranquil stream with steep wooded heights on top of which are the three fortified villages of Berjou, La Canet and Le Hamel. The objective now given to 214th Brigade was a track winding obliquely from near the railway station (400 yds west of the railway bridge) leading up to the village of Berjou on the crest, then 2 miles south-east to Point 237. The crossing of the river had to be made in two places, one near the Berjou railway station at Les Bordeaux, the other beside a factory at Le Rocray. The river was 20 yds wide, about 3 ft deep – thus impassable for vehicles. The divisional gunners were situated at Grand Beron and to the rear of Les Bruyères-de-Clecy. The historian of 179th Field Regiment RA: 'We crossed the River Noireau which was a gunner's nightmare. All the bridges had been blown so our OPs had to go on foot, working their way up the wooded slopes of the opposite bank – however, it was done, and after a very nasty two days the enemy were in full retreat.' And BSM Fred Fowler, 94th Field: 'We move again to cornfields, weather very hot. We are driving for the Orne at Athis, still colossal concentrations, barrages and smoke screens.' The Worcesters were to take the high ground around Berjou on the right (west) and 7th Somersets were to cross at Le Rocray and then concentrate on Le Hamel to the left (east). H-Hour was to be at 1800 hrs with 5th DCLI as brigade reserve. 8th Middlesex with heavy MG and mortars were of course involved in the heavy fire plan. At daylight on the 15th 'C' Squadron of the Recce Regiment moved out on the left flank towards St Marc d'Ouilly. No. 9 Troop reconnoitred towards Condé and No. 10 towards Pont Erembourg. Progress was much delayed by mines and several armoured cars and carriers were blown up. Lt. Norman Jackson was with 'A' Squadron:

> Heavy casualties suffered in earlier actions had depleted the strength of the Assault Troop. The Squadron Leader's orders were – No. 2 troop on right to capture Berjou, 3 troop on left to drive through the forest, work round east of the high ground. The armoured cars and carriers crossed the Bailey bridge. . . . Almost simultaneously the enemy's heavy shells and mortar bombs rained down – accurate and damaging. Lt. A.B. Schofield OC 2 Troop was killed by a shell burst in the trees above his turret. The radio message 'Sunray oboe two killed' was a profound shock. Alan had been with us for three years. It was a bad start to the day's work.

The Worcesters started off at 1830 hrs and waded across the river near the blown railway bridge under the heavy barrage. Despite a shower of mortar bombs 'A' Company pushed up the steep track through woods that very hot midsummer evening, clearing Teller mines on their way. William Gould wrote:

> At the river crossing Jerry brought down on us a most heavy bombardment of shells and mortars and the casualties started to mount. It was more than flesh and blood could take to go through this fire screen and panic was much in evidence.

My team of (signal) line layers indicated it would be wise to withdraw. Maj. Souper, CO 'A' Coy, a splendid half-miler having been an Oxford blue, seeing the danger walked calmly forward in the middle of the road, urged us forward. Up to this point I had been trembling in my shoes. Responding to such bravery I forced myself alongside him and my chaps backed me up. In a flash we had crossed the stream and were on our way.

Two other companies followed up and the battalion position was consolidated but Maj. Matthews of 'C' Company was wounded.

Brig. Essame described the attack on the left flank: ' "D" Coy under Maj. S.C.W. Young carried the mill in the face of lively small arms and mortar fire and established a small bridgehead on the south bank. "C" Coy under Maj. D.M.B. Durie, also caught in Spandau and mortar fire from the far bank fought their way forward across the railway towards a commanding bluff. The battalion dug in under harassing fire on a 1,000-yd perimeter.' The next day they saw evidence of the tremendous support fire put down by 8th Middlesex 4.2-in mortars and MMG – several hundred German dead were counted in the area.

The Cornwalls now followed up behind the Worcesters as George Taylor reported:

. . . with 'D' Coy leading, David Willcocks (IO) and our artillery BC, Tom Brewis and (Maj.) John Fry we went over the broken bridge, up the road past the railway station, through the gardens at the foot of the river bridge. The enemy mortar bombs exploded with deafening roars 200 yds to the right. We waded across the shallow river and moved into the gloomy wood, still burning from the bombardment: the acid smoke caught in our lungs.

By darkness George Taylor had made contact with Maj. 'Doc' Watson of the Worcesters and 'the Cornwalls dug in forming a solid triangle on the edge of the plateau. Six companies were sited cheek by jowl only 80 yds away from the enemy. They harassed us with mortar fire and losses among the Worcesters began to mount.' But no artillery support as the heavy wireless sets could not be carried up the hills, no vehicles, no tanks, and no anti-tank guns had yet crossed the Noireau. The river crossings were under constant enemy fire but the divisional sappers, as usual, did their stuff. 553rd Field Company built a Bailey bridge across the site of the demolished bridge and 204th Field Company with a waterproofed bulldozer, three tipper lorries of flexboards, four landing-stage units and two boat units, built a tank ford and three trestle bridges, having had to clear dense minefields including booby-trapped mines and the discovery of the lethal TMIZ 43 igniter. The CRE, Lt.-Col. Pike, was severely injured when his recce car overturned in the darkness, and 204th Field Company lost a complete section to gun fire and mines. Several trucks and tracked vehicles were blown up. It was a long, hard, cold, moonless night with everyone drenched by a thunderstorm at 0200 hrs.

On the morning of the 16th determined enemy rearguards of the 986th Grenadier Regiment launched – predictably – counter-attacks, as George Taylor recounts:

> The BRRRRRRRRP of the deadly fusillade of MG 42s sited in depth – the sound of a giant tearing up monstrous playing cards in his powerful hands. They began with an infantry attack on the left-hand company of Worcesters. Maj. Matthews, their CO, was badly wounded in the arm. Casualties were mounting among the DCLI and the Worcesters and a steady stream of men were being evacuated from left to right in front of the wood. The edge of the wood became a death trap. The Germans attacked on the extreme right of 'D' Coy. They could now cover the crucial track leading down the hill. Communication to the rear was cut off. Just in time a welcome roar from behind as the leading tanks of the Sherwood Rangers under Lt.-Col. Christopherson arrived. So too did Cpl. Northcott the Mess corporal who had braved the battle to get hot food to us. All at once there was a picnic atmosphere.

But Leslie Skinner, padre with the Sherwood Rangers, noted in his diary:

> During the nine-day costly struggle in Operation Blackwater the Sherwoods had fourteen KIA and twelve wounded, of whom seventeen were in 'C' Squadron. The view from Berjou looking down on the deep valley of the Noireau and countryside was beautiful indeed. It was easy to appreciate why mortar and shellfire had been so accurate. The Germans could see every move that we had made.

The gunner FOOs were now on the top of the hill so the two battalion commanders, Osborne-Smith of the Worcesters and George Taylor of the Cornwalls, hatched their battle plan. The Worcesters would capture Berjou where an entire enemy company were dug in with twelve tanks or SP guns while the Cornwalls would clear the left edge of the ridge including a troublesome hump which dominated the whole area – as George Taylor relates:

Brig. Essame approved my plan, said increased fire power would be available to support the Worcesters' attack. 'A' Coy took the ridge (Les Monts) supported by tanks. A large number of the enemy were killed or captured in the process. In a farm on the plateau lay the bodies of five of our men. Around them were nineteen dead Germans. Covered by the great artillery barrage the Worcesters swept forward, taking Berjou and a considerable number (sixty) of prisoners.

It was a perfect attack across 400 yds of flat tableland backed by the Sherman BESAs and by 1730 hrs the village was taken. Two rare species – German officers – were captured but the gallant 'old man' of the Worcesters, RSM Hurd MM, who took in thirty prisoners himself, was killed by an 88-mm shell. Sixteen Worcesters lie buried beneath the calvary on Berjou ridge. Pte. Dutton wrote: 'Although we were only half a battalion in strength we put that attack in with as much effort as possible, thinking after this one we may have a few days rest out of the fighting.'

The Cornwalls too had suffered that day, losing sixteen killed, seventeen wounded and two missing. Since 26 June they had lost thirty-seven officers (120 per cent, as George Taylor pointed out) killed and wounded, and 508 other rank casualties – the brunt being borne by the rifle companies, as usual.

On the brigade's left flank 7th SLI with Sherwood Rangers tank support fought their way through a group of small villages south of the Noireau; many prisoners were taken and by nightfall they had linked up with the Cornwalls 2 miles south of the river. La Bijude, Le Bas Hamel, Le Vardon and La Batonnière were strongly-held hamlets but at 0800 hrs on 17 August 'C' Company entered them and took ten prisoners, and the Pioneers started to clear yet more minefields. 'A' Company ran into serious difficulties near Le Canet, but tanks and infantry worked together in a half-hour battle and then continued along the road east to La Bijude.

Brig. Essame paid tribute to the French resistance movement, particularly the Raymond 1929 group operating from St Remy under M. Raymond Pierre, who supplied detailed information about the enemy's dispositions, minefields, state of the crossings of the rivers Orne and Noireau, and provided guides with local knowledge of roads and tracks.

The battle for the crossing of the River Noireau and the capture of the Berjou–Le Hamel ridge was over. The Recce Regiment, which had a busy and dangerous three days, advanced to St Honorine-la-Chardonne, Segrie Fontaine on the River Orne and on the 18th reached Athis and linked up with the Inns of Court of 11th Armoured Division. 5th Wiltshires occupied St Honorine-la-Chardonne to the sound of church bells, and 4th Somersets had a similar welcome in La Fertie. The division had its first taste of the enthusiastic days of genuine 'liberation' when the population gave them kisses, embraces, wine, calvados, flowers and fruit (often thrown), which will always be remembered by those who were there.

Ron Garner, 5th Wilts, wrote in his journal:

St Honorine-la-Chardonne was the first inhabited village we had liberated, the population was about four thousand. As the first troops entered the village, the church bells began ringing and men, women and children ran into the streets to greet us. The pavements were lined with the inhabitants offering us buckets and buckets of cider, calvados and abundant fruit. The German troops had left two hours before. A French liaison officer arrived to take charge of the administration. This village turned into a rest area for us. We had cinema shows and ENSA shows for entertainment.

A few miles further south the bulk of the German 7th Army was about to be trapped in the triangle around Trun, Chambois and Argentan. The famous Falaise – Argentan gap was never quite closed by the British, Canadian, American and Polish forces there converging. But backed by the full ferocious weight of the Allied airforces for five days the most appalling slaughter took place. On 22 August Gen. Model, the new C.-in-C. Army Group West, ordered a general retreat – the day before Gen. Montgomery in a personal message to all troops announced 'a definite, complete and decisive victory.' 130th Brigade moved to the Chambois area on the 22nd and could see some of the dreadful carnage at close

Montgomery visits 43rd Divisional HQ with Maj Gen Thomas (second from right) and his ADC, Pat Spencer Moore (extreme left).
(Imperial War Museum B12107)

A battered church in Cheux. *(Author's Collection)*

Hill 112: the Crown of Thorns. *(Author's Collection)*

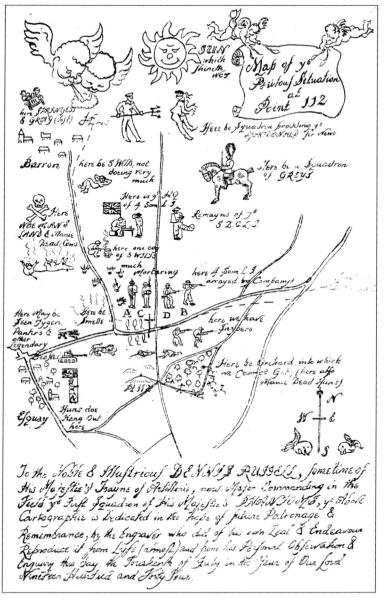

An unusual cartoon viewpoint of Operation Jupiter. *(Author's Collection)*

The Wyvern memorial on Hill 112. *(Author's Collection)*

Bloody Maltot. *(Author's Collection)*

The advance towards Mt Pinçon showing a knocked-out German tank.
(Author's Collection)

A Class 9 raft lands on the far side of the River Seine below the ruined road bridge. *(IWM BU197)*

A German column retreating from Meersen on 7 September 1944. *(Doug Proctor)*

Men of the 5th Wiltshires wait in the streets of Nijmegen before crossing the bridge and continuing the advance towards Arnhem. *(IWM B10274)*

Driel church tower was used as an observation post by both sides in September 1944. *(Doug Proctor)*

Neder Rijn: the factory and high ground near Oosterbeek were the objectives after the Dorsets' crossing. *(Doug Proctor)*

In the mud: a Limber and Quad of 94 Field Regiment RA. *(Douglas Goddard)*

General Crerar with some of his Divisional Commanders in Cleve during the Canadian Army offensive, February 1945. Left to right: Brigadier Elrington, 53rd Division; General Thomas, 43rd Division; General Horrocks, XXX Corps; General Barber, 15th Division; General Crerar, First Canadian Army; General Spry, 3rd Canadian Division; General Simonds, II Canadian Corps; General Matthews, 2nd Canadian Division.

Germany at last: a Bren Carrier of the 5th Wiltshires enters Bauchem. (*IWM B11946*)

Monty inspects men of the Somerset Light Infantry. *(WM BU8270)*

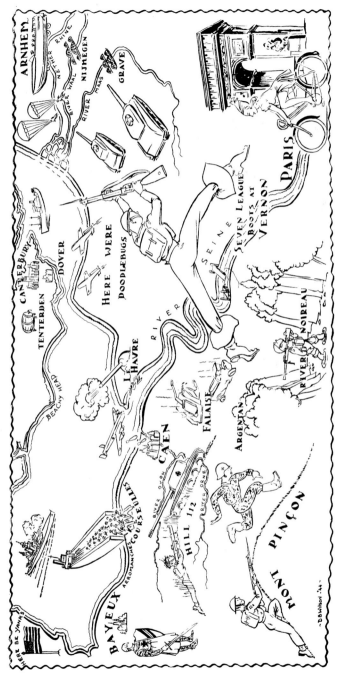

Fighting Wessex Wyverns' Christmas card, 1945.

The 5th Dorsets in the battle for Cleve. *(IWM)*

The 4th Wiltshires entering Cleve with 224 OP of 94 Field Regiment RA.

Prisoners captured by the 43rd Recce Regiment in Materborn.
(Author's Collection)

The 5th Dorsets cross the Rhine in Buffaloes. *(IWM BU2452)*

Victory parade, Bremerhaven. The 5th Dorsets march past Lt-Gen Brian Horrocks. (*Maurice Edwards*)

quarters. Ten thousand German troops were killed and fifty thousand more put in the bag. But a third of Model's Army escaped to fight another day.

Sgt. Sam Beard, 179th Field Regiment RA:

We fired 600 rounds per gun into the Falaise pocket. The observation and reconnaissance vehicles returning to our lines were washed down with disinfectant to remove human and animal debris from them. Dead friend and foe alike – for there were many French civilians trapped in the area – lay in heaps, their bodies mixed together with horses and domestic animals, filling the sunken lanes where they had sought shelter. So intense was the carnage of man and beast, that all the dead animals could not be buried and later these piles of rotting flesh were bulldozed into heaps and set on fire with petrol.

5th Dorsets moved in TCVs to St Eugenie to prevent infiltration by stragglers from the Forêt de Gouffern and to help seal the Falaise 'gap'. Maj. Maurice Edwards in his regimental history wrote of 'the miles and miles of burnt-out tanks, cars and vehicles – many of them loot from France, carts with the horses dead in the traces were ample evidence of the death of the German 7th Army in this valley of death and destruction.'

Wally Caines, battalion signals sergeant 4th Dorsets, wrote in his diary:

22 Aug. Near Falaise, massed slaughter had taken place by Typhoon Fighter Bombers. The recce party passed through this area. We travelled one road and actually our vehicle travelled over the top of many crushed German dead bodies . . . how that lot looked and stunk, dead bodies were running over with maggots and flies – it was indeed a ghastly sight seeing these dead Nazis bursting in the blistering heat of the day. The road was about 1½ miles long. Never before had I seen or smelt anything like it.

The battle for Normandy was over.

30

OPERATION NEPTUNE

The Seine Crossing

The Wyverns had a few days of relative peace at the end of nearly eight weeks of savage fighting. Some reflected on the future. Lt.-Col. Tilley, 4th Dorsets, wrote home to his wife on 21 August: 'I feel we will receive one or two bloody noses yet in our chase as the Hun is a damned good fighter. The German prisoners from SS units still seem as arrogant as ever.' He was quite right. Although optimists talked of the war being over by Christmas, the realists knew that there was a lot of fight left, far more than anyone really expected. On the same day Lt.-Col. George Taylor wrote in his memoirs: 'On a peaceful sunny day we buried our dead behind the little farmhouse on the eastern edge of the ridge. Padre Gibbons conducted the simple moving service and the haunting notes of the Last Post sounded, carried over the fields ripe with corn for the harvest.'

The division had one sinister task to perform. The legacy of widespread minefields around the River Noireau basin had to be cleared laboriously. Lt.-Col. Dent, CO 110th LAA Regiment, was unfortunately killed when his jeep went over an uncleared mine. But for most of the Wyverns decent hot meals, clean uniforms, baths, swimming in the River Noireau and entertainment restored morale. 'Before we left Berjou we were given a few days of marvellous rest and refreshment,' recalled William Gould, 1st Worcesters. 'I was elevated to the rank of corporal and given a special honour. A few of us were taken back to Arromanches and were entertained in a barn by ENSA. Mr Pastry was the star of this outfit and a very nice man he proved to be.'

On the evening of 22 August Maj.-Gen. Thomas visited XXX Corps HQ near Moulins-sur-Orne. Gen. Horrocks was determined that the pressure of the hot pursuit of the defeated German Seventh and Fifth Panzer Armies must be maintained. The next great barrier was the River Seine. He therefore selected the Wyverns to force a crossing at Vernon, some 50 miles from Paris. 'Nobody in the British Army', he wrote in his memoirs, 'had given more detailed thought into the problem of crossing rivers in the face of opposition (than Gen. Thomas). For two and a half years before D-Day he had exercised troops on this most exasperating and complex type of operation, including the crossing of the Medway, the Rother, and the aptly named Reading Sewer, preferably in the tidal reaches, and by night, in heavy rain and midwinter.' Nearly half of those superbly trained crossers of water had already become casualties in the ferocious battles of Hill 112, Maltot, Mt Pinçon and the River Noireau. Gen. Thomas made a point of addressing all the fighting Wyverns and stressed the vital importance of the early capture of the V-bomb launching sites in the Pas de Calais, which since June had been causing death and destruction to the people of southern England and London. An excellent motive to continue the battle.

Wally Caines, 4th Dorsets, diary: '24 Aug. The boys in the companies did a bit of bayonet training, thoroughly cleaned their weapons, replenished ammo. Later we met a charming young French girl with her mother who came to greet us . . . gave us flowers, black coffee, after a quiet chat, a bottle of rich wine saved for the day of liberation. Our vehicles were all decorated with bunches of flowers.' When the Cornwalls knew that the advance to the Seine was 'on', Col. George Taylor wrote: 'We celebrated with a party and the noise of singing and jollification was heard far into the night. Sgt. Frank Grigg being the star performer.'

Horrocks' memoirs continue:

With the forcing of the crossing at Vernon in the teeth of enemy fire of one of the great rivers of Europe over 650 ft wide, with a strong current and muddy bottom, his (Thomas') hour was about to come. He was instructed to force a crossing of the Seine on or about 25 August. To cover the construction of a Class 9, a Class 40 and Class 70 bridge. To form a bridgehead of sufficient depth to allow passage through of the remainder of XXX Corps (i.e. 11th and Guards Armoured Divisions).

Operation Neptune was the appropriate codename given to this nautical venture.

Gen. Thomas and his GSOs retired to his caravan to produce their operational plan. Vernon was 120 miles away to the east-north-east. Army HQ had provided 1/50,000 and 1/25,000 scale maps of the area plus one large-scale vertical air photograph, as well as much topographical, technical and engineering data. It was known that US 19 Corps had already reached the west bank of the Seine and their patrols were thought to be in Vernon. But to get there the 3,300 vehicles of 43rd Division plus cumbersome bridging equipment (stormboats, pontoons, etc.) would have to cut across the American lines of communication on the route Argentan– Breteuil–Pacy. Negotiations at Army level produced three timespans for the Wyverns to push their traffic through towards Vernon: (a) 25 August 0800–1200 hrs and 1400–1800 hrs; (b) 26 August 1300–1800 hrs.

For the assault crossing Thomas chose Brig. Mole's 4th Somersets, 4th and 5th Wiltshires of 129th Brigade plus a borrowed squadron of 15/19th Hussar Cromwell tanks from 11th Armoured Division. The brigade would cross on a two-battalion front in stormboats and DUKWs (which had to come all the way from the beachhead). 4th Wiltshires would occupy and secure the town of Vernon, immediately opposite to the smaller suburb of Vernonnet across the river. The two bridges were known by air photographs to be totally or partly destroyed. The railway bridge 800 yds downstream (north) certainly had been destroyed but the old stone bridge linking Vernon and Vernonnet, demolished in 1940, had been cobbled together with a metal structure by the Germans. It had one long girder blown out of position by the FFI either to prevent any German counter-attacks or to prevent the crossing of German transport fleeing from the Falaise 'pocket'. In theory it was just passable for infantry in single file but they would be completely exposed to hostile fire. In the meantime the FFI in Vernon, a charming well-laid-out town of ten thousand inhabitants, a popular Parisian summer resort, had liberated the town with some élan. Behind the suburb of Vernonnet was a steep 300-ft chalk-faced escarpment dominating the river and both river banks. Two roads from Vernonnet passed through the escarpment, one north-west to Gisors and Les Andelys and another south-east to Gasny and Giverny. Beyond the escarpment the huge dense Forêt de Vernon, criss-crossed with rides and tracks, provided excellent cover for German reinforcements likely to appear from Beauvais. There were of course to be many problems. A number of submerged islands in the middle of the river were, according to the optimistic FFI 'pas de problème', but according to maps and photos they posed a distinct problem. The furthest span of the wrecked railway bridge ran over a 'cut' which according to the FFI was also 'pas de problème' for crossing troops. Unfortunately this was quite untrue. The western verges of the river bank were so steep that DUKWs could not get down into the water except over a new man-made ramp or ramps. And so on!

The actual advance to the Seine was a miracle of superb staff planning. The integration of the order of march of recce cars, infantry, engineers, gunners, signals and armour on a single main road through three separate timespans of passage 'rights' demanded immense experience – and a great deal of luck. The Luftwaffe, say a couple of ME 109s or Focke-Wulfes, would have nearly 15 miles of nose-to-tail Wyvern vehicles as prime targets – overloaded DUKWs with dust-coated infantry, jeeps, carriers, 3-ton lorries, Hussar Cromwells, pontoon and bridging transporters. At Pacy-sur-Eure, 8 miles south-east of Vernon, the Recce Regiment discovered that the river bridge was blown and boobytrapped. The village of St Acquilin-de-Pacy was so heavily cratered by RAF bomb holes and a line of burned-out vehicles, as to be almost impassable. But one way or another these considerable obstacles were overcome or bypassed.

Sgt. George Drake, 'C' Squadron Recce Regiment, noted: 'There seemed to be a great deal of Calvados in every village, enough to fuel a rocket to the moon. It was very powerful stuff.' At one stage he and his Able 3 Troop spotted a vehicle coming along a lateral road and trained their 37mm guns on it. It turned out to be the GOC's Ark: 'I spotted the passenger had a red general's hat.' Pat Spencer Moore, ADC to the general, was map reading in that Ark: 'One of the most exciting trips I have ever had in my life. It was a marvellous summer morning and we were swanning through the countryside of France, the horrors of Normandy were all left far behind. . . . En route I took a wrong turning and went straight towards a German group. Gen. Thomas was NOT pleased, very angry with me. The only time his wrath descended on me. Soon passed!'

Early on the 24th the Assault Group started off via Ecouché, then to the dreadful ruins of Argenton, east to L'Aigle, east-north-east to Breteuil in drenching rain, Damville, St André and Pacy-sur-Eure. The Recce Regiment led and 'C' Squadron reported the blown bridges at Pacy. No. 7 troop were closely followed by RE recce parties and the GOC. At Pacy the Americans there agreed to bulldoze a crossing over the railway bridge via the railway station and No. 11 Field Company RE hastily built a Bailey bridge over the

Eure. Work went on through the night of the 24th and the road to Vernon was open by 1015 hrs on 25 August. The timeframe given by Gen. Horrocks was slipping!

No fewer than 1,600 vehicles passed through the American check point in the four-hour span allocated to the Wyverns. 'B' Squadron Recce and the 4th Wiltshires arrived in Vernon at noon, wound down the steep and winding road into the town to a tumultuous reception by the populace and extrovert Maquis. The Wiltshires dug in their rifle companies, hid their vehicles under trees, beside buildings and then acted as traffic police. Everyone was under strict orders to give the enemy across the river no inkling of the brigade attack to come and to pretend that Vernon was in the hands of the French assisted by a small American patrol. So 'C' Squadron 15/19th Hussars kept their Cromwells under cover at the top of the hill. The Wiltshire historian wrote:

> 25 August. In Vernon everybody was parading the streets, asking questions, accepting cigarettes, giving fruit and advice with charming lavishness. Every male and most females were armed with a variety of weapons of all makes. Some wore uniforms of a kind, most seemed to be in their Sunday clothes. German troops were plainly visible sunning themselves on the cliffs above the river. Below the cliffs in the suburbs of Vernonnet six German posts could be seen without binoculars; the demolished rail bridge and bombed road bridge in ruins though with difficulty still passable to infantry. An American patrol had attempted to cross by it. It was heavily defended by automatic weapons, which covered its whole length. Our DUKWs drove through the trees behind the buildings almost at water's edge and the stormboats were offloaded and carried down by large fatigue parties.

At once on arrival the recce armoured cars scurried out on patrols along the Seine north, opposite to Les Andelys, and north-west towards Louviers. 94th Field Regiment and 121st Medium Regiment brought their guns into position on the edge of the Forêt de Bizy. The Tour des Archives, a seventeenth-century castle near the town's fire station, provided the best observation post of the panorama opposite. Soon the heavy Vickers MGs and large 4.2-in mortars of 8th Middlesex were in firing positions. Eric Codling's carrier had seized up on the way to Vernon, blocked the main road and caused congestion: 'The divisional GOC, breathing fire, arrived in his armoured car, ordered a large recovery vehicle to push my carrier off the road.' By now 'Codger' Green and Eric were the only original members of 14 Platoon left from the landings in late June. Eric was not a happy man on his arrival in Vernon: 'How many of those prosecuting youngsters sporting their FFI armbands had actually engaged in combat with the Germans?' The women were being shorn of their hair for consorting with enemy soldiers, always a distressing sight to Tommies passing through. By 1600 hrs TAC HQ and the bulk of the Assault Group were also in harbour in the Forêt de Bizy and the villages of La Heunière and St Vincent-des-Bois.

Intelligence sources credited the opposition as being about 250 strong in and around Vernonnet and a further 250 at Giverny, 2 miles upstream. Both garrisons of the battlegroup Meyer were part of 49th Infantry Division with reserves at Beauvais, 35 miles north-east. They were armed with MG and 20-mm dual purpose Flak guns. Some of their manned slit trenches could be seen in and on the chalkface cliffs opposite. There did not appear to be tank support since most had failed to get clear of the Falaise 'gap', few 88-mm guns, and few of the dreaded 'Moaning Minnie' mortars. But the wide river and commanding cliffs were natural barriers that must make a crossing hazardous.

Lt.-Col. Evill, the CRE, reported that suitable launching sites for the DUKWs were hard to find. So stormboats would be used until the sappers had built ramps on the Seine verges to launch the DUKWs. There was little time to brief the men in the use of stormboats. Each held eighteen men (i.e. half a platoon) but were long and heavy and needed thirty-six men to carry one. A journey of 100 yds down to the river's edge was exhausting.

There were to be two simultaneous battalion assaults with H-Hour at 1845 hrs. Lt.-Col. Bill Roberts and 5th Wiltshires would attack on the right 300 yds above the old road bridge and Lt.-Col. Lipscombe and 4th Somersets on the left near the damaged railway bridge. A distance of some 600 yds separated the two battalions since a direct attack on Vernonnet would have been courting disaster. The covering fire plan involved fifteen minutes' bombardment, followed by ten minutes of smoke shells to create a screen, which was to be maintained until nightfall.

31

D-DAY, 25 AUGUST

The 5th Wiltshires' Attack

Pte. Fred Greenwood, a signaller, overheard his officers talking: 'They seemed to think that the crossing was going to be a piece of cake. The enemy was supposed to be very weak along the Seine consisting of old men and those unfit for front line duty. (The enemy opposite had not in fact fought in Normandy.) We were going to dash across the river with no trouble at all. It worried me to hear them talk about the coming battle as though it were just a game.' Within the next thirty-six hours Greenwood was to be wounded and taken prisoner. 'A' Company started to cross the river with 18 Platoon leading. The first two boats grounded on the submerged island only 30 yds from the far shore. Twenty-four men out of thirty-five were killed. Sgt. Mackrell:

> The smoke started to lift as we got under way and we could see the opposite bank. Then the MG opened up on us. As we neared the far bank we got stuck on a sandbank. Several men in the boat were hit. I shouted to the men to jump off the boat and wade ashore. We were in 4½ ft of water. As the men got on to the bank they spread out to gain cover and I lost touch with some. The boat was swinging in the river with two Royal Engineers – the crew – hanging on. I managed to get one wounded man on board again and with the REs swam the boat back to the other bank. There were no survivors in Lt. Selby's boat. By the end of an hour only one of the eight boats survived.

Ron Garner wrote: 'The company continued to cross in the remaining stormboats until they became wrecked or stranded. Eventually 60 per cent of 'A' Coy crossed.' Lt. Drake and his men made for their objective, a house on the road about 200 yds from the bank.

Sgt. Ted Gardner was originally with No. 8 Beach Group, landed at Juno Beach with 3rd Canadian Division and joined 'A' Company after the Mt Pinçon action:

> In the middle of the river we were hit at rear of craft, two men wounded. We managed to get to the high east bank. Lt. Miald led the attack towards houses some 300 yds away. Our own smoke shells were falling around us. The Germans put in a strong counter-attack as it got dark and 'A' Coy was virtually wiped out. Myself and a Lance-Corporal lay in the bottom of a foxhole, later scarpered back to River Bank. Only thirty-three of us had got across the river including Coy CO Maj. Milne who was later taken prisoner.
>
> L/Cpl. Coster about 2 ft on my left was hit by an empty 25-pounder smoke cannister and was killed, as we made for a White House across the water meadows (recalls Pte. J.V. Webb). During the defence of the house there were twenty of us of whom sixteen were wounded at about 3 a.m. on the 26th. All night our signaller was calling for reinforcements. All night we were told that other companies were on their way. Eventually we ran out of ammo. The enemy were close enough to lob hand grenades through a large hole blasted in the front of the house. The company lost twenty-five dead and twenty taken prisoner in that one night. From the private soldiers' lowly view it looked like an absolute disaster but at least some of us survived.

Pte. Webb was captured and spent the rest of the war in a Stalag.

Cpl. Vic Coombs landed farthest upstream on the extreme right: 'We made a detour upstream. Then heads down and run like stink for the road towards a group of houses out of sight of the Germans. Lt. Drake was killed there.

The disaster to the stormboats now forced Lt.-Col. Roberts to use the DUKWs. Ron Garner: 'At 2230 hrs his four DUKWs were launched and three were grounded immediately. We now only had three left which continued to operate and ferry the remainder of the Bn across. "C" Coy the next company to cross was commanded by Lt. Holly and all his platoons were commanded by Sergeants.' By 0300 hrs 'C' Coy largely due to CSM N.L. Haines were across without loss and reached the top of the ridge. With 'B' Company now on the right and 'D' on the left, the first bridgehead had been secured. Sgt. Norman Smith, 'D' Company, recalls: 'My 18 platoon consisted of mainly South Staffs and some Royal Berkshires, but not a single Wilts! On hands and knees we crawled up and found the caves in the side of the hills. A crowd of women and children came forward. They must have recognised my Brummy Accent.'

D-DAY – THE 4TH SOMERSETS' ASSAULT

If much of the problem on the right-hand attack was due to ill-judged assessment of the 'submerged' islands, now another misjudgement landed 4th SLI in trouble. 'A' Company under Maj. Acock embarked in stormboats at 1910 hrs and established their initial bridgehead. 'C' Company under Maj. Mallalieu followed up quickly and advanced inland. The watercourse between and under the railway bridge and the distant mainland was not dry as expected. It was 60 ft wide, with steep muddy banks containing deep water and depths of soft mud and silt. Capt. Hancock was the 94th Field Regiment FOO:

> On the dot we heard the dull thud-thud of the guns in the rear and in a moment the opposite hillside was carpeted with mushroom-like puffs of smoke intermingled with tracer and HE from our tanks along the river bank. Two minutes before the assault, 468 Battery began to lay a smokescreen. (Later) After some hours of confused fighting which included the melancholy discovery that my battalion had landed on an island, we dug ourselves in for the night in our bridgehead of about 150 yds by 100 yds.

Brig. Mole was obviously deeply concerned about the mishaps to both lead battalions and now ordered the Worcesters to attempt to cross by the broken road bridge. So 'A' Company moved to the foot of the bridge to be greeted by a shower of mortar bombs from Vernonnet. The leading platoon under Sgt. Jennings climbed up and on to the partly destroyed bridge and at the far end set off a booby trap of egg grenades. Although badly wounded he managed to withdraw his men. Hails of Spandau fire swept along the bridge from a large concrete pillbox 50 yds from the bridge and 2-in mortars and 6-pounder fire failed to silence the enemy machine guns. 'A' Company then withdrew to nearby houses to have a hot evening meal! Pte. T.C. Dutton described the 'broken down

foot bridge, looked like a switchback at a fun fair. All pylons
had been blown away giving it several W shapes.'

By midnight the GOC and Brig. Mole at TAC HQ were faced with
the failure of the three attacks. 5th Wilts had lost 'A' Company
and the rest of the battalion had not yet crossed. 4th Somersets
had two companies marooned on an island near the railway
bridge and it was stalemate for the Worcesters on the broken
road bridge. Pat Spencer Moore, the GOC's ADC, recalls: 'I could
see that Thomas was a little agitated and caught snatches of his
conversation with Brig. Mole. He seemed to be trying to get Mole
to move the 4 Somersets to a new site and prodded the map,
saying "Have you tried to get in round there?" The plan was
obviously going wrong.'

D+1, 26 AUGUST

Lt.-Col. Lipscomb, 4th SLI, had already decided to land his 'B'
Company under Capt. Hutchinson in DUKWs 300 yds upstream to
the right of the island where 'A' and 'C' were still marooned. One
DUKW grounded on a mudbank and the other sank at the foot of
the new ramp just constructed by 260th Field Company
bulldozers. But the rest of the company crossed in stormboats,
without difficulty, and made a new bridgehead downstream, left
of the road bridge. Then they cleared the ground between
Vernonnet and the river.

Leo Davis in the Signals Platoon 4th Somersets, wrote:

We did not normally consider ourselves as 'fighting' soldiers.
For once, at Vernon, this altered. We had to cross the river
and each group had to clear certain houses in view on the
other side. . . . I was given eight men to carry out the assault,
two of three of my own signallers, a couple of company
runners and two Regimental Police. For advice on how to
conduct the assault, I consulted the company runners,
riflemen of course. They told me 'The leader dashes up to
the door, kicks it open, and sprays the inside with his
machine gun and the rest follow him in.' The leader was me,
I was plainly told. On the way over the boat engine
spluttered, stopped and refused to restart. We wallowed
helplessly. I had a sudden brainwave. 'Take out your
entrenching tools and paddle like hell.' It worked beautifully.

Leo arrived on the far shore, jumped and landed face down in mud which blocked his Sten. According to his battle drill, at the house he kicked the door open and fired the Sten. 'Out came just one dull thud which was just as well as the house was crammed with thirty to forty women and children refugees.' Meanwhile two RE field companies were busy constructing the Class 9 bridge 'David'. Thirty-four rafts were assembled and the bridge approaches bulldozed under 20-mm AA gunfire, mortar bombs and Spandau. Cliff Roberts, 553rd Field Company said: 'We had to manhandle the cumbersome rafts around the back gardens to get them down to the river all the time under sniper fire. The atmosphere was electric.' It took 500 sappers twenty-eight hours to construct the 40-ton Bailey bridge called 'Goliath'. It spanned 684 ft and was opened to traffic forty-eight hours after the first assault. Twenty sappers were killed or wounded in its construction. Sapper Jim Collins was a young lad with 584th Field Company RE, part of 15th Kent GHQ Troop Engineers. They had trained on the Isle of Wight in April and May with landing pontoons, part of Mulberry Harbour for the D-Day landings. 'With 582 and 583 companies we began the task of building the third bridge over the Seine, a Bailey codenamed "Saul bridge". Whilst we were building it our drivers recovered an assault boat from the middle of the river and buried its occupants from the Wiltshire regiment. We had been blooded into real war.'

Vernonnet was still held in some strength although the Somersets had knocked out two MG teams on the outskirts with hand grenades in the dark. And from the west bank 15/19th Hussars' Cromwells had fired across the river and eliminated another gun crew. Soon a number of prisoners of 148th Grenadier Regiment were being put in the 'bag'.

32

D+1, 26 AUGUST

The Worcesters' Attack

At dawn the Worcesters made a second head-on attempt to cross the battered road bridge and, to their amazement, the Spandau teams had vanished, probably under threat from pressure by 4th Somersets. Divisional 'management' must have been much relieved to find the greater part of three attacking battalions were across the river but without anti-tank guns or tank support. Three 6-pounder A/Tank guns and three carriers were ferried across upstream to back up the Wiltshires. The General now decided on a 'deception' programme as Col. George Taylor recounts: 'Capt. Anslow and his carrier platoon (Cornwalls) was instructed as part of a divisional plan to make a diversionary attack 10 miles north-west opposite Les Andelys to draw the enemy's reserves. His small force consisted of a 25-pounder, a 3-in mortar plus the carriers.' They went downstream to simulate a crossing at Gaillon. In addition Brig. Heath, the CRA, ordered ostentatious registration of divisional artillery targets up and down the river to confuse the enemy. They failed to counter-attack in strength that day. The overall battle was now going rather better. 5th Wiltshires sent out two patrols from 'B' Company under Sgt. Clarke which destroyed two troublesome MGs in the cliff-face who had been raking the sappers below building a new bridge. By early afternoon the Wiltshires had consolidated east of Vernonnet taking 100 prisoners. John McMath, their signals officer, noted:

> The CO and I crossed the river in the dark using a DUKW. On the other side lying flat on our faces in the long grass with me 'sotto voce' trying to make myself heard over the 18 set whilst being told by the CO 'Be Quiet'. We had made many attempts under fire to get a cable across the river but had to wait until the cold light of dawn after a night of continual fighting before I was able to take a cable party over the remains of the demolished bridge and establish a direct telephone link across the river.

On the left flank Maj. Garner led 'D' Company of 4th
Somersets, who had disembarked before first light, to clear the
gardens and houses at the northern end of Vernonnet. Doug
Proctor, section leader 18 Platoon:

> At the O group Lt. Jary informed us of the calamities that
> had befallen the other three companies. It was obvious that
> 'Gen. Chaos' was in command. We clambered into the
> stormboats and with engines roaring we commenced moving
> across the wide expanse of the river, 17 Platoon first,
> followed by us, then 16 Platoon. The noise from the engines
> was terrific and encouraged the German defenders to greater
> efforts. Flak guns on the escarpment and numerous
> Spandaus snarled defiance.

Lt. Jary later stalked into a small cobbled village square in
Vernonnet 'inviting the enemy to show their presence by firing at
him. It was a foolhardy thing to do – our young commander was
thoroughly enjoying his war. Danger, like a drug, filled him with
exhilaration. He was an example to all of us.' By early afternoon
'Lippy's battalion was dug in along the spur 1,200 yds north of
Vernonnet, having captured four 22mm dug-in Flak guns and
taken thirty prisoners. Vernonnet was found to be full of enemy
dead.'

1st Worcesters were across the damaged but undefended main
bridge by 0800 hrs and then advanced north-east to capture the
high ground inland from Vernonnet. Pte. T.C. Dutton with 'A'
Company: 'We continued down the battered main street, forward,
with the church on our left up through the churchyard and
cemetery to an open field beyond. We progressed over open
moorland passing a demolished factory.' The gunners were firing
smoke shells ahead and the empty smoke containers fell around
Dutton and his mates. 'At least you could see them whizzing
down, even if they were our own!' With his mate 'Dosey' Denby,
Cpl. William Gould 'reached "A" Coy who had dug themselves in
round the church. We informed the CO anxiously waiting on the
Vernon side for news that all was going well. He was delighted
and sent the rest of the Bn over. "B" Coy came first and we teed
on to the existing line. . . . Dosey Denby in his droll aside said we
should both be given the Military Medal.' Dosey was a regular
soldier who had served in India for eleven years, a hardened
veteran.

We were pinned down by MG up the hill from Vernonnet, my best friend Joe Cartwright (recalls Albert Kings), a Birmingham chap, was killed, a bullet went through his helmet, he gave a violent twitch, he was dead. During our encounter Bert Smith, a Dudley man, was wounded. As he was being picked up by stretcher-bearers, a machine gun opened up killing all three of them, no wonder I was angry. We were to fire from the top of a hill in the direction of an unseen enemy. The anger and venom with which I fired my Bren that day still amazes me to this very day. Maj. Grubb had a personal duel with some jerries, killing them all with a grenade.

War photographers were now busy on the Vernon waterfront taking many photographs of the bridges being built and DUKWs being launched. Pte. Illsley, 'C' Company 5th Wiltshires, recalls:

Sgt. Stevenson and I crossed back over the river by the old bridge to collect two twenty-four hour Ration boxes for 13 Platoon. On our return journey we were asked by a photographer if he could take a photo of us taking food to the troops over the river. As we had barely eaten for twenty-four hours this request did not go down too well! The following morning Sgt. Stevenson was hit by rifle fire. There was a large explosion and I was sent back to the RAP and later Hospital suffering from shock and internal bleeding.

Brig. Mole now ordered 4th Wiltshire across the damaged road bridge in the heat of the day to clear the area south of Vernonnet between the river and the escarpment. Many deep caves were located and accurate fire from them continued to cause heavy casualties to the REs building their bridges below. After an advance of 1,000 yds, deployed on a three-company front, 'A' Company in thick undergrowth discovered an enemy platoon with two card 'schools' playing behind a cordon of sentries. 'D' Company disturbed several light enemy SPs in the woods and tried to stalk them with PIATs. By evening the spur 1,700 yds south-east of Vernonnet had been reached.

The sappers of 553rd and 204th Field Companies finished the rear trestle and approach and started to move out the rafts to form the pontoon bridge. The machine gunners still surviving on the escarpment had easy targets. In a short time only a third of the crew of each raft survived. Sgt. Hicks and Cpl. Sutton did brave work but by midday only half the bridge had been completed. The heavy casualties and damage to material forced the CRE, Lt.-Col. Evill, to order the work to be halted temporarily.

Les Trimmer was a sapper with 553rd Company:

> For me one of the worst few days of the war. My friend Ted Lawless was hit in the back by a mortar shell fragment. He was a fine musician and spoke German. Sgt. Burns also died that night which was dark and raining. Owing to intermittent shellfire we were forced to build some of the rafts of the bridge upstream and float them down into position. The bridge was completed by midday only to have a shell land right in the middle of it. Our Sgt. Pietre walked out on the bridge and carried a wounded man back. 27 August. The bridge was repaired and by 2000 hrs vehicles were passing over.

Eric Codling, 8th Middlesex, was rather scathing: 'Unfortunately the REs were not seasoned in battle conditions. When the enemy artillery opened up they suffered a heavy toll due to their inexperience.'

The General now ordered 214th Brigade across the river to expand the bridgehead. The scout patrol of the Cornwalls radioed back at 1545 hrs that they had reached the centre of the Forêt de Vernon due north of Vernonnet without opposition. The Cornwalls were to go first, followed by 7th Somerset, the troops across the broken road bridge and vehicles by the new Class 9 bridge 'David', now at long last finished, by 1730 hrs. George Taylor wrote:

> Our advance was turned into a festive occasion by the villagers of Vernonnet who pressed wine and cider on the heavily laden infantrymen. Three miles further on 'B' Coy under Maj. Hingston took up a position left of the high ground near Pressagny L'Orgueilleux. Maj. Parker's 'A' on the right in front of the forest edge and 'D' blocked the cross tracks 500 yds south-east; 'C' Coy did not exist due to the Normandy casualties. A/Tank guns were sited and Bn HQ was in a chateau, a home for orphan boys run by a bearded unfrocked priest! All was quiet and peaceful. Our bliss was to be short lived. In the middle of the night 'B' Coy was over-run and an enemy force was in the village. (A German patrol had unknowingly linked up in the darkness with a Cornwall patrol.) It became a deadly

game of hide and seek. At dawn the Germans moved up through a field of corn in superior numbers, swept out of the early morning mist and quickly over-ran the few defenders. The survivors fell back to the 'A' Company positions by the forest edge. Firing rifles and light automatics, throwing grenades the enemy stormed through the gap. A strong party outflanked 'A' Coy platoons dug into their slit trenches.

CSM Philp killed several of the enemy 148th Grenadier Regiment with his Bren gun. Harry Parker and Col. George Taylor quickly agreed a DF fire programme on top of 'A' Company! 'The first salvo sent the enemy scurrying into the woods. We suffered only three casualties from the artillery fire but two prisoners taken by the Germans were murdered in cold blood.' Now 'D' Company came under attack from two enemy companies. 'A small detachment held them up for a short time in a bloody little action but after inflicting losses on the enemy, they were over-run and every man killed. For a while there was confusion among the men of 'D' Coy and stragglers fell back to Bn HQ.' The situation was so desperate that Col. Taylor issued a special Order of the Day to be circulated to and including all section commanders: 'The battalion WILL defend the LEFT flank and by defend I mean TO THE LAST MAN and the LAST ROUND. In this close country the enemy may infiltrate behind you but remember – if you hold your FIRE he can't locate you and if he can't locate you he'll walk straight into your trap and if he walks into your trap every bullet you fire will kill a German.'

Several armoured cars from the Recce Regiment and later some 4/7th Dragoon Guards' tanks arrived to stabilise the situation and the Cornwalls then moved to occupy the village of Pressagny. But all three rifle companies had taken heavy casualties, dead, wounded and POW.

33
D+2, 27 AUGUST

The Corps Commander, Gen. Horrocks, arrived in Vernon on 17 August:

I had set 43rd Div. a difficult task. There is no doubt that Gen. Thomas had every right to be extremely proud of his division. I saw the situation for myself. I had not realised what an almost impossibly difficult operation this had been. The whole town and two broken bridges over the Seine were completely dominated by thickly wooded hills on the far bank, so every movement on the bank of the river and in Vernon itself was visible to the enemy. Thomas told me they had been opposed by tough experienced German forces.

At the main river crossing all through the morning of the 27th the engineers worked on their bridge building under more or less constant fire. Although the clifftop MGs and 20mm Flak guns had been silenced by now, an enemy gun firing from the south caused trouble during construction of the Class 40 'Goliath' and the Class 9 'David'. One direct hit on the latter sank boats and destroyed two of the floating buoys, closing the bridge for nearly two hours. Another shell fell on 'Goliath', wounding or killing twenty sappers working on it. Even the GOC and his brigadiers came in for special treatment and shells fell extremely close to them. Lt.-Col. Tom Lloyd, 7th Army Troops REs i/c construction of the Bailey Class 9 'David', noted: 'Stray shells were still dropping on the town and each company in turn reported casualties but there was no "stonking" . . . Vernon, the nicest little town we had seen in all our travels, a fine slow river just asking to be bridged.' Later watching Goliath, 'it was being built to the accompaniment of the same back-chat used by Shakespeare's soldiery . . .'. By 1715 hrs the first vehicle, a bulldozer, crossed Goliath. By 1930 hrs the tanks of 4/7th Dragoon Guards and 15/19th Hussars were crossing to give urgent support to the infantry on the far side.

Brig. Essame, having reinforced the beleaguered Cornwalls with the first rafted tanks over the river at 0800 hrs on the 27th, now ordered 1st Worcesters to advance on Tilly, 6 miles north-east inland from Vernonnet, and 7th Somersets to move on their left through the thick Forêt de Vernon south of Panilleuse, some 5 miles due north of Vernonnet.

Despite receiving reinforcements after the Noireau crossing, the Worcesters were much under strength. The total battalion mustered only 533 all ranks: the rifle companies averaged sixty-five and now only had two platoons each twenty-five strong, plus enlarged Company HQ with LMGs and mortar. At 0810 hrs they set off. 'Nipper' Dutton, Sgt. Sid Potter and their new 2nd Lieutenant and three others went off on a tank-hunting expedition: 'At the end of the woody part of the high ground, in the bright sunshine, no more than 50 yds away was a German Tiger tank. As we all looked, it began to drive away along the hedgerow away from us. Sgt. Potter said to our officer "It looks like he might be buggering off like his mates have been doing all night, Sir."' The patrol returned and soon after:

. . . shouts of 'Tank Alert', this anti-tank gun of Sgt. Jack Guest was loaded and ready. The tank rumbled towards us round the bend and was just half visible. The order came to fire. The first shell was a hit. As the tank tried to wriggle back to safety more shells were fired into it, setting it on fire. As the crew bailed out they were dealt with by the lads of the Platoon. It was at this time another tank appeared in the field by the side of the road. There were infantry with this one. The verges were being fired upon by the second tank's MG. Lots of shouting from the German infantry up on the high ground. We were ordered to withdraw down the road to the next company's position. No order was ever obeyed as quickly as this one. With bullets at our heels we were jet propelled. Then we came upon one of our Majors on the side of the road shouting 'Stop, Stop!' We halted and he ordered us to go up the slope where we were to meet the attack. There I was struck by a German bullet and became one of sixty-five casualties from this action (twenty-six were KIA, sixty-five wounded).

Battle Group Schrader was counter-attacking with four companies forward, backed by three Tiger tanks, handled with great skill, fighting in dense woods. The confused battle went on all day with the close-packed column of carriers, jeeps and anti-tank guns continually under fire. Maj. Benn, the 2 i/c, and Pte.

C. Long by his side, were killed by bullets from the second tank as was Cpl. W. Bratt, commander of one of the two 6-pounder A/Tank guns knocked out. 'D' Company casualties were so severe that they had to withdraw. Capt. P. Mather was killed and Lt. Trimnel wounded. But two stretcher-bearers, Ptes Durkin and Kilby, had an extraordinary time; they were captured and set to work in the enemy RAP, but later walked back with their captors – an officer and thirty-six ORs – as captives!

Stan Procter was sent by the Worcesters' adjutant, Capt. Leadbeater, to take his signal remote control on foot to a bend to advise RHQ of any tank movement: 'That day will be etched on my memory for ever. The trees were in full leaf, a racket of guns firing and the noise of tank tracks. The infantry ahead were fighting on the right and suddenly they came back in a bit of a hurry towards our White scout car alone on the road. I saw the Maj. (Benn) shout out "Come on you buggers, follow me", waving his revolver and led the men back up the hill. He was killed almost at once.' The next morning Stan saw a long line of men sleeping under their groundsheets. There had been heavy thunderstorms. They were all dead Worcesters.

Maj. Algy Grubb's batman earned the MM for knocking out an enemy MG, as William Gould recounted: 'He suddenly slipped away into the trees, not seen for ten minutes, merely answering the call of nature. On returning he said "Sir, we can get forward now, I have dealt with the machine gun."' He had stalked the MG crew from the rear and thrown two grenades into them.

I was the Brengunner in the leading section moving up the hill from Vernonnet. Suddenly a Spandau opened up. I heard a cry behind me (recalls Albert Kings); someone had been hit. Bert Smith was lying there wounded and calling for stretcher-bearers. Two came ambling up the road in no time, armed only with a stretcher and their red cross flag. The German machine guns fired on them, killing all three. No quarter was expected and none would be given. My best friend Joe Cartwright and another chap were both shot dead right across the road from me. Sgt. Kerrigan was also killed when a burst from a MG hit him across the chest and throat. (Later) We got to our objective, charged across the road shouting with guns blazing: the birds had flown.

Eventually the Worcester battle was stabilised with the arrival of two tanks from 4/7th Dragoon Guards, up the steep winding road.

On the left flank of 214th Brigade's advance the 7th Somerset LI moving forward through thick forest had an equally difficult time, not only because of the terrain. Brig. Maj. Bill Chalmers took part in a conference in Vernon with the GOC, Brig. Essame, and the unfortunate Lt.-Col. J.W. Nichol, CO of 7th Somerset LI. 'Thomas visited Bd HQ to discuss the plans to move inland with Brig Essame. He picked on the fact that 'A' Coy was being held back in reserve and not being used. Thomas insisted that ALL the companies should push through the forest of Vernon, clear the woods, make for the village of Panilleuse. Col. Nichol was ordered to move 'A' Coy to a set of crossroads in the middle of the forest.' The battalion had the usual four rifle companies, all well below strength with only two platoons each, with the three sections having about six men instead of ten men, i.e. at half strength. Capt. John Newmark was 2 i/c 'A' Company and wrote:

Col. Nichol wanted to keep 'A' in reserve. He had a perfectly good reason. Our strength was very low, many of the men were new. Most importantly our own Company Commander was new. He was Major G., had spent nearly all the war in the Colonies, had no battle experience in any theatre of war. More out of kindness and common sense, Col. Nichol deemed it wise to introduce him gradually to battle conditions. There should always be troops in reserve. Even a lance-corporal would know that. Depleted 'A' Coy with a brand new CO was thrown in at the deep end. Incidentally the Gen. was known as 'The Butcher'. 'C' Coy under Maj. David Durie were behind 'A' Coy in the advance. We duly advanced through the forest for about a mile and dug in round an abandoned house by a set of cross tracks. The forest was almost a jungle. Visibility was down to yards and waist-high bracken made it impossible to use our rifles or Bren guns from the trenches unless the men stood up. Maj. G. always ensured we had men on guard and men on patrol. I sent a radio signal to Bn HQ to report our arrival. (Later) At early stand-to the next morning followed by a breakfast of haversack rations – another warm day. The Major said 'I have an idea,' strode out of the door, talked to the men.

Maj. G. then led a patrol on a short recce to establish that 'A' Company were in the correct position, since the maps were so unreliable. Shortly afterwards Company HQ came under attack; shots were fired; Joe Guest, the signaller, was shot through the neck. John Newmark informed Battalion HQ and asked for mortar fire on a MG position which he judged to be about 40 yds along one of the tracks. He also asked for tank support and for stretcher-bearers:

> I heard voices outside the house speaking in German. To my astonishment there was most of 'A' Company lined up in two rows with the Major at one end, all being searched by a German officer and other troops standing around in menacing positions. I was totally baffled. Had they put up a fight? I felt sure they would not have surrendered meekly. After all they were fighting soldiers. What on earth could have happened?

John was one of sixty Somersets captured that morning. His friend, L/Cpl. Bill Baron told him that 'the patrol with Maj. G. came to an open area of grassland, suddenly they were fired on. A sergeant and the company clerk were killed seconds later. Our men were overwhelmed by scores of German troops, weapons removed and escorted back to the farmhouse.' Their captors were a group of nearly three hundred. The GOC duly fired Lt.-Col. Nichol for allowing 'A' Company to surrender in the forest, despite his being vigorously defended by Brig. Essame. Nichol, a small dapper man, possessed of a clear mind, crisp and to the point, was a brave and popular leader, who had won the DSO at the attack on Le Plessis Grimault. He was well liked and the men had confidence in his leadership, but 'Butch' Thomas fired him in spite of Essame's protests.

On the far right sector of the divisional front were 129th Brigade. 214th were on the left in Pressagny L'Orgueilleux and the Forêt de Vernon and 130th Brigade in the centre pushing up the road east to Tilly.

Guided by the Maquis 4th Somerset LI plunged into dense forest to advance on the village of Bois Jerome St Ouen, 2 miles inland from Vernonnet. 'D' Company led and soon got into a dog-fight against infantry and two dug-in tanks. Five hundred yards west of the village was an enemy-occupied chateau. Capt. Hutchinson was OC 'B' Company who had captured it by midday (on the 27th) only to be thrown out by a sharp counter-attack supported by some armour. Fortunately the enemy later pulled out and the chateau was empty! But the enemy were still clashing vigorously. Lt. Peter Ost, survey officer with 94th Field Regiment, described the scene:

> We soon got to 129th Brigade HQ and were directed on up the road to 5 Wilts. Here Maj. Le Quesne (BC of 94th Field) told us that things were going very slowly because of 88s and Spandaus and the densely wooded terrain. We then went through the glades of the forest leading to Bois Jerome until we reached the Somersets RAP. The only sound of war was the occasional plop and crump of a mortar and the sharp burst of Bren and Spandau in the distance. A Boche 20-mm opened up with an unholy racket, at very close range down the track by which we were parked and its shells were bursting in the trees on either side. Bill Stockton the signal officer, was slightly wounded and the RSM's language was incredible. Unfortunately at this very moment Maj. Sir John Backhouse, 2 i/c 179th Field Regiment arrived, dismounted from his scout car when the Boche gun opened up. He fell at once hit in the head. Gunner Stickley and his driver raced to his assistance oblivious of the fire. A Somerset carrier moving up in an attempt to knock the gun out, received a direct hit and burst into flames.

Eventually the Somersets knocked out the 20-mm cannon. Maj. Concannon wrote: 'Lying close by the gun was the German four man detachment, all had been killed at their posts. Around the site were great piles of empty shell cases serving as a testimony to the terrific fire they had put down and which had caused us such trouble. They were very brave men sticking to their task as they did, even though they were hopelessly outnumbered and surrounded on all sides.' Led by Maj. Concannon, the survey partly chopped down trees and cut a way out through the wood.

That evening the Somersets took part with tanks in a night attack with 'A' Company leading behind an artillery barrage. Cpl. Doug Proctor with 18 Platoon under Lt. Jary: 'We penetrated through to the north edge of Bois Jerome and it was obvious that the village was undefended – once more they had slipped away. Discretion and a dislike of night fighting had caused them to withdraw.'

The two other battalions, 5th Wiltshires and 4th Wiltshires had started at 0800 hrs on the 27th pushing down the roads to Gasny and Giverny, south-east and south respectively. Ron Garner, 5th Wiltshires, recalls: 'We came up against heavy opposition from light flak guns, used in a ground role. An artillery stonk shifted them. The bn set up for the night in a wood. All night there was 3.7-cm flak fire despite the torrential rain. The night was so cold and wet that a rum issue had to be made. This entailed a trip of about 30 miles each way to get the rum.' The 4th Wiltshires, aided by 15/19th Hussars' Cromwell tanks from the 11th Armoured Division (who were shortly due to pass through on the Great Swan) soon reached the outskirts of Giverny with little opposition. Maj. D.M. Robbins, OC 'C' Company 4th Wilts, was told to outflank the village of Giverny and give supporting fire to the main attack.

34
D+3, 28 AUGUST

The whole division was now firmly established across the Seine and the General gave orders to push the bridgehead out as rapidly as possible. Despite torrential rain every night, rations (and rum) came up more or less on time and morale was quite high! On the extreme left 1st Worcesters had relieved a battered 5th DCLI in Pressagny, now supported by Sherwood Ranger tanks, as Col. George Taylor, Cornwalls, wrote:

We were relieved by tired Worcesters who, with the Somersets had been involved in heavy fighting. We plunged into the forest with orders to capture Panilleuse some 4 miles away, which was necessary to complete the bridgehead. The trees and undergrowth were thick and we were forced to advance in a long 'snake'. I felt that we were in danger of being ambushed like Gen. Braddock's Red Coats were in the American War of Independence. (Later) I sent in 'D' Coy under Maj. John Fry supported by tanks of the Sherwood Rangers after the softening-up barrage to take a large farm. Then 'B' Coy were to spearhead the attack on Panilleuse who swept with great dash into the village through our own shell fire which wounded Lt. Bishop and four privates. The enemy were caught unawares by this onslaught. (Later) A house to house search was hampered by French civilians thrusting flowers upon our men, kissing them, plying them with wine.

On the right flank of the Cornwalls, 7th Somersets' objective was the spur between Panilleuse and Pressagny, which they reached without difficulty helped by the Recce Regiment.

In the centre 5th Dorsets pushed slowly through the woods and cleared the villages of La Queue and Heubecourt, taking the first at 1730 hrs and the latter, one and a half hours later.

Maurice Edwards wrote in the 5th Dorsets history:

'A' Coy (Maj. Allen), 'C' Company (Maj. Pack) were to bear through the woods on the right of the road towards the village of La Queue d'Haye which was 'B' Coy's objective (Maj. Mead), whilst 'D' Coy (Maj. Hartwell) with two troops of 4/7 Dragoon Guards cleared the road as far as the edge of the woods. 'D' stalked an A/tank gun, took forty prisoners whilst 'A' and 'C' managed to flush out from the woods the DAA and QMG of 130 Infantry Brigade (Maj. D.G. Pascall) who was lost!

La Queue d'Haye was void of enemy and the tanks went on to Heubecourt which was also empty.

The 7th Hampshires also put in an attack on Tilly, 'B' Company on the left, 'D' on the right and the village was taken by 1400 hrs with the capture of ninety-five prisoners. But the Hampshires had met scattered but persistent resistance on the way.

On the very far right 4th Wiltshires cleared the village of Giverny despite sniping and SP guns – a slow and difficult attack by 'D' Company – then the battalion took the high ground to the east of the village and moved into Le Pressoir. At the same time inland 5th Wiltshires on the right, 4th Somersets on the left were ordered to attack the village of La Chapelle-St-Ouen just off the road east to Gasny. The Wilts advanced under a barrage across open fields and orchards. 'B' Company suddenly came under fire at short range from MGs in cornstooks in front of the village and all three section commanders were killed. But the enemy quickly surrendered and 160 prisoners including many Poles were taken, for the loss of thirty Wiltshires. All the haystacks were set on fire by the Germans, which the Wyvern engineers extinguished with a trailer pump! Sgt. Smith of 'D' Company remembers how angry the French farmers were: 'They were hopping mad. We had killed one of their cows. I said to a farmer "cut it up for meat" – he went berserk – the cow must have been the village pet!' One of the lads was a butcher in civilian life. While a feast was being prepared in a farmhouse, Sgt. Smith remembers: 'There was an almighty burst of laughter coming from under the floor. In the cellar were a crowd of young German soldiers and girls who all cheered "Viva La" something or other. I thought "Stone the crows. All they wanted was to get out of the war!" '

4th Somersets were then directed on Haricourt. Sydney Jary recalled 'a classic attack with 25-pounder stonk advanced over open farmland in immaculate formation, consolidated exactly on time. Total bag – one dazed German, one dead German and one dead hare. The whole affair was preposterous.'

The next day the Wiltshires advanced 7 miles to Gasny but the enemy had flown. 'Our tank support 13/18th Hussars and carrier patrols fanned out and about another eighty prisoners were brought in. They were in a terrible state of fatigue. Their clothes were in rags, their boots down at heel,' wrote Ron Garner.

The Recce Regiment spent a busy, brisk and often dangerous four days at the Vernon bridgehead. Initially they explored and probed the riverside flanks to observation posts opposite Les Andelys on the Seine and Louviers on the Eure, often finding US recce units, German stragglers from the Falaise pocket and occasional enemy tanks bereft, fortunately, of petrol. Lts Scarr and Jackson tried to ferry their cars across, became badly bogged, but made the crossing at dawn on the 27th. 'A' Squadron crossed over the bridge under heavy shell fire and lost six casualties on the far side. 'B' Squadron probed north towards Les Andelys and north-east towards Tilly, lending fire power to the infantry, although Sgt. Barraclough's car was knocked out by a Tiger tank. Meanwhile 'A' Squadron pushed south in the opposite direction towards Giverny where Lt. Edge in his first action was killed by a sniper. 'A' also supported 5th Wiltshire in their advance towards Gasny, where Sgt. Smailes won the MM for knocking out an A/Tank gun and crew. And Lt. Howe helped out 4th Somerset LI by bombarding the Chateau of Bois Jerome with withering fire. Lt. L.S. Baker carried out his own troop 'war' at Notre Dame de L'Isle, north of Pressagny. His leading cars covered the road and his carriers went right-flanking, forcing the enemy left towards the river. He then went on foot along the river bank engaging enemy with his Sten, killing one, wounding another, capturing two others. All told his troop captured the village with fifty Germans dead, wounded or prisoners. A splendid effort for which he earned the MC. Every enemy occupied village was sharply probed by the Recce Regiment – Tilly, where Lt. Shutler's car was hit by an 88-mm gun, Gommécourt, where a crater in front of the leading car was filled in by enthusiastic French civilians, and Haricourt, where our tanks got there first only to be held up by A/Tank guns.

BSM Fred Fowler's diary reads:

We (94 Field Regiment) advance about 60 miles through Argenton, had to be seen to be believed, absolutely devastated. Then through Pacy-sur-Eure, people going almost mad. Fruit and wine everywhere. We still drive on to go into action 4,000 ft short of the Seine. Our division is to make an assault crossing at Vernon. Weather still very hot. Still very heavy firing smoke screen. Kept going continuously to enable sappers to bridge the Seine, thousands of rounds expended. Observation plane shot down by ME on our position. Pilot killed. The plane is an awful mess. Our chaps have crossed the river, bridges (three) are under construction. We are over. Jerry beat it in a hurry. The 2nd Army sweeps over our crossing.

Ken Storey's 217th Battery, 112th Field Regiment, was sited close to a shoe factory on the outskirts of Vernon:

What little footwear still inside was ALL for left feet. The guns were firing smoke a lot of the time to screen the bridging process. On crossing the pontoon bridge on the 27th in the OP carrier one was immediately in awe of the huge cliff dominating the town from the east bank. Large caves were cut into this cliff as defence positions, others where a lot of the population sheltered during the shelling and fighting.

By the end of the 28th – D+3 – the Seine bridgehead was firmly established. Control of the bridges passed to XXX Corps, and the 11th Armoured Division's tanks, half-tracks and SP guns began to rumble across. The author was one of the young officers who passed over Goliath and failed to realise at the time the sacrifices the Wyverns had made to bridge the Seine.

In the four-day battle the division suffered 550 casualties. The main sufferers were the 5th Wiltshires (159), 7th Somersets (100 including 60 of 'A' Company taken prisoner), 1st Worcesters (93), the sappers (about 80) and the 5th Cornwalls (about 60 at the fierce action at Pressagny). About five hundred German prisoners were taken and several hundred killed.

It was a famous Wyvern battle honour.

35

REST IN RURAL FRANCE

After the battle for the Seine bridgehead, which allowed the great armoured charge to liberate northern France, Belgium and parts of Holland, the Wyverns had earned some days of rest in rural France. For two weeks the division started to make life-long friends with the people of Vernon and the outlying villages. Feet under the table, cafés, shops, dances at the 'Salle des Fêtes', a boar hunt by Maj. Hingston of the Cornwalls in the Forêt de Vernon, all kinds of sport, concerts by the Life Guards Band, 'grenade' fishing in the Seine and boating on the river, ENSA parties (Kaye Cavendish, Flanagan and Allen, Florence Desmond et al), church parades, and, above all, leave parties to 'Gay Paree'. Ken Storey, 112th Field Regiment RA: 'I had my nineteenth birthday on 29 August, and remember the charming little café on the main route to Paris. The patron was a leading figure in the local FFI and his lovely daughter Jeannette and niece Jaqueline, evacuated from Brest.' In St Pierre-de-Quelet, BSM Fred Fowler met 'English speaking French woman and her husband in FFI, have dinner with them, most interesting, they give a concert and dance in our honour (94 Field Reg RA) and an address by the Mayor. We are addressed by the CRA. Any hitch-hiking to Paris gets brought back, bad luck, pictures and ENSA daily. Div. Commander gives out decorations, Col. Bishell DSO, Maj. Greenshields MC.' The Q Department of 179th Field Regiment had problems with the shortage of cap badges, many given away as souvenirs to new friends.

Among the many reinforcements were infantrymen from 59th Division recently broken up after its Normandy battles. Bill Hudson was a Canloan officer who joined 5th Dorsets with his pal Harold Matthews, at Heubecourt. 'We were welcomed by Lt.-Col. Aubrey Coad the CO. I was posted to "C" Coy and Hal to "A" Coy. I wondered at the time what kind of reception a Canadian officer would receive from members of his platoon. Extremely fortunate that Ted Chivers was the platoon sergeant, very helpful in "breaking in" a green platoon commander. We all got along well.' A complete company ninety-four strong from the South Staffs regiment now arrived to become the 'new' 'A' Company of 7th SLI. 'Into my section came Ptes Minnis, Dobson and Flude', Doug Proctor, 4th SLI, wrote: 'The first two were "Geordies" from the Argyll and Sutherland Highlanders. Flude was a young cockney lad who was just nineteen. The three made a comical trio. Dobson was well over 6 ft tall, broad with it. Minnis was short and slim, well educated. George Flude was as cocky as only cockneys can be. All three were on the same wavelength. We luxuriated in peace and quiet at Le Mesnil Milon.' Each unit could send twenty-six men per day to Paris on leave.

A divisional padre, walking down the Champs-Elysées, probably unofficially, was spotted by Gen. Thomas, who sent his staff officer across the road. 'Padre, what are you doing here?' Back came the quick answer: 'Buying Communion wine, Sir.' Pte. O'Connell, 7th SLI, wrote: 'We did rejoin the human race in Vernon where good feeding, good resting and good enjoyment put the deeds of bridging the Seine and what happened after into the background of our thoughts. We did think ourselves as real good old stagers. We did come the acid with the reinforcements sent us, just out from England. But we did welcome them as friends, soon the best of chums sharing our fags and tea with them.' Ron Garner, 5th Wiltshires, recalls how in Gasny he and his mates organised a dance in 'a large room of a public house. Place was crowded. This was the first dancing the French here had had for some years. The men taught them the modern dances. The French resistance cut the hair of women collaborators behind the Mayor's house, out of our sight.'

Pte. N.L. Francis joined 'C' Company 4th Dorsets as a reinforcement from the South Lancs of 50th Division:

> We had never heard of the Dorsets and were not even sure where that county was. Our cap badges instead of reading ICH DIEN (I SERVE) in German now sported the motto PRIMUS IN INDUS (FIRST IN INDIA) in Latin! We joined on 30 August at Tilly and soon swam in river much to the amusement of the local women admiring the Tommies desporting themselves. Our new Sgt. Abberley told us NOT to take any prisoners but to shoot them! We looked at each other realising 'Playing Soldiers' was over.

John McMath, 5th Wiltshires:

I established my Signals Office in the village bakehouse. The smell of fresh baking bread gave me a sense of well-being, peace and quiet. In delightful peaceful Gasny we had ENSA shows, our own battalion concert, football matches, swimming and even trips in Rommel's motor boat – his HQ had been nearby. But the River Seine was the main attraction, on a quiet stretch, using a rowing boat we enjoyed some marvellous swimming in the fresh warm, soft and healing water. After the thick, cloying dust of Normandy this was the life!

The 4th Wiltshires stayed in Giverny, Battalion HQ in the Mairie and absorbed a large draft of reinforcements from the Royal Berkshires and Beds and Herts. However, training started almost immediately, weapons accuracy was tested, field guns and mortars were recalibrated, stormboats and DUKWs were taken out on the river for future crossings, and there were wood clearance exercises. The GOC held cloth-model field exercises in a large hall in Tilly and as usual pounced on every error. Brig. Essame wrote rather ruefully: 'real battles were much less tense, the enemy gave one more time to think'. Three investitures were held by the GOC, one for each brigade. Only twenty-eight of fifty-five officers and men appeared on parade; the rest were dead or wounded. Pte. Albert Kings, 1st Worcesters, was detailed for a burial party: 'We recovered our dead including Joe Cartwright and Sgt. Kerrigan. We dug a grave for four bodies on the side of the road, side by side covered with gas capes. After four days in the sun they were covered with maggots. I wept.'

Col. George Taylor: 'After a tumultuous welcome in Vernonnet, there was great euphoria at that time which was general to the British Second Army. . . . One felt that the war had not long to run.'

First to move were the Recce Regiment. 'C' Squadron moved from Lavacourt on the 6th as local protection to TAC HQ. Second Army moved 150 miles north via Arras and Douai and on the 9th entered Brussels on the heels of Field Marshal Montgomery amid crowds of cheering people. They were based on Perk, a few miles north, for some days, but one troop helped liberate St Nicholas, south of Antwerp.

The Hampshires spent eleven days at Tilly and then were dispatched as mobile reserve and garrison for part of Brussels.

On 9 September they arrived at the Hospital St Jean, a German barracks in the city. Their duties were escorting prisoners to the rear, guarding food, wine, petrol and coal dumps, map depots and clearing the Bois de la Cambre and Forêt de Soynes of German stragglers. The Palace Hotel was set up as an officers' transit hotel. Since 22 June the battalion had had thirty-five officers and 450 ORs killed or wounded. Maj. Gordon Viner spent a week in Brussels – his jeep besieged by excited citizens of all ages and sexes enjoying their liberation. His onerous duty was guarding a depot crammed full of Moet et Chandon champagne. He 'rescued' fifty cases and put them into the cellar of Baron d'Asche's house and drew a line across and said firmly 'Right 50–50?' Just in time before NAAFI officially liberated the depot and confiscated the bulk of the 'champers'. Ernie Bolton was part of the Defence Platoon of TAC HQ: 'As I was driving my Bren carrier in total darkness along the route to Belgium, we discovered the badly damaged caravan of the GOC. The driver who was unhurt had crashed into a road block.' So Ernie and Co. towed the vehicle painfully and slowly to Diest, on the hill seeking assistance from farmers with their cart horses!

There was one story that Monty offered Gen. Thomas the opportunity for the Wessex Wyvern Division to be the garrison for Brussels. The General answered 'Not bloody likely, we're a fighting division,' or words to that effect. In a truly democratic world, Thomas might have consulted his troops, who would have produced a very different answer.

After the Hampshires, the divisional sappers followed the route north through Gisors and Beauvais, crossed the Somme at Sailly Laurette, then went through the First World War battlefields around Albert, Bapaume, and Arras past the Vimy ridge on to Lille and Roubaix into Belgium. The week before three magnificent armoured divisions had swept north on the Great Swan, 7th Armoured to Ghent, 11th Armoured to Antwerp and Guards Armoured into Brussels. Brig. Essame recalled the move to rejoin XXX Corps east of Diest by last light on 15 September:

The long column filed past the red, yellow and black frontier posts of Belgium. A densely populated country of small houses flush with the streets, estaminets (where many trucks and carriers happened to 'break down' or get 'lost' and require advice and sustenance), slipshod villas, steam trains still running, the coal mines were working. The Belgians were free but they were hungry. Bottles of brandy and Burgundy appeared. Bearded priests and nuns came out to cheer. Crowds of children swarmed round the cook's lorries, clamoured for cigarettes and sweets.

Mesdemoiselles from Armentières and other well-known places swapped kisses, as their mothers had done thirty years before: 'All the villagers were out in force waving banners and bunting (wrote Cpl. Doug Proctor), lavishing on us gifts of fruit and wine. We were travelling (4th SLI) in DUKWs, ideal vehicles for showing us off as "Conquering Heroes". Many of the locals clung to the sides of our vehicles, handed us bottles of wine. We travelled almost non-stop for about 250 miles.' For Sgt. Jim Kingston it was a moving experience – the First World War names of Amiens, Albert, Cambrai, Mons, where his father had fought and died. In Linkhout young Lt. Sydney Jary commandeered the local brothel without realising at the time what it was. However, friendly nuns suggested the soldiery be berthed in their convent instead! Col. George Taylor's battalion HQ at Briane le Conte was in a monastery school: 'the monks told us stories of the SS troops who had retreated through the town on bicycles.'

The fine weather now broke and heavy rain fell on the Wyverns as they learned of the dramatic – and ambitious – plans for Operation Market Garden.

36

MARKET GARDEN

At 1100 hrs on 16 September in the little mining town of Bourg Leopold, Gen. Brian Horrocks, XXX Corps Commander, held his 'O' Group in the cinema opposite the station. All officers down to the rank of lieutenant-colonels and including brigade majors, had to attend the vital briefing for one of the most daring and audacious military operations of the Second World War. This was to be called Market Garden – Market for the Airborne dropping operations, Garden for the link up and relief by XXX Corps. Brig. Essame remarked on the amazing array of rainbow sartorial styles of the officers attending and the fact that Horrocks made the comment to Gen. Thomas: 'Hullo Von Thoma, how is the Wicked Wyvern?' He also said before his very detailed brief: 'This is a tale you will tell your grandchildren . . . and mighty bored they'll be!' As Col. George Taylor recounts:

> The object was to secure a bridgehead over the Rhine. This entailed the crossing of three great rivers, the Maas, the Waal and the Neder Rijn at Arnhem. The airborne troops of three magnificent divisions (101 US Airborne under Maj.-Gen. Maxwell Taylor, 82 US Airborne under Maj.-Gen. Gavin and 1st British Airborne under Maj.-Gen. Urquhart) were to pave the way by forming a 'flying carpet' and seizing the great bridges at Grave, Nijmegen and Arnhem. (A 60-mile thrust through Eindhoven, Veghel and Uden known as Club Route.) The 2nd Army with XXX Corps as its steel spearhead was then to connect up with the airborne troops with the utmost speed. Guards Armoured was to lead XXX Corps and 43 Division was to pass through after the capture of Arnhem and reach the Apeldoorn area, blocking the escape routes of the German armies in Holland.

> On the right 8 Corps was to protect the east flank of the corridor and 12 Corps was on the left. The main task of the airborne divisions was to seize and hold the vital bridges at Arnhem, Nijmegen and Grave. Information about the enemy

dispositions was unclear. The enemy had 719th Division backed up by battlegroups of SS, paratroops and airforce units and their rearguards around the Escaut canal had infantry, SP guns and Tiger tanks.

The two key problems were the lack of information about the enemy and the fact that the whole Corps advance was effectively astride a single road with a 'frontage' of perhaps 600 yds for the whole of the 60-mile advance. Cpl. Doug Proctor, 4th SLI: 'The magnitude of it all left us stunned and apprehensive.' Pat Spencer Moore, the General's ADC: 'I was present at the "O" Group. Horrocks openly castigated – but nicely of course – G.I.T. the "Wicked Wyvern" in getting hold of the commander of 52 Lowland Div. on their first commitment and getting him to agree to lend G.I.T. their divisional artillery support for 43 Div. advance up to Nijmegen. G.I.T. was good at wheeling and dealing – until found out.' By the afternoon of 19 September Guards Armoured had reached the southern outskirts of Nijmegen. News of the British 1st Airborne's precarious situation began to filter through. They had landed 6 miles to the west of Arnhem but unfortunately two German Panzer divisions had recently been moved into the area to refit. This proved fatal. Maj. Frost and his gallant battalion held the main river bridge against all odds until overwhelmed four days later. The American airborne divisions had secured their three most southerly objectives – the bridges over the Wilhelmina and Zuidwillemswaart canals at Son and Veghel and over the River Maas at Grave – but the great bridge over the Waal just north of Nijmegen proved to be too strongly held for 82nd Airborne to take by themselves.

The ground battle of Garden had started on the afternoon of the 17th when 5th Guards Armoured Brigade, backed by a heavy barrage, and Typhoons of 83rd RAF Group burst over the Escaut canal and captured Valkenswaard over the Dutch frontier. On the next day Eindhoven was found to be strongly held. Eventually a triple attack by 101st US Airborne from the north, 32nd Guards Infantry Brigade from the east and 5th Guards Brigade from the west and Grenadier Guards group from the south finally overwhelmed the enemy. And there was heavy rain.

On the 19th Guards Armoured made an excellent advance of 35 miles and made contact with 82nd US Airborne at Grave, crossed the River Swang right to Heuman, then north towards Nijmegen and made a hasty but abortive attempt to seize the road bridge there with 82nd US Airborne.

On the evening of the 19th Brig. Essame was writing: 'The situation of 1 Airborne Division at Arnhem was critical; need for speed over-rode all other considerations. Owing to bad weather, re-supply had failed.' And on the morning of the 20th: 'Contact had been made by wireless. Their situation was critical in the extreme. What was left of the division had been compressed into a tight perimeter at Hartestein, where it fought on, weary, hungry and sadly depleted in numbers.'

In these three crucial days the divisional artillery was in action most of the time. 94th Field Regiment were at Overpelt, supported the main Guards attack on the 17th, and after dark the 12th Corps attack on the left when their gun position was mortared. The next day they were supporting both flanks of the main attack and in the evening thirty Luftwaffe bombers hit the gun positions. On the 19th Maj. Concannon, FOO with the Guards, reported he was well beyond Eindhoven. BSM Fred Fowler's diary: 'Crossed the Leopold canal at Hasselt into action 500 ft from the Escaut canal at Neephelt, very easy digging in sand: two pubs on edge of gun position, nice beer and sherry but soon sold out. We get plastered from across the Escaut 90–100 casualties, Jerry only 500 yds away. Fair amount of firing, we are waiting don't know what for. I see Monty in his open car and get a salute returned.'

It was after two frustrating days, on the morning of the 20th, that the Wyverns started to move along 'Club Route' through Hechtel. The Recce Regiment led the divisional column of 3,300 vehicles, followed by 130th Brigade, 214th Brigade, the Royal Netherlands Brigade (under command) and 129th Brigade. 8th Armoured Brigade, 147th Field Regiment and 64th Medium were also under command. The whole morning was spent static in an immense traffic jam as 107th Panzer Brigade's tanks and SP guns had cut the centre line at Son, 5 miles north of Eindhoven. Passing many knocked-out Guards Armoured Shermans Brig. Ben Walton's 130th Brigade reached the Grave bridge by nightfall. The Recce Regiment with 12/60th KRRC were ordered to protect the right flank against a possible counter-attack.

Whilst assembling at Hechtel we could see V-2s being launched about a mile away in woods from where we were. They were being fired desperately before they were over-run. Fired straight up then angling off towards their target. I (R.F. Hall) was then 2 i/c 'C' Coy 4 Dorsets under Tony Crocker. When we reached the bridge at Nijmegen we were stuck with tanks in front and the rest of the Brigade behind. We could see the tidy Dutch collecting up German corpses in carts and dumping them in the river!

Lt.-Gen. Horrocks and the GOC met at Malden on the road from Heurnan to Nijmegen late on the 20th and as a result 4th Dorsets were sent to protect the Grave bridge and a company were sent to Neerbosch, while 7th Hampshires and 5th Dorsets were sent to help clear Nijmegen. The two bridges, road and rail, were intact. One theory was that the Germans planned to counter-attack from Arnhem due south and retake Nijmegen. 'This was quite the most fantastic operation; far from finding any Germans lurking in the town, it was with the greatest difficulty that any progress could be made through the excited occupants who festooned the troops with flowers, filled their pockets with apples,' wrote Maj. G.R. Hartwell of 5th Dorsets. By early afternoon on the 21st they had established a bridgehead on the north bank of the Waal, covering both road and rail bridges, while the Hampshires took over responsibility for the south bank. The Grenadier and 3rd Irish Guards plus Gen. Gavin's 82nd Airborne had done a fine job in capturing the great Nijmegen bridges. Now the Wyverns guarded them.

On the night of the 20th 214th Brigade had only reached Eindhoven because of the slow-moving traffic on 'Club Route'. Later on the 21st Col. George Taylor met Gen. Horrocks, who told him and Brig. Essame and the other two COs, that the enemy was stubbornly holding a line north of the bridge and preventing the Guards from breaking through to reach Arnhem. Gen. Model's first priority was to block off the approach of the Guards. 'Horrocks said "What would you do, George?" I said "Do a left hook and use the DUKWs to cross behind the enemy holding Oosterhout." I did not believe they had much depth behind that village. This proved to be so.' The area between the Waal and Neder Rhine was called the Island. In his memoirs Horrocks wrote:

With its dykes, high embankments carrying the roads and deep ditches on either side it was most unsuitable for armoured warfare. It was perfect defensive country in which the anti-tank gun hidden in the orchard was always master of the tank silhouetted against the skyline. I pinned my hopes on the 43rd

Infantry Div. which had been ordered up from the rear. Their move had been much delayed by congestion, along our one and only road, caused to a large extent by the increasing enemy pressure which was coming in from the flanks. On arrival they would push through the Guards in the morning (of 22nd). I hoped this fresh infantry division would succeed in joining up with the Polish Parachute Brigade who had dropped on the 21st near the village of Driel. Together they would be able to bring succour to the hard-pressed Airborne.

The German 9th and 10th Panzer Divisions were now putting intense pressure on the narrow corridor – 1,000 yds wide at most – from the west, and furious counter-attacks were coming in from the Reichswald Forest to the east on Gen. Jim Gavin's 82nd Airborne. Gen. Urquhart in Arnhem wrote ruefully: 'It means that Horrocks was already some 30 hours behind schedule!' Communications with the beleaguered Airborne were minimal. 64th Medium Regiment RA was now 11 miles south of Arnhem and had targets fired into the Market area selected by the airborne brigadiers Shaw, Hackett and Hicks. Curiously the civilian telephone exchanges were still working and Dutch civilians in Nijmegen were still talking to their friends in Arnhem, but the sophisticated British Army was unable to communicate effectively over that fairly short distance! 'I wandered into a cottage and found some Dutch Resistance chaps,' remembers R.F. Hall, 4th Dorsets. 'I asked them what was happening in Arnhem. They picked up the phone, asked their friends in Arnhem and told me the position.'

Brig. Essame pointed out: 'The country ahead (north of Nijmegen) was a maze of orchards. No viewpoint (for gunner OPs) could be found. The enemy held firmly the grid-iron of roads south and south-west of Elst in considerable strength. His west flank clearly rested on the maze of houses, orchards and trees around Oosterhout. This the two Brigadiers (Essame and Norman Gwatkin of the Guards Armoured) must take with all speed to enable the advance to be continued.' Unfortunately 7th Somerset Light Infantry had been delayed getting through Nijmegen.

How clean and wholesome were the Dutch houses, red-tiled, red-bricked, clear shiny windows, close-cropped neat lawns. When the Dutch discovered we were British, the barriers went down, hugging and kissing all round, every vehicle in the column had a Dutch Fan Club. Woodbines, Gold Flake and Senior Service fags were brought out by us. We held those Dutch people in high esteem. My Sergeant said if the women could have been better looking he might even fall in love with them (wrote Pte. D. O'Connell, 7th SLI. Later) A muck-up in a Dixie occurred. The column in front got separated from the rest. . . . I became the front carrier in a dash across the road bridge. At one part of the town was love, kisses, fruit and flowers: on the other there was a barrage of bullets. A motley group tailed behind us, light AA guns, some anti-tank guns, some Pioneers, another tank or SP gun and a few more ragtag and bobtail.

Eventually Lt.-Col. Hugh Borradaile, the CO, who was the fifth commanding officer since D-Day, gathered his scattered battalion together and crossed the railway bridge, which could bear the Shermans of 4/7th Dragoon Guards. They then advanced 2 miles to set up an attack on the village of Oosterhout. The GOC ordered his third brigade, 129th, still some way behind on 'Club Route', to advance over the road bridge on the right – and then both 214th and 129th would set sail for Arnhem. Weather conditions were awful, rain and thick mist, so RAF support was nil. Ammunition for the divisional artillery was rationed because of the acute supply problems on the centre line. In any case FOOs could not easily identify targets. 130th Brigade in Nijmegen was to be relieved by 69th Brigade of 50th Division, with the defence of Grave bridge handed over to the Royal Netherlands Brigade. The only concrete road on the 'Island' was the main road from Nijmegen to Arnhem running through Elst, and the Guards simply could not get past the tank and anti-tank defences, hence Gen. Thomas's left flanking attack (and that of Col. George Taylor). For the set-piece attack on Oosterhout the Somersets had much support. Maj. Sidney Young's 'D' Company led and were soon pinned down on the southern fringes of the village by a tank, 88-mm and infantry defences. Young was mortally wounded and died later. He was known to Pte. O'Connell and others as 'Gun Cotton Joe' for his love of explosives, loud bangs and hell for leather charges. 'I was front carrier and had to pick him up and drive him to the RAP where he died a few hours later. We were saddened but that was life or death and we had to move on.' The Somersets then tried to turn the right flank and failed, so Brig. Essame ordered a set piece attack with H-Hour at 1520 hrs, a barrage of four field regiments, a medium regiment, heavy 4.2-in and 3-in mortars – the lot. By 1700 hrs 'A' and 'B' Companies reported that the village was clear, 139 SS prisoners were taken for the loss of twenty-two casualties including three KIA. Five small AA guns, an 88mm gun and three tanks were captured or destroyed but Gen. Urquhart was dismissive: 'wasted most of a day, held up by a tank and some infantry'. The Corps artillery was now down to three rounds per gun. And Horrocks sent the Somersets a personal message of congratulations.

The Recce Regiment probed the north-west sector of the 'Island', scouting into De Hulk, Andelst, Zetten and Randwijk. 'C' Squadron patrolled towards Hien. The enemy encountered were elderly gentlemen of the Luftwaffe dressed in smart new uniforms, who had been manning searchlight or AA Flak sites in occupied Holland. They were on their way to Utrecht and were not amused to be put in the bag. Regimental HQ was set up in Slijk Ewijk.

Now it was the Cornwalls' turn. Col. George Taylor in the dusk quickly formed up on the road north-east of Oosterhout, an 'armoured column' with ammo and medical stores intended for the airborne survivors and, at the rear, Maj. Parker's 'A' Company with carriers and mortar platoon. The rest of the battalion under Maj. St George Martin was to follow on foot. The objectives were to reach Driel on the banks of the Neder Rijn, link up with the Polish gliderborne troops and make contact with the airborne. After the spirited defence of Oosterhout by the Germans it appeared a tall order. Off they set at full tilt, roared ahead on the bund (riverside track), and reached Slijk Ewijk 'tracks clanking, motors roaring, dashing headlong ignoring the danger of ambush and mines, we were soon in the streets of Valburg. The Dutch inhabitants astonished at the eruption of armour and men, went wild with joy, shouting and cheering. The light was fading rapidly as the head of the column reached Driel. The journey of about 10 miles had been completed in under 30 minutes. We felt that even Gen. Patton would not grumble at this,' were Col. Taylor's words. An equally exciting drama was happening in the rear of the column as CSM Philp, DCM recounts: 'Maj. Parker was leading 'A' Coy's group in his jeep travelling much faster than my carrier. Halfway to Driel I was 600 yds behind. In the distance I saw Maj. Parker passing a tank on the fork roads between Elst and Driel. Within 100 yds I saw they were a column of tanks marked with the black cross. We could not stop but charged on hoping to get through.' CSM Philp shot the leading tank commander and he and his carrier baled out in a muddy ditch with Pte. Tucker and Rogers, and they lived to tell the tale.

Maj. Harry Parker then returned with PIAT reinforcements and laid an ambush at the De Hoop crossroads.

We now heard the Tiger tanks shooting up 'B' Coy. A German dispatch rider came up the road from Elst, blew up literally on our No. 75 mines. We then heard the tanks returning headed by a DR. He also blew up. The leading tank was firing Very lights every 30 seconds, obviously 'windy'. There were five tanks. As the first tank reached the .75 mines I gave orders to fire. There was a tremendous explosion and six PIAT bombs hit the tank, put him completely out of action. The next tank hit the mines, received the same treatment. The third tried to back out but hit a string of mines which had been pulled behind it. He came to a halt. Every time he tried to move another mine went off. Pte. Brown went within a few yards of the tank, fired his PIAT. The tank was knocked out but Brown lost an eye. As he was put on a jeep later he said 'I don't care, I knocked the bugger out.' The two remaining tanks panicked, tried to back out and ditched themselves. The crews escaped into the woods. Although shelled by 'friendly' fire CSM Philp dropped grenades down their turrets making them incapable of further action, despite being wounded by a shell splinter.

So the Cornwalls had an exciting night, and Pte. Brown was awarded the MM.

Contacts were made with the HQ of Gen. Sosobowski, the Polish commander, a proud, very independent character. The GI of the Airborne Division had swum the river and reported that their losses were so great that they had scarcely enough men to guard their perimeter under attack by tanks and SP guns. For thirty-six hours no news had been received of Maj. Frost's heroic battalion holding Arnhem bridge. The attempt to get the DUKWs laden with ammo and medicines failed. The big awkward vehicles, top heavy and clumsy, ran off the slippery road into the ditch and were stranded. The Recce Regiment was now guarding Slijk Elst and the Worcesters had come up in DUKWs to guard the Valburg crossroads.

While the Somersets and Cornwalls were successfully beating their way forward on the western flank, 129th Brigade with 4th

Wiltshires leading, supported by 13/18th Hussar tanks on the eastern flank, headed due north towards Elst. Maj. Hans-Peter Knaust, the German CO at Elst, was handling his battle group with skill. The terrain was described by the Wiltshires as

> . . . dead flat polder, dotted with thick apple orchards, an intersected maze of drainage ditches 5 ft wide filled with water and thick mud. The ground was impassable to tanks because of ditches and few crossing places. The church spire at Elst stood out – the best OP on the island. Co-ordination between 129 Bde and 214 Bde was 'lacking' and 'A' Company attacked 7 Somersets in the orchards 500 yds away to the left! (Finally 'A' Company under Maj. A.D. Parsons found their 'real' enemy.) Violent close quarter fighting took place in the orchards and ditches against well dug-in, concealed enemy.

Tank and mortar fire rained down on the Wiltshires, 'desperate section battles took place, stalking Spandaus up ditches, waist deep in mud and water trying to rush them. All the head-on attacks failed.' 'B' Company tried to move through to clear the crossroads but two Mk IV tanks held them up, causing heavy casualties. Two Shermans of 13/18 Hussars were soon knocked out and at last light four more were lost in one minute. The mortars had to be man-handled into place and often had targets only 100 yds ahead. Capt. Bedford and Lt. Hardiman were killed and the Wiltshires took thirty-seven casualties on that black day. 'Not for want of trying, Elst was not reached, we achieved next to nothing!' Night fell with both sides dug in 50 yds apart.

On their way through Nijmegen on the night of the 22nd, Ron Garner, 5th Wiltshires, recalls:

> All along the bridge, high up in the struts were dead Germans, snipers who had climbed perilously in the steel girders to try and stem the advance. We made contact with the American 82nd Airborne and Bn HQ was established in Lent on the north side of the river. The rifle companies moved forward to take up defensive positions. 'A' Coy was counter-attacked. Our CO, Co Roberts, spent so long with them, we thought he had become a casualty. That evening a brengun carrier exploded setting light to a 15 cwt and two DUKWs. 25 pdr ammo exploded in all directions setting light to surrounding buildings. Our casualties were four killed and fourteen wounded. Next morning (22nd

'C' Coy was attacked and in the evening 'A' moved forward to make contact with the 1st Welsh Guards. During 23rd enemy fighters numbering over a hundred attacked the Nijmegen bridge but some of their bombs fell too close to be comfortable.

For twenty-five hours 'Club Route' had been cut by a German force of thirty tanks and two hundred vehicles from Erp on the right flank astride the centre line north-east of Veghel. 32nd Guards Brigade had to be sent back to re-open the road. Gen. Dempsey and Lt.-Gen. Horrocks, who had met at Veghel, saw at first hand the very determined German attacks. At this stage they must have realised that there was no likelihoood of getting the whole of 43rd Division across the Neder Rijn and thus reinforcing the battered airborne troops. The GOC now ordered 130th Brigade to advance at first light on the 23rd along the Bund to Slijk Ewijk, via Valburg, to link up with the Cornwalls in Driel, while 214th Brigade were to capture Elst from the west, that is, from Valburg. Led by 5th Dorsets, 7th Hampshires and 4th Dorsets in sleet and driving rain, the column set off at 0600 hrs, supported by 13/18th Hussars, in another mad dash for Driel. Bill Hudson, Canloan officer with 5th Dorsets: 'Going through Nijmegen, Ted Chivers told me to remove my rank badges and to carry a rifle so as not to be an obvious target for snipers. "Farmer" Jewell of our platoon stood on the edge of his slit trench, firing back with a Bren at an ME 109 which was strafing us, shouting "I'll do you, you bugger."' Despite the column being cut in two by enemy tanks firing from Elst, 5th Dorsets reached Driel by 1130 hrs and contact was made with the Cornwalls and the Poles.

By 1645 hrs 4th Dorsets had reached Homoet with 7th Hampshires on their left near Heteren. Gen. Urquhart in Oosterbeek received a message: 'leading infantry 43 Div. have arrived south bank. Hope they will be able to cross under mist.' He also wrote in his memoirs: 'Gen. Thomas ordered a comparatively junior Brigadier (Ben Walton) of 130 Brigade to take the Polish brigade under command and attempt a crossing into the perimeter at night. The plan was not going to produce a crossing of sufficient strength to be of any real use.'

Meanwhile the Cornwalls had laid on a fire plan from the south bank from tanks, MGs and 3-in mortars to distract the German troops surrounding the airborne perimeter. The Wyverns received a considerable amount of 88-mm shells, airburst and mortars in return. Col. George Taylor asked Brigade for a supply of assault boats so that if necessary his Cornwalls could cross the river. A few boats were brought up and given to the Polish Brigade.

It was mid-afternoon before the follow-up 214th Brigade managed to deploy across the Valburg crossroads under constant 88mm and MG fire. Their Battalion HQ was in the local pub near the crossroads. As Gen. Thomas arrived for an 'O' group with Brig. Essame a fierce 88-mm stonk greeted his arrival, smashed the pub windows and killed several men outside. A second salvo arrived and 'Von Thoma' vented his wrath, not on the Germans, but on the person responsible for siting Brigade HQ in an obvious target site! Eventually just before dusk the attack started on Elst, held by Waffen SS, under a divisional barrage. On the right (southern) flank, 7th Somersets had to move cross country with their tracked vehicles and supporting tanks separated on the main road. Pte. Len Stokes:

'B' Coy was reduced to only two platoons. The attack on Elst was to be made along the axis of the road – behind the back gardens of the houses. We set off in heavy rain and had gone three-quarters of the distance when we were halted by heavy fire from the crossroads. The two company signallers were just behind me. They called for artillery fire but must have made a mistake with the map reference as the 3-in mortars fell right on us – causing casualties. I was the sole survivor of the HQ group I was with. I was running towards an ornamental goldfish pond 9 ft away when a mortar bomb landed between me and the pond. After this shambles we had to retreat to our start line and in pouring rain started the attack again and took the objective.

Capt. Meredith, signals officer 'D' Company, got on to the main road at Elst and 'bagged two German DRs, a 20-mm AA gun with crew, a towing vehicle, one artillery officer and one ration truck. The night was quite a "bit of a party". "D" Company were alternatively fighting the Boche trying to withdraw from Reet to Arnhem and those trying to get reinforcements down from Arnhem towards Nijmegen. The saving factor was that the enemy's information was chaotic.' Pte. Sweby was in 18 Platoon 'D' Company. 'Our company position in Elst was situated alongside the main Arnhem–Nijmegen railway line. Behind our positions was a crossroads, dangerous because of enemy shelling. About 100 yds from the crossroads was the village church damaged by our bombardment and also by German shelling. The tower was used by both sides as an OP. From our dug-in positions to the north we could see the St Elizabeth hospital with huge red cross on its roof.'

The Worcesters had a more difficult time. Peter Hall had arrested a jackbooted Dutch policeman in Nijmegen ('Christ! A German officer!'), reccied a wood and heard two German vehicles colliding. 'There was an explosive shout of "Dumkopf"', and then he fell through a trapdoor in a barn, 15 ft on to hard concrete. So he went back to 'A' Echelon 'to get my muscles back into trim.' William Gould: 'My platoon suffered with the rest. One lad from Nuneaton died from wounds from mortar fragments. For two hours I sat with him in a garden shed but he never regained consciousness.' Gould recalled that:

> . . . a Panther tank had ditched itself and its fire was directed at an angle above the Worcesters. Four young Hitler Youth soldiers surrendered in the RAP. The Provo Sergeant G. Ridler and five ORs were killed by shelling at Valburg crossroads. The village of Elst was only partly taken by the night of the 23rd and it was not until the morning of the following day that it was properly taken. Every house contained Boche with MG and grenades and the Worcesters took many casualties. Panthers caused havoc and Maj. Souper, OC 'D' Company, and Maj. Gibbons, OC 'A' Company, were killed by 88-mm and mortar shells.

'On Sept 24th No 12 Platoon assembled to take its final objective. We could muster only seven men and Mr [Rex] Fellows the Platoon Commander. On the way in, a burst of machine gun fire spat the earth at my feet; the toe cap of my boot was shattered and I was bleeding badly. I made my way behind a Sherman tank for cover and then over a road and a fence into the arms of two men of 10 Platoon. Lady luck had at last deserted me, my war was over.' Pte. Albert Kings, 1st Worcesters, was flown back to the General Hospital in Nottingham.

Back at the river's edge near Driel the stout-hearted Poles were ferried across the fierce current in sixteen assault boats by 204th Field Company RE and the 5th Dorsets. Although supported by every weapon 130th Brigade could bring to bear, they were unfamiliar with this type of operation and suffered heavy losses. They left the assault boats on the far bank where they were shot to pieces during the day. Maj.-Gen. Urquhart noted: 'By early hours of Sunday 24th a total of 200 Poles had managed to cross. Some were killed before they could be put into position by Hackett.' The General made no comment about the reckless bravery of the Poles trying to go to the rescue of the Airborne. Pat Spencer Moore 'attended a caravan HQ meeting with Polish Brigadier, G.I.T. (the GOC) and Gen. Horrocks. On our way up to the meeting we passed the Polish (survivors) coming back. They looked exhausted and done in. G.I.T. told me later that Horrocks had told the Pole to get his Brigade remnants back out to rest. Pole, standing very erect and fierce. "I will continue in battle, General." Horrocks, "You will do as I bloody well tell you." Pole, "General Horrocks, I will do as you bloody well tell me."'

On the 24th Lt. Jary, 4th SLI, near Reet 'found the Dutch family Witges, father, mother, son and daughter riddled by Schmeisser fire. They lay in awkward posture of death amidst their ransacked home. The charred wreckage of an American Dakota, and the torn and burnt bodies of the 82nd Airborne troops littered the orchard like charred and mutilated rag dolls. Attached to a front window of the remains of the cockpit was a tiny teddy bear. In one garage was a pile of British equipment, complete R/T set, Radio Telephone waveband set for all major units in XXX Corps.' Leo Davis, signalman 4th SLI, 'rode my motorcycle on the way to Elst and stopped at greenhouses on the way back to fill a pannier with ripe tomatoes. Repair of continually broken telephone lines was a nightmare. The supply lines were cut. We lived on German rations for several days. We did not like black bread and liverwurst. Fortunately 'our' kitchen was well provided with a huge pan of preserved eggs, a side of bacon and a churn of sugar.'

Col. George Taylor: 'There was great air activity this day (24th). The attempts to drop supplies were tragic, but a wonderful spectacle of courage and devotion by the air crews, both American and British. Halifaxes and Dakatos flying in compact groups against angry black bursts of flak shells. Only a small percentage of the parachute containers fell in the target area. Our air losses were heavy.' Horrocks, Thomas, and Col. Taylor climbed the church tower in Driel and made a thorough reconnaissance of the ground, the position of the enemy and our own troops. The area occupied by the airborne troops had no military value. The enemy held the high ground overlooking the river and its approaches. Bridging to put a brigade across was obviously impossible. Horrocks ordered Thomas to prepare an urgent evacuation called Operation Berlin. Cornelius Ryan's book *A Bridge Too Far* mentioned that Brig. Ben Walton's orders to Lt.-Col. Tilley were 'to broaden the base of the perimeter' and then 'hang on until reinforced' with food and ammunition for three or four days. Shortly after 1800 hrs Walton told Tilley there had been a change of plan, 'the whole operation – the large scale crossing – was off'. Tilley was to take 'only enough men to do the job', approximately four hundred men and twenty officers. At the St Oedenrode conference with Horrocks and Gen. Browning the plans were made to withdraw the Airborne Division. Maj. James Grafton, the Dorsets' 2 i/c, was told 'I'm afraid we're being chucked away.'

Brig. Essame wrote: 'To get a firmer grip on the river bank on the far side 130 Brigade were ordered to pass over 4 Dorset on the left with a further party of Poles – on the night of the 24th/25th. The crossing site was the ferry (non-working) at the western end of the perimeter, but overlooked in daylight by mortar and MGs. A factory about 600 yds inland was selected as the battalion's objective.' The current was likely to increase rapidly after midnight so zero hour was provisionally fixed for 2200 hrs. A huge defensive fire plan by the divisional artillery, plus all of 8th Middlesex MMG and mortars, 13/18th Sherman tanks, and from the Hampshires on the left, 5th Dorsets on the right, was planned. But the actual assault boats intended for the crossing had not arrived although twenty had been promised. It is an unfortunate story. In the darkness two lorry loads of boats took the wrong turning at Valburg and drove into the part of Elst still held by the enemy. Two more lorries slithered off the muddy road into a dyke and could not be rescued. The fifth lorry reached the Poles but they had no paddles. Since the Poles were being unco-operative, Brig. Ben Walton commandeered their surviving assault boats. Most of the DUKWs available stuck in the mud or sank or were damaged by shell and mortar fire. The unfortunate CRE, Lt.-Col. W.C.A. Henniker later wrote to Lt.-Col. Tilley, CO 4th Dorsets, 'We only met for a few moments in the dark in that orchard where your start line was, for crossing the Middle Rhine. I joined the Division the day before. After that frantic box-up, in every possible way, your last words to me were "Tell the Brig. that everything is OK. Thank him for his arrangements." Everything went wrong. You paid the price. You need have no qualms about emphasising the sappers' failures.'

At 1930 hrs 4th Dorsets moved off under murderous fire and at

2130 hrs arrived at Driel. Maj. Grafton, 'A' Company, and Maj. Whittle, 'B' Company, were to lead the first flight of assault boats; 'C' Company under Maj. Crocker and 'D' Company with Maj. Roper, were to follow. 'S' Company with supplies, was to cross last. Maj. Whittle wrote: 'We spent three unpleasant hours waiting for the boats to arrive, due mainly to the energy of Capt. Dawes of 5th Dorsets.' Pte. N.L. Francis, 'C' Company:

> We came under shellfire from Jerry SP (large gun on tank chassis). We abandoned our vehicles, dived into ditches at road side. Shellfire was frightening like express trains coming at you, we sheltered behind tufts of grass. When it slackens off amusing to see Cooper, a big lad, with his not inconsiderable arse stuck in the air. Proceeded in DUKWs at full alert. We blacked up, issued extra ammo. Sgt. Abberley arrived with whisky and rum. Davies and I had a sip of whisky. He asked me to go and see his mother if anything happened to him; promised to do the same for me. Prepared ourselves in battle order, pack, pouches, gas mask, gas cape, entrenching tool, water bottle, bayonet, steel helmet, rifle, two bandoliers of 100 rounds of .303 ammo, spare Bren gun mags, grenades and pick or shovel down the back of your pack. I got a pick as No. 2 on 2-in mortar had two containers of bombs to carry, not much compared to First World War lads but enough to stop record attempts on four-minute mile. NCOs like mother hens, 'Keep up lads, close up, lads', original fear of going into action was subsiding, very cold and cheesed off. At start point allocated canvas boats. Follow white tapes down to the river, all hell let loose. First our guns to the rear of us, then heavy MG firing tracer, parachute flares which illuminated the scene. Jerry joined in and we just blundered on through shit, shot and shell while both sides attempted to outdo each other. Took what cover we could behind canvas boat until urged on: came to river, launched the boat, balanced flat bottomed craft as best we could, paddled with rifles, spades and hands. If we had gone into the river we would have had no chance at all with all the impedimenta we carried.

Capt. R.F. Hall was 2 i/c 'C' Company: 'My job was to supervise the loading of our company boats. By the time when I should have crossed there were no boats at all left for our battalion. They had all been sunk or swept away by the current. The enemy were firing mortars and 88mm guns into the river as well as on the banks and machine guns everywhere. I saw the CRA and CRE in their white macs, soft hats and swagger canes walking up and down discussing what they could do to help. A wonderful British sight!'

Maj. Mike Whittle:

Two of the ten boats in my Coy group were holed badly before reaching the bank. A strong current swept my two leading boats rapidly westwards where the Factory 400 yds downstream was ablaze. We were beautifully silhouetted. By using spades as well as inadequate paddles we eventually landed 100 yds east of the factory and got ashore without much trouble. Moved forward to edge of trees 50 yds from river bank but only two further boatloads joined us. Three had been holed before launching, one was swept downstream and landed below the burning factory, four crossed with us, other two sunk during the crossing. On the spot strength of 'B' Coy was two officers (Whittle and Lt. Macdermott) and less than thirty ORs. Where the trees started was a steep bank about 100 ft high and the enemy were well dug in on the top of it. We started an assault and met very heavy opposition. The Jerries rolled grenades down on us. We gained the top with 50 per cent of our strength. We occupied the trenches at the top with about fifteen men. We were joined by the CO (Lt.-Col. Tilley), Maj. Roper and about twenty men of 'C' Coy. They set out to the right to try to contact 'A' Coy and ran into opposition immediately. The CO's party advanced up wooded slopes, were soon surrounded and forced to surrender.

Maj. Grafton's boat caught fire before leaving the south bank so he set off in another. Halfway over he realised his was the only surviving boat in that wave. Of the 420 officers and men of the Dorsets who set out for the perimeter, only seventeen officers and 298 ORs reached the northern bank. Maj. Grafton and his FOO eventually reached the Hartenstein perimeter near the lower Oosterbeek church with the withdrawal plan codenamed Berlin. By 0330 hrs the Dorsets were across the river in small groups. 204th Field Company RE managed to get three out of six DUKWs across the river with supplies, only to stick in the mud on the far side, so their RASC drivers swam back.

Meanwhile Pte. N.L. Francis with 'C' Company was fighting for dear life on the far bank:

We jumped clear of the boats on to the bank which shelved upwards. Jerry MG were now firing over the ridge as we took cover. Suddenly a young Lieutenant jumped on to the ridge, shouted 'charge' – nobody moved. He jumped down again – it seemed a miracle that he wasn't hurt. After a moment or two, he was up again 'come on, lads, charge.' There was a bit of shuffling – no charge. The Lieutenant waved his revolver and shouted 'If you don't charge, you bastards, I'll shoot you.' When the next lull came we mounted the ridge, flung ourselves into the black night punctuated by gun flashes and tracers and a fire in the background. I felt at a disadvantage carrying the mortar bombs. Here I was like a bloody pack-mule, stumbling along, swearing, whilst blokes called out as they were hit, but we jogged on, on and on. (The fighting went on all night.) We fired at any sound or movement. Two well-thrown grenades blew jerries firing Spandau out of their trench in a vivid flash, etched on my memory like a picture on a camera negative.

Francis captured a German Red Cross man and gave him some Sharp's caramels. Dawn came and a German armoured car appeared on one of the pathways so Francis and a corporal shot him up with a Bren gun:

. . . he just bowled off without returning our fire. We pooled our spare ammo, were running short. Where were our lads? Why didn't they reinforce us? If they didn't come soon, some poor buggers were going to get hurt. To our astonishment our officer Lt.-Col. Tilley shouted to us all to 'cease fire'; he continued 'our position is hopeless. Our mission was to draw the Germans away from the paratroopers for three hours whilst they were rescued.' We had been in action for six hours and our ammo was nearly exhausted. There was no way back or hope of relief. His orders were to surrender. We were stunned. We had expected the might of the British Army behind us to reinforce the bridgehead we had made . . . and then relief, perhaps we were going to live after all. (The captured Red Cross prisoner was then sent back to his lines with a message.) Shortly afterwards the jerries of Herman Goring SS Division came out of the woods swinging their Schmeissers from side to side. They marched us off. We were joined by captured paratroopers, airborne and glider pilots, marching in good order, singing 'Green grow the rushes O'. Our singing upset Jerry.

Privates Francis and Davis and the other captured Dorsets (thirteen officers and 200 men were killed, wounded or captured) arrived at Stalag XIIA at Limburg, ' a sea of khaki-clad bodies', and then in October were sent to Stalag IVB, Hut 24B.

Maj. Mike Whittle continues his story:

I took two men to try and contact the other companies, leaving the other small group under Lt. MacDermott. We failed to make any contact, ran into enemy patrols and positions. Almost light, returned to the landing point, found twenty others. I called in the remainder of 'B' Coy, searched for others in nearby trees, dug in behind a bank halfway between river and trees. My strength was about thirty, a few of 'B', 'C' and 'D' Coys, about ten of 'S' Coy and an Airborne MO. We remained in the position all day (25th). Trenches fired on by snipers and a German patrol attempted to attack us. Two well-meaning Spitfires strafed us. A German, speaking reasonable English, did his best to make us surrender. I gave the order to withdraw to the river bank and at 2300 hrs we found one sound boat, so wounded and non-swimmers pushed off in it. The rest swam back. I arrived back at Brigade HQ in Driel with about fifteen men at 2330 hrs. 'A' Coy landed even more scattered than we did; eventually Maj. Grafton and a few men got through to Airborne bridgehead and were evacuated. Maj. Crocker was badly wounded during the landing and the CO and Maj. Roper both captured just before dawn.

Maj. 'Henry' Hall got across with orders for the Dorsets and was later awarded the MC.

I was at Brigade reporting back about my trip over the river when Mike (Whittle) arrived. The Brigadier (Ben Walton) congratulated him on his success and wanted to put him up for a MC. The Div. Commander (Butch Thomas) was also there – he wanted to courtmartial Mike for retiring in the face of the enemy without orders. I witnessed a stand-up row between the two of them. The result was the Brigadier was sacked (Aubrey Coad, CO 5 Dorset took over) and poor Mike got nothing! . . . For the following two or three nights I repeatedly crossed the river in a rubber boat I had found and brought back a few Dorsets and Airborne and beat up more Germans again.

Pte. Jackie Matthews and Pte. Caliendo, nicknamed the 'Duce', were signallers attached to 'C' Company HQ, 4th Dorsets:

> We started to cross the river, but a mortar shell hit the first boat, two comrades were wounded and had to be evacuated. We tried again later in a second boat, halfway over the officer i/c shouted 'Turn back'. He was wounded and the boat riddled with shrapnel and bullet holes. We then transferred to another boat for the third time. The Major was wounded but refused to be left behind. After many minutes of horror, toil and sweat, reached the opposite side. 'Duce', the company runner and I started to make our way to the RV through dense woods in absolute darkness. We suddenly stopped, looking down the barrels of German rifles. I quickly turned the tuning dials off frequency on the radio set. We were blindfolded and marched away to a house. I was terrified. After being interrogated and asked many questions, all our personal belongings were taken away. We were thrown into a cellar and left for several hours – frozen stiff. The Jerries gave us some water and tiny pieces of bully beef. The following night intense artillery and air bombardment started and Jerry started to retreat. (Later they escaped, found a shattered boat and, using tree branches as oars, reached the south side. They found a military policeman and were taken back to the RSM and CSM of HQ Company.) A miracle we had returned after four days of hell. We then learned of the colossal loss of our comrades, either killed or captured, wounded and missing.

Operation Berlin – the withdrawal from Arnhem and Oosterbeek – was finally approved by Monty at 0930 hrs on Monday the 25th. 'Club Route' was cut again north of St Oedenrode and was closed to XXX Corps for nearly thirty-six hours. Three enemy divisions had been identified east of the axis and two more west across the Schelde. It was obvious that the Island was soon to become a salient. Levels of ammunition were running down, the RAF no longer had air supremacy and the weather was deteriorating rapidly. The GOC was responsible for Berlin. Elst, where two Tiger and six Panther tanks were accounted for, had finally been captured.

Thomas was ordered to protect the west flank, and the east flank from Elst to the south bank of the Neder Rijn and keep a brigade group in reserve and supervise the dangerous return journey of the Airborne and remnants of the Dorsets. From 2200 hrs on the 25th 130th Brigade was to be responsible for the river withdrawal and the CRE, Lt.-Col. W.C.A. Henniker, was in charge of the actual ferrying operations. There were to be two crossing sites: 260th Field Company RE and 23rd Canadian Field Company opposite the Airborne perimeter, and 553rd Field Company RE and 20th Canadian Field Company a mile downstream, where 4th Dorsets had crossed. At each site would be twenty-one stormboats and sixteen assault boats. A divisional barrage would be fired to cover the withdrawal and tracer fired on fixed lines to guide the boat crossings. Cpls Eric Levy and Don Linney, 'B' Company 8th Middlesex, recalled:

> For many of the Somersets it must have been the first time they had been under fire. Some of them looked young enough to have just about finished their basic training before being sent out as replacements. We were cut off more than once on the Island. We were issued with captured German rations which did not do our guts any good. It was all confusion, nobody seemed to know what was really happening. Perhaps it was just as well. We were lucky not to have the whole of XXX Corps in the bag. I spent my twentieth birthday being driven up and down the river – lower Rhine – firing a Vickers over the heads of the Airborne as they withdrew – still wearing their red berets when they came up from the water.

Eric confessed that the local huge greenhouses contained enormous, luscious, magnificent peaches! 5th Wiltshires plus empty DUKWs, pontoon and bridge lorries were sent ostentatiously to Heteren, 2 miles west, to stage a feint attack. Ron Garner: 'an operation "Roberts Party" went into action composed of our carriers, mortars and machine gunners – to Zetten to act as a decoy. We took a large amount of transport to make it look as if we were going to cross the river. We put up a fairly heavy stonk, were rewarded with some retaliation.'

On the south bank 5th Dorsets were responsible appropriately for Operation Berlin. Special cooking centres were set up and ambulances marshalled for the wounded. A large barn in Driel, lit by jeep headlights, was a main reception centre, where tea and hot stew, rum and blankets were readied. The AQMG, Lt.-Col. McCance, had forty jeeps equipped with stretchers, as on the narrow slippery roads jeeps were the only vehicles likely to get through.

At 2100 hrs the divisional covering barrage opened up and in heavy rain and pitch darkness the sapper crews carried their boats over the dyke walls and down to the water's edge. Lt. Bevan taped the route from the assembly area to the embarkation point. Maj. G.R. Hartwell's 'D' Company were in and around the reception centre and Maj. H.C. Allen's 'A' Company on the right at the junction of the road and the railway embankment. No lights could be used, but the enemy harassed the area with shell and mortar fire. The boat crews suffered many casualties and Sgt. Rigler's Pioneer Platoon was called in to help and made several crossings. 'D' Company were kept very busy regulating the flow of traffic. At one stage 150 exhausted casualties were lying in the company area. In the space of half an hour 200 mortar bombs fell there. Pte. H.K. Cuffs remembers: 'We had some Paras coming through who had swum the river; some were dressed in ladies' clothes which they had found (in Arnhem).' The strong current carried some boats downstream but the first flight of boats brought back a hundred men. The burning factory flames were fanned by the strong wind. Back and forth the brave sappers went, and by first light 2,000 Airborne and a few 4th Dorsets had been rescued. But at dawn the enemy could see what was happening and rained down 88-mm shells and mortar bombs and set up machine guns in the reeds on the far bank. Despite gunner smoke screens, the CRE called a halt to the ferrying operation after Maj. W.A. Vinycomb of 260th Field Company made one last trip in a stormboat, loaded it with men and came back under heavy fire.

On 25 September Col. Lines the ADOS came to me for what army battledress, mess tins and blankets I could spare for the wounded of 1st Airborne (recalls Maj. Ben Vigrass, 43rd Recce Regiment), who were going to be evacuated from Arnhem that evening. I gave him what battledress and mess tins I had, but blankets I had none. So I went to every man in 'B' Echelon and collected one from each and gave thirty-two blankets. (Bringing up supplies by 'Club Route' was usually rather dangerous.) With Trooper Waring driving the ration 3-tonner we decided to run the gauntlet over the Nijmegen Bailey bridge with the enemy bombing around it. We went across as fast as we dare, when our guns opened up and those red Bofors shells came flying over our lorry from front, back and sides. It was amazing we were not hit. Everyone knew Trooper Waring, an excellent driver, always very cheerful. He would say things bluntly and outright in his lovely Gloucestershire accent. A grand chap.

As they (the Airborne troops) passed through our ranks at Driel they looked like stunned zombies and one wondered if such devastated men would ever recover their sanity and respect. For them at least a respite, but for us the battle would go on. They had been in a very severe battle (wrote William Gould, 1st Worcesters), but it had lasted a mere nine days, whereas those of us who fought on – some of us at any rate – had already endured almost four months of continual action and were to endure another six months before there was any respite.

And Ken Storey, 112th Field Regiment wrote: 'A steady trickle of men (Airborne) in various forms of dress or undress. Perhaps just a blanket. A passing through from the river to somewhere beyond. I think most of us felt despondent to see this exodus. Had we let them down? Mark you, it was no picnic on our side of the river – the "Island".'

Out of 8,905 Airborne plus 1,100 glider pilots who had landed at Arnhem, 2,163 were rescued, together with 160 Poles and 75 Dorsets. Another 200 were making their escape plans north of the river. Sgt. Wally Caines, 4th Dorsets, returned to his unit on 2 October after being taken ill with malaria:

Several of my comrades had been killed and captured. Lt Birch, Signal Officer was missing, believed captured, our CO too. At the CP I met the Adjutant, Capt. Tony Cottle, and new CO, Maj. Eyre, our former 2 i/c. He informed me that men were still expected back from across the River Lek. Every night someone managed to improvise a raft and crossed the river. I was to take command of the signal platoon immediately and re-organise it. We moved back to Nijmegen to a village nicknamed the Holy Land, models of Calvary, Jerusalem, model churches.

On the 5th 103 reinforcements joined the Dorsets but they were still well under strength.

On 4 October Sgt. F.A. Eyers, commanding 18 Platoon 'A' Company, 4th Wiltshires, earned the DCM. With ten men he attacked a large burned-out house about 50 yds ahead and, after a desperate struggle, brought in ninety-eight prisoners, including four officers. Since 29 September the battalion had lost eighteen KIA and fifty-two wounded.

Operation Market Garden was over. Maj.-Gen. Urquhart obviously thought that XXX Corps had not done enough to rescue or better still link up with his beleaguered troops in Arnhem and Oosterbeek. Although in his memoirs Urquhart wrote: 'Thomas could sometimes make me very angry. Having worked with him before, however, I knew that he would do what he could to help us.' And he did. Gen. Horrocks wrote in his memoirs: 'It would have been better to have committed 43 Div. on a different axis, ordered Gen. Thomas to carry out a left hook across the Lower Rhine much further to the west and so attack the Germans attacking 1 Airborne Div. from behind. The failure at Arnhem was primarily due to the astonishing recovery made by the German armed forces after their crippling defeat in Normandy.'

37

ON THE ISLAND

For the next ten days the Wyverns stayed on the Island fending off many severe counter-attacks from elements of 2nd, 9th and 116th Panzer Divisions and part of 1st SS Panzer Division plus 108th Panzer Brigade. Gen. Model's main objective was to recapture Nijmegen and force XXX Corps out of the Island. The shortage of ammunition continued and everyone complained of the German rations which, perforce, had to be eaten: very peculiar tea, nasty carroway-flavoured biscuits, tinned black pudding and hard black bread, although some fortunates secured brandy and 'Genever' Dutch gin. Gen. Horrocks sent encouraging messages to the troops: 'We have burst through the enemy's defences and secured a passage over two of these rivers. . . . I want all ranks to realise that the German is putting up a stubborn resistance as we approach his frontier . . . very soon I hope we shall be advancing into Germany and carrying on the war on German soil.'

On the 26th and 27th the Recce Regiment was guarding the division's west flank. Their front was nearly 2 miles in length. On a dark moonless night one of 'A' Squadron's listening posts reported Germans digging in behind them on our side of the river. Sgt. Taylor, manning a Bren gun on the dyke bank was amazed to see six Germans putting an A/Tank gun into place just in front of him. Confused fighting went on during the night and at dawn on the 27th Maj. Scott-Plummer ordered all troops into action. With machine guns and 2-in mortars they destroyed two 20-mm guns and accounted for many enemy. However, a hornets' nest had been disturbed, and bazooka bombs and shells began bursting among the armoured cars. Some enemy broke through into Randwijk and 'C' Company 7th Royal Hampshires were ordered, with a troop of 13/18th Hussars, to contain and 'mop up' this strong patrol. The fracas developed into a sizeable battle. Three or four Wehrmacht companies plus a company of SS had crossed the river in rubber boats under cover of darkness. Their engineers intended to build a bridge across, the start of a large-scale counter-attack. On the 27th the GOC summoned 7th Somersets to the rescue from their comfortable billets in Herveld. Mounted on 'A' Squadron 4/7th Dragoon Guards' Shermans, they charged down the road to Zetten and Randwijk. Maj. D.B.M. Durie MC wrote:

> Elst was still smouldering after days of bitter fighting. The Germans had crossed the River Lek at Rustenburg with 300–600 men. With a troop of tanks 'C' Company were to capture the dyke road commanding the ferry that the Germans had used for their crossing. We debussed from tanks at Hemmen canal bridge, passed through 12/60th KRRC (part of 8th Armoured Brigade). No information about the enemy: 'A' Coy on our right, nobody on our left for 2 miles. Usual Dutch scene – ditches, willows on either side of road, lone farms, houses, orchards. Boche were well dug in, concealed. Best to move up wet ditches rather than flanking attacks over very flat ground on either side of us. Sgt. Wood, Pte. Pomeroy 13 Platoon, with Bren guns firing from the hip cleared a strong point, killing three enemy, taking twelve POW. We were attacked by fifteen or twenty low-flying Luftwaffe Messerschmitts, but no casualties. At 2030 hrs after 500 yds advance reached short apex of large triangular orchard. We could see the high ground on opposite river bank. It was dusk in heavy rain, given orders to return. The 18 set was damp, out of action. We consolidated near the orchard, and the final attack was planned for dawn (on 28th). Heavy mortar fire, A/tank solid shot, smoke bombs, parachute flares, greeted the CO Lt.-Col. Borrodaile who arrived: 'now imperative to secure ferry crossing *that* night.' So the Div. artillery saturated front of the orchard. 'C' Company with rain-soaked maps amid the burning farm buildings, followed the barrage, 'leaning on it'. At times the Mediums were falling behind us. Ten minutes later objectives taken, the newly dug weapon slits empty, patrols to rivers edge made no contact. Dawn broke on our position completely overlooked from the high ground across the river. Lots of demoralised Boche came in to surrender. A SS officer crept up to 13 Platoon's weapon slits, wounded three men with pistol before their carrier driver Pte. Bennett riddled him with a Bren.

Throughout the long dark wet night Capt. Ian Bridges, 179th Field Regiment, brought down DF targets in front of the Somersets. But on the right flank Maj. L. Roberts and 'A' Company headed for Randwijk and the river bank in the late afternoon of the 27th:

We were pitifully exposed to torrential rain, journeying towards the canal on Sherman tanks and in carriers. Flat expanse of marshy ground up to the southern fringe of Randwijk village, visible some 800 yds away. Our gunners fired smoke trying bravely to conceal our nakedness. As their 88-mms would kill our tanks they supported us with indirect fire. The bedraggled 9 Platoon with Canloan Lt. W.B. Mottram, was in the vanguard hugging the hedgerows. All the time pouring with rain, the 88s were sharply barking from the opposite bank, their shells exploding near us. Some carriers had run the 800 yds gauntlet prancing out of the way of shells. Two Messerschmitts swooped, strafed road with MG fire. Amazing how troops disappear. A ditch or hole leaps to the eye – legs propel with piston-like urgency – a flying leap, wait and hope, panting with fear and thrill. Cpl. Pete Maskell's patrol brought back exact position of enemy, a strong platoon each side of the road. We shelled the wretched Germans mercilessly whenever they made the slightest move. At 0630 hrs our attack went in with a Div. artillery concentration and our 3-in mortars. A great success owing to tremendous weight of artillery. The enemy in slit trenches experienced a foretaste of hell, many Germans totally dazed. Some SS evaded our mopping up and waylaid our transport. A lively battle by our drivers and the SS escaped. Randwijk mopped up after a gun duel around the church. The enemy lost six killed and 130 POW. 'A' Coy only seventy strong lost two killed and five wounded.

Joined now by 'C' Company of the Hampshires the village was finally cleared and there was a final tally of 150 POW. The enemy bridgehead south of the Neder Rijn was effectively destroyed.

Gen. Horrocks now entrusted the defence of the Island to Gen. Thomas, lending him the 5th Guards Brigade who were holding the maze of polders and orchards east of the Arnhem–Elst road. Brig. R.Y.C. Knox with 69th Infantry Brigade (50th Division) held an area south-east of Elst. Brig. Mole's 129th Brigade controlled the line of the railway embankment to the junction with 130th Brigade on the Neder Rijn. Brig. Essame's 214th Brigade continued to hold the river area around Randwijk while 43rd Recce remained in charge of the north-west river frontier.

8th Armoured Brigade was still under command with Sherman squadrons supporting all Wyvern battalions in the line.

Gen. Thomas' southern boundary included Oosterhout, where the Cornwalls were in reserve, and the vital bridges at Nijmegen. The LAA Regiment was there to fend off the Luftwaffe but failed to do so early on the 28th. Lt.-Col. Henniker, the CRE, was entrusted with overall control of the 'close bridge garrison' with 'B' Company of 8th Middlesex and two batteries of 73rd A/Tank Regiment under command. A boom was placed across the river but no one contemplated an attack on the bridges by water. No searchlights illuminated the river.

> I was standing on the southern end of Nijmegen road bridge at five o'clock in the morning when there was an almighty bang leaving a hole in the road of the bridge, followed by another explosion from the railway bridge. One end of the centre span of the rail bridge dropped into the river. We had spent all night watching for frogmen (wrote Leslie Trimmer, 553rd Field Company RE). We failed to spot them in the dark night and so did those watching at a Navy boom constructed further up river. The frogmen were captured, the road bridge repaired and the rail bridge was used as a footbridge.

On the morning of the 29th a large group of German 'frogmen', German Navy trained in Venice, in grotesque grey rubber suits, placed explosive charges which damaged the road bridge and destroyed the railway bridge at Nijmegen. It was a brilliant performance although most, if not all of them, were shot or captured.

George Searle, 43rd Recce Regiment, relates:

> The Div. Cdr. arrived and came into our (RHQ) lean-to tent. I was on set with Trooper Bernstein, a brilliant operator never out of touch and always 'on net'. The GOC drew the CO, Lt.-Col. F. Lane-Fox (a dedicated and brave regimental leader) to the situation map and they began talking. During the conversation which I could not hear properly owing to my headset, I thought I heard the Div. Cdr. say 'One squadron', then dead silence. The CO turned and said 'Would you two leave us'. Their conversation continued and sounded slightly heated. The GOC came out, jumped into his vehicle and drove off. The CO then said to me: 'Tell my batman to pack my kit, I am leaving

tonight.' He looked shattered. I knew him well. He had been my Squadron leader in the Blues previously when I was an NCO in that regiment.

When the GOC wanted to cross the river he had to take a Dutch tug – no wonder he was irascible.

On the morning of 1 October the expected major counter-attack to recapture the Island and Nijmegen came in from the east. The brunt fell on 69th Infantry Brigade and 5th Guards Brigade who fought a really savage battle south of Elst against fresh troops, plus armour and intense artillery fire from the Germans. In the costly two-day battle some ground was lost south of the Waal. The Wyverns suffered too. The 4th Somersets were defending Elst, as Cpl. Doug Proctor recalls:

There were far more enemy to our immediate front than we had supposed. On numerous occasions we had to repulse large-scale attacks. They approached under cover of the dykes and were in the orchard before their presence was suspected. Again, they seemed to have an abundance of ammunition and countless Spandaus with which to fire it. The German Spandau was a deadly accurate weapon, capable of spitting out death at a far superior rate and accuracy than our own Bren. Young Biddle who had joined us at Le Mesnil Milou was killed outright in his slit trench – shot through the abdomen by an enemy sniper in the orchard.

Capt. Hancock, a FOO with 94th Field Regiment: 'Elst church tower was a lively spot for FOOs from all batteries. It was the only possible place for an OP in our area and got a lot of attention from the Hun. Often fifteen to twenty hits a day, but very thick walls.' And Lt. Sydney Jary, 4th SLI: 'Shelled by heavy artillery, SPs with airburst 25 ft above Coy HQ. The casualties mounted. CSM Sammy Jones, Spot Martin the jeep driver, two Bren-gunners in 16 platoon slit trench died, but L/Cpl. Jack Lee, Pte. Peter Filmer were buried in their trench, dug out unharmed, remarkably cheerful. Morale was always higher during an attack. Sitting around being shelled is not an occupation to be recommended.

The Somersets lost 150 casualties in the two-day battle but took over eighty prisoners and inflicted many more casualties.

To the left of the Somersets along the railway embankment 5th Wiltshires had an equally vicious battle around a level crossing halfway between Elst and the river. Maj. Wheatley's 'D' Company was there while 'A' and 'C' guarded the left flank. Maj. E.R. Norris with 'B' were in reserve 300 yds behind in some farm buildings. Capt. David Hadow, their FOO, 94th Field Regiment: 'I had my OP in the station buildings astride the railway line and could see the enemy positions dug into the far side of the embankment. Since the guns were 8,000 yds away and at right angles to the embankment, the angle of descent made it impossible to get within 30 or 40 yds of the Hun.' Sgt. French then brought his 25-pounder up into Elst: 'One of the few occasions when the OP could actually see the casualties being inflicted. Their commander was last seen heading rapidly in the general direction of the Reich!' At 1000 hrs on the 1st over a hundred 88mm shells landed on 'B' and 'D' Companies but the Wiltshire mortars saw off the infantry attack. Two hours later they came again. 'There are more Germans than I have ever seen in my life – about 50 yds away.' But Hadow's DF plans broke them up and tanks were knocked out by the Wiltshires. The GOC was worried enough by the counter-attacks on the Wyverns to ask for, and get, two RAF medium bomber raids early on the 2nd, which undoubtedly deterred 3rd Panzer Division. Nevertheless at 0300 hrs the enemy appeared in large numbers and, as Brig. Essame remarked, 'advanced as if drugged, flashing hand torches to see the way.'

'Enemy tanks came up to the railway and were engaged by our 5.5-in mediums. PIAT teams also went out from our 17-pounder platoon and bagged a Panther. 'B' and 'D' Coy HQs were shelled and set on fire. A personal order was captured by another unit signed by Hitler that the 43rd Division was to be annihilated at all costs. By 1400 hrs 2 October we had suffered a large number of casualties in killed and wounded and 'B' and 'D' Coys had to be combined into one company under Capt. Rudd,' wrote Ron Garner. All the 'D' Company officers were casualties so CSM Jones took command, but seventy-eight prisoners were taken.

Capt. Hadow: 'During 2 and 3 October I had to shoot on no less than three counter-attacks, the first at 0330 hrs on the 2nd, when 'B' and 'D' Coys were virtually surrounded and the level-crossing platoon was driven in; another at 2245 hrs on the 2nd and the third at 0120 hrs the next morning. This time my OP was burnt out.' But Hadow's CO, Lt.-Col. Bishell, was hit by a shell fragment at Brigade HQ and mortally wounded. On the next day a bold counter-attack by Maj. D.I.M. Robbins, 'C' Company 4th Wiltshires captured thirty-three POW including a rare officer. A few days before 4th Wiltshires had found an abandoned German train laden with Luftwaffe winter clothing, fleece-lined boots and coats. And a jam and crystallised sweet factory manager, Mr Taminao, in their battalion area in Elst, sold them many Christmas presents for the folks at home!

Further on the left, a party of fifty men of 116th Panzer Division came over the railway embankment and attacked 'B' Company 5th Dorsets. Their Bren gunners had a crafty ploy; they crawled out to a wood 300 yds away, fired noisily at the enemy and then returned. The enemy regularly shelled the wood assuming it was the 'B' Company position! Across the river Germans could be seen through periscopes wearing articles of British equipment, using British weapons, eating British food, all captured from the luckless Airborne, while on the Island German rations were being reluctantly consumed and German weapons and equipment used.

A strong enemy patrol came across the river on the 1st and occupied a factory in front of 'B' Company 7th Hampshire, and despite six counter-attacks over four days fought them off. The SS Hermann Goering troops sheltered from the artillery bombardment inside kilns in the factory. The 500 yds of marshy exposed ground, despite heavy river mist was swept by well-sited MG fire, and violent hand to hand fighting took place in the tangle of factory buildings. Attacks by Typhoons merely resulted in severe casualties to the Hampshires. Capt. Anaka, Canloan officer, 'D' Company, attacked a machine gun single handed and was mortally wounded. Pte. Barlow, a sniper, killed four of the enemy with his Bren but fell to a grenade. In the four days of severe fighting the Hampshires suffered 150 casualties including Capt. Ward, Lts Hope and Jenkins. They were thankful to be relieved on the night of 4 October. That same day 5th Dorsets were attacked by strong patrols and on the 5th had a very tricky operation handing over to the Americans, leaving their mortars, carriers and A/Tank guns for them.

The Cornwalls meanwhile were in reserve at Andelst and then Oosterhout but not before Maj. Harry Parker was hit in the stomach by an 88-mm shell splinter. He later recovered from his wounds and added a MC to his MM. Maj. John Fry, the hero of Cornwall Wood on Hill 112 was slightly wounded and sent back to Battalion HQ. The RAP was demolished on top of him by three shells. When he recovered he was awarded the MC and posted as G3 to 43rd Division staff. David Willcocks, the IO, entertained with his piano playing and composed popular songs: 'The sleepy dreamy Waal' and 'Oosterhoot, a song of Arnhem'.

On the 5th and 6th 101st US Airborne Division relieved the Wyverns and brigades withdrew south of the Waal – except for the Cornwalls who had to fight one last battle. Opheusden is a village on the Neder Rijn west of Randwijk, which was occupied by 506th RCT (Regimental Combat Team) American battalion backed up by Scots Greys Shermans. But a strong enemy build-up was detected late on the 5th so the Cornwalls, as divisional reserve, moved to Andelst railway station in case they were needed. They were. The Americans, having eliminated 200 Germans the previous day, were now pushed back to the eastern outskirts of the village. 'Col. Sink and I decided', wrote Col. George Taylor, 'that the best policy was a combined Anglo-American spoiling attack along the road (westwards) to the village church with the Cornwalls on the left, Americans on the right, supported by a thin artillery barrage and mortar fire. The Scots Greys were to capture a small bridge and open up the road. It was a nasty, savage little battle that went on for many hours against A/Tank guns, mortars, MG and small arms fire from a determined enemy. The many evil-smelling irrigation ditches were just one hazard. The radios all failed to work. One of the Scots Greys tanks, having knocked out about thirty enemy troops was itself 'brewed up' and the road blocked. The village mill was crammed full of American, British and German wounded. Sgt. Baron MM and Lt. Snell fired Brens from the hip and threw grenades. Maj. Kingston, Capt. Spencer and Lt. Snell were wounded. The Americans ran out of ammunition and had to withdraw. Lt. Welsh and Sgt. Baron were killed amongst the seventy Cornwall casualties that day. 'Company losses were severe, the men could make no further headway. But they put down enough fire with Brens, mortars to hold the enemy in a deadly stalemate', wrote Col. George Taylor. 'All the battalion jeeps under Lt. Birchenall, the Pioneer officer, late that night ferried out all our wounded, American and British. A new fresh US battalion relieved us, digging in further to the east. Maj.-Gen. Maxwell Taylor, the American divisional commander, personally thanked the Cornwalls who 'attacked on schedule with vigour and determination in the face of withering enemy fire. Their courage was an inspiration.'

38
OPPOSITE THE REICHSWALD

Early Winter

For nearly five weeks – 7 October to 10 November – the Wyverns found themselves in a role of static defence in an area east of Nijmegen between the rivers Maas and Waal. Just west of the Reichswald on the German border, it was a country of sandy heathland, small farms, woods and uncleared American minefields. 82nd US Airborne Division had dropped in the zone around Groesbeek, Malden, Mook, Knapheide, Cuijk and Molden Hoek where 129th Brigade first arrived on the 8th. Their responsibility was for Molden Hoek and the pontoon bridge at Mook over the Maas, which was, shades of Nijmegen bridge, to be heavily guarded. 214th Brigade then arrived to take over from 3rd British Division south-east of Mook, and on the 10th 130th Brigade relieved 505th RCT of the 82nd US Airborne east of Groesbeek. The GOC put his HQ in the orchards near Hattert and the divisional artillery deployed their gun positions in the wooded sandhills just east of the Maas. 'The policy of 5th DCLI during this time', wrote Col. George Taylor, 'was active defence, patrol raids and harassing fire on a four days on, four days off routine. Much of our time out of the line was spent on training.'

Pat Spencer Moore recalls: 'G.I.T. resuscitated the Divisional Battle School with (Maj.) Algy Grubb and (Maj.) Ken Mead – both had come through unscathed and had been instructors at Sandwich. G.I.T. was very enthusiastic about these two young officers. Both company commanders, they got on, without fuss and got stuck into their job. No whingeing and stood up for themselves if needs be. They remained doing these NCOs and officer (3 /2 day) courses up to and after the war.' The GOC directed that every available daylight hour away from fighting should be devoted to military work, mine clearing, house-to-house fighting, Bren and mortar firing. 'Back to battle drill' was the General's slogan, 'the motto of 43 Div. has always been that nothing but the best will do'. The battle school was in Haute Heiuvel, in the Nijmegen suburbs.

Both GOC and the Corps commander were anxious to keep up morale, always difficult in dreary, winter defensive positions. Lt.-Gen. Horrocks lectured audiences of officers and NCOs in the village hall at Hattert. He told them of the wider aspects of the war, the battles in the Schelde to clear Antwerp, the full story of the Arnhem campaign and some of the plans to invade Germany. News from home about the continuing V-2 'Doodle Bug' campaign was discouraging, but it might have induced resolve to get the war over with. Pte. O'Connell, 7th SLI wrote:

It was nasty, cold, eerie and wet in the middle of those woods, trees dripping with rain in that windy forest. I lost a good friend killed by an airburst to which there seemed no protection. Sounds seemed magnified, many a rifle was fired at an imaginary enemy or a flitting 'Ghost' that seemed to dodge among the trees. It would have taken a group of top comedians and indeed dancing girls to have lifted our morale any higher than two degrees above rock bottom. (The first German jet plane appeared and) it certainly cleared the bods from above ground into their slit trenches. The sound was indescribable.

We move to a pine forest at Malden and dig in, taking over from another division (3rd British). Everybody gets below ground and make themselves comfortable. We move to and from HF positions every six days, shelled pretty bad. CP hit and a LAA Sgt. killed. One shell arrives at breakfast time, some casualties. Bill was killed about this time. I get a crack on the head. Good thing I was wearing a battle bowler. I've been to the OP. There seems to be hundreds of gliders there. These lads held the Nijmegen bridges (US 82nd Airborne).

These were Fred Fowler's diary comments. Bill Garnham's LAA battery was deployed around the mining town of Brunssum. 'The gunpit we inherited was well constructed with a small dug out with stove.' Bill was billeted in the local headmaster's large house. 'Leo had five children, two Russian lady servants and kept chickens in the attic.' 179th Field Regiment RA guns were dug in around Mook. On 10 October a ceremonial salvo of shells was fired on to German soil. Sgt. Stewart's gun section won first prize for best-dug gun pit – a barrel of beer.

A solitary shell landed in 218th Battery area (94th Field Regiment) at breakfast time. The cook's truck was destroyed and nine men wounded. These unfortunates were all on the point of going to Antwerp on forty-eight hours' leave. 'Worst of all', said Sgt. Holbrook, 'I saw three rum issues and twenty bottles of gin go up in flames.' Most of the day-to-day gunners' shooting was done from a 'harassing fire' position in a lonely spot about a mile away from the main gun positions. 'One afternoon', said Lt. Chater of 218th Battery, 'there were half a dozen airburst overhead. During a lull some reinforcements arrived. There came an ominous whistling, the guns were straddled by a twelve round stonk. Detachments, reinforcements, kit and everything else scattered. Before they were all under cover another batch arrived followed by 150 shells peppering the battery in a perfect bracket. The Hun was certainly no novice at airburst-ranging.' The Hun was also quite innovative with his propaganda leaflet campaign depicting possible 'Dear John' scenarios back at home involving well-heeled American suitors. 'Why should English be killing Germans when both should be fighting Bolshevism?' was another doubtful ploy. But the kindness of the many Dutch families to the young Wyvern soldiers – many to become lifelong friends – gave much cheer, although the female bath attendants in the commandeered public baths were a source of comment! Parachute silk was a most acceptable present to the young Dutch ladies and was also useful for making slit trenches more comfortable.

Lt. Sydney Jary, 4th SLI, was one of the Wyverns' experienced leaders of patrols. 'In a firefight between a German and a British platoon their MG 34 and MG 42 won hands down against our Bren and Sten. We were amazed at the crushing fire of these very rapid firing guns – their infantry seldom used rifles, carried an endless supply of boxes of light MG ammo. As the nights lengthened the hours of "stag" lengthened too and with them the mental and physical fatigue of the company.' Sydney, and many others, were always full of praise for their 25-pounder field gun support. 'I doubt if any experienced infantry officer would deny that the Royal Artillery during the Second World War were the most professionally competent people in the British Army.' Sydney, Lt. Alliban, Cpl. McQuillan and Lt. Priani (the PIAT specialist) all led daring and successful night patrols.

Sgt. Woodhouse, 7th SLI, was in charge of a sniper section. From Mook on 9 October his patrol came under fire from 3 MGs in a forest ride, so he fired many shots from the hip while his men got under cover. He was an 'old' soldier, with many years service, a boxer, heavily built, rather bald with a slight stoop. He also snored loudly at night, so slept alone. One night in Groesbeek a Boche patrol crept up to his trench 'attracted' by his heavy snores and fired a burst of Schmeisser at him, which missed. Nor did he wake up. On another occasion he was chasing two pigs which ran into a wood in the enemy lines. His men could hear the Germans laughing at him!

Maj. Durie was going round the posts of his 'C' Company after dark. He approached Lt. Eves on a lonely stretch of road doing the same thing. The two shadowy figures at the same moment dived into ditches on opposite sides of the road. A pause as revolvers were extracted from holsters. Both heads came up. 'Psst – who's there?' Heads both go down in case the answer should be bullets. No answer. Pause. 'Psst. . . . Who are you?' 'British'. 'Then what's the pass-word?' Neither of course knew it, but they recognised each other, and walked off together laughing (not very loudly). From the 5th Wiltshires Lts B.A. Tarrant, M. Stapylton Cotton and Sgt. Mackrell distinguished themselves. Ron Garner's diary:

> 13 Oct. The enemy we were up against in this area (near Middelaar) were nicknamed the 'stomach' battalion since most suffered from stomach ailments. Although we did not attack, we kept up incessant shell and mortar fire. Every night there was extensive patrolling co-ordinated with intricate fireplans which kept the enemy awake and alert. We had quite a few deserters come over to our lines. Our battalion snipers had some good times when they went out. Nearly every expedition was a success and kills reported. When we moved to Groesbeek we came under fire from rocket projectors nicknamed 'Moaning Cows'. The local monastery was used frequently as an observation post.

On one occasion a monk lingered too long at an open window and was killed by an enemy sniper.

James Brind, the 2 i/c and temporary CO of 4th SLI said to Sydney Jary:

> 'See if you can bring me back the German CO's pyjamas tonight from Middelaarhuis.' With a smile he gave me a bottle of gin. The patrol of six men included Cpl. Doug Proctor, Williams and Filmer with Bren gun and seven magazines. Plus

three armed with Stens and grenades. Jary carried a Colt revolver, 4 grenades and a large umbrella. After three patrols he was awarded the MC. Monty said to him 'Patrolling is bloody, isn't it?' To which Jary answered 'Why is it always the same people chosen for patrols?' The Field Marshal answered with a twinkle in his eye. 'One day you will command a battalion and you will understand the problem.'

Every regimental history has one or more pig stories. This is the tale of Sgt.-Maj. Laurie Symes, 7th Royal Hampshires. On the Island 'C' Company HQ was in a farm building where eight small pigs were discovered, so a lot of roast pork was on the menu. Arriving at Groesbeek, Maj. Braithwaite said to Laurie: 'We should have brought a couple of those pigs with us.' So the next day the pig patrol set off to Heteren – 'myself, the butcher and two of the lads in the company carrier'. The remaining pigs were now firmly owned by the American airborne troops who had relieved the Hampshires. A bottle of whisky changed hands as did the ownership of a pig. A German counter-attack came in so 'getting the butcher to grab the pig we jumped into the carrier and were away like the devil, the pig screaming all the way'. On their return 'D' Company were forming up for their meal. 'The butcher let go of the pig which ran across to the mess line. The lads made a fuss of it, scratching its back and feeding it from the swill bin – well that was it, no longer pork chops but a pet. Before long a sty was made, a collar and lead made and it was taken for walks round the company area. It was on parade the next day with corporal stripes painted on each side. The CO came to scratch its back.' After all it was now 0001 Cpl. Grunt (Pig). It got fatter and fatter, but you can't roast corporals!

Cpl. William Gould, 1st Worcesters, acquired American repeating rifles discarded by the American paratroopers in their dropping zone near Mook. Taking over from the Warwickshire regiment of 3rd Division he commented: 'They had been very slack over their line-laying. We had to lay out a completely new system. I was given the job in torrential rain under Monty's artificial moonlight.'

Sgt. Wally Caines, the 4th Dorset diarist:

9 October take over from US 82 Airborne at Groesbeek. Their Brigade HQ personnel – 90 per cent were chewing gum, their personalities were unchanged, the 'Hi ya bud' stuff was all very

amusing! The Bn front is 1,800 yds or so, usual front half this much. 15 October. Pte. Paddy O'Leary was chirping away on his mouth organ. The boys spent much of their spare time playing cards for money or writing letters to the folks at home. At night time line maintenance always carried out. 16 October. Charlie Bolton and I chased, shot and roasted a pig. . . .

Leave was now on the cards – Brussels was the favourite. Eric Codling spent three days there in October in the Hotel de Colonnes: 'the luxury of padded chairs, soft beds with sheets, tables set with cloths and china, not least of all BATHS. A visit to a hairdressing salon, trip to a photographer – comfort, food, drink and entertainment.' Stan Procter, 1st Worcesters, had a forty-eight hour pass to Antwerp and was 'given' 1,500 francs. There the young innocent listened to New Orleans jazz, had his portrait painted and resisted the lures of a blonde girl with a wide-brimmed hat who suggested 700 francs for the night. Back at Mook in civvy billets he managed to see an astonishing number of films. *We Dive at Dawn* and *This Happy Breed* were two favourites. ENSA shows were also available, the Wyvern mobile library appeared, and the Wyvern country club was opened at the hotel in the market square in Veghel. The Officers' Club in Nijmegen was very popular until hostile shelling closed it down. NAAFI now ran seventeen hotels in Brussels and tram rides there were free. Luxuries unheard of in drab war-weary Britain were widely available and the 'Bon Marché' store attracted all the 'liberators'. The food was rather good with local livestock helping out, and Belgian beer and rum rations cheered everyone up.

Brig. Essame now produced an extraordinary order deriving from the First World War. Specifically for 214th Brigade, every gun was manned and fired non-stop in the approximate direction of Germany for one minute at 1915 hrs on 21 October. Supporting tanks fired BESA, the Middlesex fired mortar and MMG, the field regiment had a sixty second regimental target and every Bren, Sten and rifle joined in. It was a 'Mad Minute' cacophony which possibly raised the morale of the many new reinforcements and certainly must have startled the opposition. Just as well no tax-payers' representatives were there to query the cost. A certain amount of retaliation from the Reichswald followed!

As part of the division's training programme, 8th Armoured Brigade were also involved.

Sgt. Wally Caines' diary of 23 October: 'All officers and sergeants attended demo on the use of tanks, but mostly for newly joined reinforcements to practise infantry moves with tank support. Free rides on or in tanks were given to us but after travelling a mile or so across rough country felt I would be an infantryman any day rather than fight in a tank.'

A number of 'management' changes were made. As Brig. Essame wrote almost cheerfully: 'GSOIs came and went. . . . Few men endured the strain of dealing with the impact of a commander of inexhaustible energy, insatiable curiosity and highly critical brain.' On 8 October Lt.-Col. W.G. Roberts took over command of 4th Dorsets and the 2 i/c of 5th Dorsets, Maj. W.A. Venour, became the new CO. Lt.-Col. C.H. Kinnersley succeeded the hapless Lt.-Col. Lane Fox as CO of the 43rd Recce Regiment and the 2 i/c of 94th Field Regiment, Maj. M.P. Concannon, became the CO. Lt.-Col. B.A. Coad was promoted to be brigadier of 130th Brigade in place of the unfortunate Ben Walton and Lt.-Col. N.C. Kenrick, who had been wounded at Baron, resumed command of 5th Wiltshires.

WESTERN APPROACHES

The Recce Regiment had been lent to 8th Armoured Brigade in the peninsula west of Nijmegen, lying between the Waal and the Maas. 'C' Squadron on the right from Leeuwen to Wamel, 'A' Squadron on the left from Dreumel to Alfen, with 'B' in reserve at Maas Bummel. By day their armoured cars manned OPs along the banks of the Waal with carrier and back up troops behind on call. At night two major strongpoints were manned at Wamel and Dreumel. With a front of 10 miles the enemy could not be prevented from landing. Small parties were dealt with, but larger forces would be expelled by 8th Armoured Brigade. Maj. Gosling's Essex Yeomanry 25-pounders were always on call from the church OPs in Wamel and Dreumel. Two hundred members of the Dutch Resistance manned river posts but their enthusiasm caused them to fire off weapons indiscriminately at night and to send out patrols without previous warning. There were quite a few adventures. 'A' Squadron HQ in Dreumel was frequently shelled; our A/Tank 6-pounders destroyed enemy boats and barges on the far banks of the Waal. On 26 October Maj. Scott-Plummer sent out a seventeen-man patrol to investigate a strong point at St Andries. It was a trap, Spandaus swept the area and only Sgt.

Oddy and three others returned. The CO's car and an ammo lorry were shot up by Spitfires causing two casualties. A barge owner in Appeltern asked for the river level to be lowered by 6 ft to salvage one of his vessels, scuttled by the Germans. The drop in the river level had a side effect, disrupting severely all the local sewerage systems. A Canadian recce regiment took over on 10 November and the Recce Regiment rejoined the Wyverns.

39

Operation Clipper

In early November the port of Antwerp was opened and Gen. Eisenhower was able to redeploy his vast army of American, British and Canadian troops. The Wyverns, as part of XXX Corps, were relieved on 10 November by 2nd Canadian Division and started to move 110 miles south through Veghel, St Oedenrode, through Eindhoven to Bourg Leopold – all towns which had been part of the centre line for the start of Market Garden – then across the River Maas at Berg and eastwards into the coalmining area of Limburg on the Dutch/German border. Divisional HQ were set up in Brunssum and by nightfall on the 11th the whole division was concentrated south-west and south of Brunssum. In this heavily populated area the two large collieries, Staatsmijn Hendrik and Staatsmijn Wilhelmina, were hard at work. Troops were quickly billeted and the Dutch miners' families proved to be ideal 'hosts'. Ron Garner, 5th Wiltshires:

We relieved a battalion of 102 US Division at Stahe in Germany and rifle companies took up forward position in the next village of Birgden. The German citizens still in the village had to be evacuated. Each night patrols were sent out carefully because of the big minefields. We did well for food in Stahe and Birgden: stocks of pigs and geese were killed. Stocks of sugar were found. Every night there was a heavy supper in every billet. Except when on guard, men lived in the cellars of the houses. Very few casualties from mortaring and shelling. We were quite happy.

The 4th Wiltshires went to Gilrath, relieved the unseasoned American troops and were amazed at their great enthusiasm and smiling faces. Each rifle company sent one officer and three sergeants to spend twenty-four hours with the Americans – 'lease-lend', in fact.

Gen. Thomas outlined the battle plans for Operation Clipper on 12 November in the Brunssum schoolhouse. Before the main offensive aimed at Cologne could get under way the town of

Geilenkirchen with its key road junctions had to be taken. This small German town on the River Wurm lay 4 miles across the German frontier and on the high ground to its east ran the Siegfried Line. Gen. Horrocks planned to encircle the town. 84th US Division (the Railsplitters) already east of the River Wurm and south of Geilenkirchen, would advance north-east and capture the high ground at Prummern. At 1230 hrs on the same day 214th Brigade plus 5th Dorsets on loan were to break through north of Geilenkirchen and cut the road running north-east, parallel to the Wurm. The next phase was for 130th Brigade to capture Bauchem, a mile west of the main town. The Shermans of the Sherwood Rangers would support 84th US Division attacking from the south, and 4/7th Dragoon Guards and 13/18th Hussars would back 214th Brigade's attack. The final phase would be for 130th Brigade to strike due north and capture Waldenrath and Straeten. No fewer than ten regiments of artillery (six field, four medium) would back the complicated attack. Gen. Thomas must have been very pleased with life. The greenhorn 84th US Infantry Division, 113rd Cavalry Group (armoured brigade), four 'Funny' squadrons of 79th Armoured Division and the usual 'big friends', 8th Armoured Brigade, were all under his command. In fact for the battle of Geilenkirchen 'Von Thoma' on German soil was commanding troops equivalent to an Army Corps. Spencer Moore recalls that 'Monty came to lunch before "Clipper" and declared: "When I am CIGS I will do . . .". He insisted on a photograph of all 43 Div. Brigadiers, plus G.I.T. and self. Monty organised it all.'

One of the problems was the lack of knowledge of the large American-laid minefields in front of the advance lines. No fewer than 1,400 mines would have to be lifted and 204th Field Company RE under Maj. Evill dug them up on the morning of the 14th, and dumped half of them near the Customs House on the frontier where 129th Brigade HQ was established. Pte. Robert Thornburrow was with TAC HQ 'Brig. Mole saw the REs unloading the mines, observed with alarm they were being carelessly handled. He stopped his jeep 100 yds away, went back to protest. The whole stockpile of 700 mines exploded, fourteen REs killed immediately. Brig. Mole and six REs were seriously wounded, sent back to No. 3 FDS in Brunssum. At Mole's funeral buglers of 4 SLI blew the "Last Post" and "Reveille".' Capt. Harry Peace, Adjutant 5th Wiltshires, wrote:

He was a big man in every sense of the word, above average height, thickset with black hair and bushy black eyebrows. His manner was naturally relaxed and his expression friendly – but his 'black looks' were very black indeed. A fighting soldier with an MC from the First World War and a DSO for leading his (Royal Ulster Rifles) battalion at Dunkirk. He went as far to the seat of action as was possible for a Brigadier. He had a great understanding of soldiers and what they were expected to do, and the cost involved. Inspired loyalty – a great loss.

Mole was also one of the few in the division who, as a contemporary of the GOC, would stand up to him.

His successor was an unusual choice. J.O.E. Vandeleur was an Irish Guardsman who earned fame at the beginning of Market Garden where a vital bridge was named after him for his dash and leadership. In his memoirs he wrote:

The other brigadiers were Essame and Coad. The GI was 'Tiger' Urquhart and CRE was 'Honker' Henniker, exceptional officer, as brave as a lion. 4 SLI CO was Col. Lipscomb, 4 Wiltshires, Col. Luce and 5 Wiltshires Col. Kenrick who had lost part of a hand in Normandy. I was given one priceless gift in Col. Michael Concannon, the finest gunner I have ever come across. Michael's regiment (94 Field) shot to perfection. My BM was Bob Levitt of the North Staffordshires and IO, John Isaac of the Green Howards.

Brig. Essame paid tribute to the two Brigade Majors – W.J. Chalmers of 214 and Gordon Reinhold of 130: 'Much of the success of the forthcoming battle was due to their detailed planning. Large-scale maps and air photographs poured into their HQs at Rumpen and Merkelbeek. The fire plan was complex. "Pepperpot" was to go on continuously for eighty-four hours.'

The diary of Sgt. Wally Caines, 4th Dorsets, reads: '14 November. Bayonet training for all, assault training, grenade throwing, rifle and MG firing practice. Signals carried out, radio telephone practice, morse sending & receiving and practical wireless fault finding. 16 November. ENSA. This cheered everyone, the boys were always delighted to see a good show with English actors, enjoyed joining in during the chorus songs. Staff of ENSA did a jolly good job of work to keep standard of morale high. 17 November. Recce to view Wiltshire position at Hatterath.'

The attack started on the 18th with two barrages. The first was that of a large posse of press photographers and the second of 250 supporting guns at 1217 hrs, who bombarded the wretched little village of Bauchem. 7th SLI led from the large sand quarries near the Gilrath brickworks. The bombardment went on for three hours. It included twenty tanks of 13/18th Hussars, 8th Middlesex 4.2-in mortars, 333rd A/Tank Battery and 110th LAA guns.

When Pte. O'Connell saw the horde of cameramen and reporters on each side of the start line, 'I thought we've made the headlines at last. For the benefit of a tubby individual we had to "take" a village and knock open doors that our boys had done twenty-four hours previously. Everything came as promised, squadrons of "Tiffys", rocket-firing planes came and did a good job. The barrage went overhead and we could hear the crump of Made in Britain shells landing in Germany. That heartened us.' Pte. Len Stokes with 'B' Company: 'We were billeted in a monastery for one week, the monks couldn't do enough for us. On the evening of the 17th the monks gave us a farewell concert, said some prayers for our safety.' The tracks to be crossed were named rather grandly Bond Street, Regent Street and Strand. At 1000 hrs hot tea and rum was served. The supporting tanks of 4/7th Dragoon Guards were bogged down. L/Cpl. S. Sheperd of 'C' Company handled his Bren with skill and by 1500 hrs the little wrecked village was taken with 120 prisoners of 183rd Division for the loss of twenty-one casualties.

1st Worcesters also started their attack from Gilrath at 1400 hrs. Cpl. William Gould:

The press photographed us from all angles. Years later I saw a picture of myself in Picture Post leading a section of my platoon. Needless to say the pressmen did not follow us into action. Within a quarter of a mile of Rischden, the nearest village, the leading carrier platoon were picked off one by one by a section of 88-mm SP guns. Every carrier was accounted for; the crews suffered many casualties (thirty-one in twenty minutes). Then the CO (Lt.-Col. R.E. Osborne Smith) was badly wounded in the leg, had to be stretchered away. The two leading companies ('B' and 'C') pressed forward with a splendid rush which took them into Rischden. The senior major (John Ricketts) took over command. In spite of the confusion, continued with the attack on Tripsrath where they dug into slit trenches in the enveloping darkness. . . . All around men ready for flight, this only averted by the extreme courage of junior officers.

'C' Company took many prisoners cowed by the ferocious bombardment. The adjutant, Capt. W.L. Leadbeater, and Maj. Ricketts, to quote Brig. Essame, 'by their courage and decisive action at this crisis saved the day'. The tanks of 4/7th Dragoon Guards were bogged down, the artillery barrage had moved on to support the Cornwalls and 5th Dorsets. The final attack on Tripsrath only 1,000 yards ahead, started at 1715 hrs with 'A' and 'D' Companies leading. A barrage of our medium guns fell 600 yds short and caused casualties among 'D' Company. Percy Huxter: 'I was with 'A' Coy under Keith James and we were to take the north end of Tripsrath and 'D' Coy under Bryan Elder was to take the east side. We advanced into the village in the dusk, very quiet, pretty well deserted, spasmodic fire and a few Germans.' Percy was sent back to contact 'D' Company. On the way he heard Germans talking on the other side of a 6-ft brick wall, 'having a heated discussion, so I lobbed a grenade over the wall, I heard a few screams, then everything went quiet.'

The Cornwalls started from Gilrath at 1100 hrs to reach their start line in Niederheide by 1500 hrs. Their two objectives were Hocheide and then Bruggerhof, cutting the main road running north-east out of Geilkirchen. Despite an immense traffic jam in Niederheide with carriers, A/Tank guns and even jeeps bogged down, Maj. Lonsdale's 'D' Company pressed on at great speed towards Hocheide and after a short fire fight with 'B' Company in the mist and smoke, took the village and dug in near Bruggerhof. 'A' Company under Maj. Holland reached the main road out of Geilenkirchen and laid an ambush. At 1800 hrs Sgt. Garnham and his No. 9 Platoon saw German infantry marching in threes southwards and killed, wounded or captured all of them. But a Tiger tank which arrived at 0300 hrs escaped the net.

The last of the day's attacks was by Lt.-Col. Venour's, 5th Dorsets, again starting from Gilrath. Again the supporting tanks of 13/18th Hussars were bogged down as they advanced south-east towards Bauchem. The approach lay across 1500 yds of open ground. Maj. Hartwell wrote: 'reminiscent of pictures of the last war as wave after wave moved forward. It was a classic attack.' By 1800 hrs it was over. Darkness had fallen and the Pioneers cleared mines on the main Gilrath–Bauchem road. For the loss of only four casualties, 182 prisoners were taken and many more killed. The savage bombardment had destroyed the enemy morale. Over ten thousand mortar bombs alone had been fired on the Bauchem defenders. By nightfall all the division's objectives had been taken. The overwhelming fire plan had been too much for 183rd Volks Grenadier Division – not one of the Fuehrer's crack units. Geilenkirchen was now encircled but no hot food got through during the night to the forward troops.

Gen. Horrocks wrote in his memoirs: 'The attack on 18 November was made with worst possible weather conditions, rain pouring down until the ground turned into a soggy glutinous marsh.' Pat Spencer Moore drove his GOC by jeep into a field: 'ARC abandoned, roads filthy, bloody wet and foul. With map clipped to steering wheel, 19 set headphones around my neck. Head down, "take that route across the field." So we did, halfway across the wheels started to sink. Deeper. Hit bottom. "We'll walk" says GIT. It took three tanks – one bogged down too – to get that wretched jeep out of the mud. Nobody exactly pleased!'

CLIPPER D+1, 19 NOVEMBER

19 November saw four main actions. 84th US Division's attack on Geilenkirchen started at daybreak. The town was strongly held but by 1430 hrs 33rd RCT had forced their way into the centre. The Worcesters were ensconced in Tripsrath and were relieved when at 0500 hrs four Shermans of 'B' Squadron 4/7th Dragoon Guards arrived. Three were immediately hit by bazookas and the fourth by a SP gun. 'C' Company found twenty Germans sleeping in cellars and made them prisoners. At the same time 104th Panzer Grenadier Regiment (15 PZ Div.) attacked 'A' Company but were beaten off with forty dead. Percy Huxter, 'A' Company: 'Just before dawn we were counter-attacked by about a hundred Germans. Some over-ran the forward platoon only to be shot when they reached our Coy HQ. For the next two to three days we were shelled continually by heavy guns from the Siegfried line.' Another counter-attack came in at 1100 hrs against 'C' Company in Rischden, 100 yds south-west. Two Tigers and two SP guns with a company of infantry emerged from a huge wood (later to be known as Dorset Wood). Fortunately the Worcesters' A/Tank guns and some Shermans had reached Rischden and took a heavy toll of the enemy infantry, and three enemy armoured vehicles went

up in flames. Sgt. Drew of 'B' Company hit a tank at 300 yds on his third shot, a unique high-angled shot from his PIAT. William Gould recalled: 'A platoon strength of Germans were marched down to breakfast in full view of our troops. Their cookhouse was in one of the main street houses in Tripsrath. We took full advantage of this sitting target. . . . On one particular night we had 2,000 shells landing on the two villages we held.' Battalion HQ was set up in a cellar in Rischden, the Signal Office alongside, which on one occasion was attacked by fifty enemy. Capt. Leadbeater, the adjutant, William Gould and his six signallers, fought them off with rifle fire until a Dragoon Guards Sherman turned up to help them.

The GOC now decided to seek control of the wood and area between Hatterath and Tripsrath by deploying 130th Brigade, and also that 214th Brigade led by 7th SLI should clear the long wood which stretches from Hocheide 2 miles north-east to Hoven. So at 1345 hrs on the left flank 5th Dorsets with a squadron of 13/18th Hussars set off under a mortar smoke screen. They began to beat the woods on either side of the main track, but in a wide clearing were caught by mortar and machine gun fire which caused several casualties. Night fell with all three companies pinned down, but though most vehicles were stuck, food and rations got through. Not a happy situation.

On the right flank, leaving the carrier platoon and anti-tank guns in Neiderheide, 7th SLI reached the southern end of Hoven wood by 1530 hrs. The wood is nearly 2 miles in length and averages 600 yds in width. A barrage by four field regiments supported the attack and an hour later the narrow neck of woods half a mile south of Hoven had been reached, with forty prisoners taken, but nineteen casualties. One of them was Pte. O'Connell: 'We had been on the fringe of a wood out in the open with our carriers when the mortars caught us out. I received a 22-carat gold Blighty wound in my right thigh. The shrapnel entered deep and after treatment in the RAP I landed up in hospital in Louvain, train to Ostende, shipped home to Sunderland.' For three and a half days the Somersets stayed in Hocheide woods. The only muddy sloping path for tracked vehicles led outside the wood in full view of the enemy. It was slippery, bordered by deep ditches, and nearly every vehicle became bogged under heavy mortar bombing. Only tracked Weasels could get through with food and ammo. The shelling became worse and worse. The huge shells fired from the Siegfried line, with a noise like express trains, rained down on the roofed dugouts where the Somersets paddled in 6 inches of water. Casualties were forty a day. Ten Somersets were killed in Neiderheide and twenty in the Hocheide woods. By the end of the third day, company strength was down to thirty-five.

Now back to the Cornwalls near Bruggerhof astride the main road, 1½ miles north-east of Geilenkirchen. About 1500 hrs on the 19th, about forty enemy infantry backed by three menacing SP guns were trying to escape.

Ptes Reynolds and Potter did well to alert Bn HQ of the situation, since their No. 18 wireless set radio aerial had been shot away. Soon the surrounding woods were being swept by machine guns of 4/7 Dragoon Guards, 3-in mortars and artillery fire. Everything possible was done to relieve the besieged 'D' Coy (wrote their CO). The battle raged for forty-five minutes. For a time it was touch and go. An enemy tank with following infantry penetrated the centre, knocked out an A/Tank gun. Lt. Williams and 8 Platoon were inflicting heavy casualties, often in close quarter fighting and No. 9 were busy accounting for the SP guns and crews. Cpl. Lynch, with great gallantry, ran over open ground defying enemy fire to contact the Americans.

Maj. Holland shot the German CO with his revolver. This was a very successful company action, as the Cornwalls only had five casualties. The enemy left thirty dead and wounded on the ground. And the CQMS produced the first hot food and rum for thirty-six hours.

CLIPPER D+2, 20 NOVEMBER

The Siegfried line heavy guns were pounding the Worcesters in Tripsrath and 7th SLI in Hoven woods. But the 5th Dorsets had perhaps the most difficult time in the woods west of Tripsrath, later known as Dorset Wood. The troops were entering their third day of battle. Still holed up in the dark dripping woods a dawn attack started with Maj. Hartwell's 'D' Company on the left flank fighting all the way to clear the wood on the northern edge. Capt. P. Aspinall led 'B' Company, on 'D's left, and by 1000 hrs the three companies ('A' and 'C' were now merged under Maj. Allen) reached the end of the wood overlooking Tripsrath. They could see open country towards Straeten and Waldenrath. The enemy now shelled with SP guns but one counter-attack was broken up by the divisional artillery. The Gunner FOO with 'B' Company, Capt. Gilders, was killed. Despite many casualties the Dorsets held on to their gains, which included 104 POW and the destruction of almost an entire enemy battalion. At 1230 hrs Brig. Coad visited and gave orders for a relief by 4th Dorsets that night. Sgt. Wally Caines, 4th Dorsets:

We took over Dorset Wood from 5 Dorsets. They had suffered badly, lots of casualties as had our 'D' Coy. Two newly joined officers, brothers, one was killed, the other badly wounded. We noticed the dead of the 5 Dorsets. Jerry had allowed the attacking infantry to get within a few yards of his MG nests, opening up, many met their death almost instantly, situated right into the Siegfried line, subjected to heavy artillery fire. Many members of the rifle companies became lost, making their way through wooded country, pitch black night, only lit up by gunflashes. 'A' Coy under Maj. Hall completely lost, and 'D' Coy missing altogether. It was a hell of a night. Everything seemed to go wrong. Transport failed to turn up, most of it had got stuck in the mud along the main route. All ammo had to be manhandled by carrying parties to the companies well forward. This operation took hours and hours to complete, the whole of Bn area under very heavy fire. Rain also fell heavily, all of us soaked to the skin, trenchs of 5 Dorsets half full of water. Signals carrier lost. No communications for Bn apart from runners. It was bloody miserable. Only remedy, a swig of the bottle.

Lt.-Col. Roberts wrote:

The area was a sea of mud, slit trenches were waterlogged, only Weasels could move, our transport and tanks of 13/18th Hussars all bogged down. Divisional REME under CREME Lt.-Col. Neilson personally supervised this difficult operation. . . . Brig. Coad came up daily, brought me shaving water duly shared out with company commanders visiting Bn HQ for 'shaving parties'. Peter Steele-Perkins, the Battery CO (112 Field Regiment) did valiant work in supporting the Bn upon every possible occasion. The QM Capt. Titterington and cooks in 'A' Echelon did their very best but most meals when delivered were cold!

'On the night of the 20th I went forward in pitch darkness made worse by torrential rain and found Advanced HQ of 214 Bd almost in the front line,' wrote Lt.-Gen. Horrocks in his memoirs. 'I met Brig. Essame who as usual had spent most of the day with the leading troops of his Brigade. The enemy were very active and only a few hundred yards away.'

Dorset Wood. It was just like the First World War. My 'A' Coy took over the top left of the wood. On my right flank, George Mead, a Coy CO of 5 Dorset was buried in his slit trench by a near miss. I was there to liaise with him (recalls Maj. 'Henry' Hall, 4th Dorsets). We dug him out. As his head was exposed the first thing he said was 'Will somebody light my pipe, the bloody thing's gone out.' On the night of the 21st in my Company HQ, a German bunker, I suddenly found myself on my back. I felt no pain. I could not see any faces. I felt hands giving me morphine and dressing a chest wound. It was my cockney Corporal stretcher-bearer bandaging me up. At the RAP the MO checked my dressing. The Padre, stupid fellow, offered me a cigarette and then wrote to my wife to say I had been killed.

CLIPPER D+3, 21 NOVEMBER

All this time the 'virgin' 84th US Division was fighting desperately beyond the River Wurm, in and around Prummern, Beek and Wurm itself. On the edge of the Siegfried line among the concrete defences – dragons' teeth – the defence was bloody and obstinate. It was decided that the Wyverns should help by capturing the high ground south-west of Hoven and the village of Kraudorf, 4 miles north-east of Geilenkirchen. The Cornwalls were selected for this operation.

With neither tank nor A/Tank guns in support, no other Wyvern units fighting on either side, and with the tired rifle companies down to sixty men instead of a hundred (except for 'C'), Col. George Taylor put his reservations about a 'solo' attack in writing to Brig. Essame, who kindly said: 'George, I am not asking your battalion to attack on its own. The Americans on the high ground will attack simultaneously in the direction of Wurm.' And 4/7th Dragoon Guards, Middlesex MMGs and 'D' Company of 7th SLI would strengthen the attack, although the Cornwalls' 'A' Company was still defending Bruggerhof. Taylor's plan was for 'C' to attack and secure the wood south of Hoven, 'B' would then leapfrog through and capture Hoven, and 'D' following up would move on to Kraudorf. From captured prisoners it was clear the 10th SS Panzer Division were the opposition, much more professional than the Volk Grenadiers.

CLIPPER D+4, 22 NOVEMBER

The attack started at noon on the 22nd – the day and night were wet and piercingly cold. The block barrage came down in front as planned.

> Then the German artillery, mortars and 88s joined in, pummelling the area around our CP; this fire caught 'C' Coy reserve platoon and destroyed it in seconds (wrote the Colonel. He sent Maj. Kitchen up to take command.) 15 Platoon had ceased to exist. Moving with difficulty, I reached 14 Platoon. They had suffered considerably. All this time we were being heavily mortared. Neither before nor since have I experienced such an intensity of fire. It was a real shooting match Bren v. Spandau.

The CO could see that the attack had failed and sent 'D' Company formed up on the right, not to attack Kraudorf, but to perform a slight right hook, move into the wood, covered by a barrage and smoke screen and then on to Hoven.

Capt. Spencer, CO of 'D', despite most of Lt. Savory's platoon becoming casualties, had by nightfall taken the hamlet of Hoven plus forty prisoners. All the tanks were bogged down, so wretched 'D' Company was now isolated without A/Tank guns: 'All the time the piteous cries of the wounded as we laboured to secure them added to the misery of that terrible night. The battalion, battered and shaken, was like a virile giant beset and wounded. I sent Lt. Bill Birchenall back to Brigade HQ with a request that 5 DCLI should either be reinforced or withdrawn.' Shades of Hill 112 all over again. Gen. Horrocks now met Brig. Essame at 214th Brigade HQ. The Cornwalls were nearly 2 miles ahead of Brig.-Gen. Bollig's 84th US Division, who were themselves having a very difficult time against the newly arrived 9th Panzer Division. Horrocks told Essame he could withdraw 5th DCLI if he thought fit. Where was Gen. Thomas? Essame argued that the Cornwalls had captured Hoven at great sacrifice and to pull them out now would be bad for morale. Essame then told Lt. Birchenall that the Cornwalls must hang on and be relieved the next morning by 5th Wiltshires. By 0400 hrs 'A' Company had arrived with ninety men under Maj. Kitchen and reached Hoven wood. In Hoven 'D' Company, now under Maj. Lonsdale, was being counter-attacked just before dawn by SS infantry and SP guns. Their wireless set was destroyed, the telephone line cut and all the fortified houses were alight. Ammunition was running out, so captured German weapons were being used. Capt. Spencer fired a PIAT at a tank 20 yds away. 'It was a misfire. The tank crew swung their gun in my direction. A great flash, blinded, hit in the head, arm and leg I crawled down into the cellar.' The fifteen survivors of 'D' plus some walking wounded made their escape back and joined Maj. Kitchen's 'A' Company. They in turn were counter-attacked 'by sixty Boche advancing in uncertain light, talking at the tops of their voices. Taken by surprise we inflicted many casualties.' Two SP guns turned up and peppered the Cornwall wood with 88s. 'But our chaps were magnificent. Pte. Everitt my batman, killed four enemy with his Sten gun at 20 yds.' Kitchen was hit by a bullet in the right shoulder and Lt. Williams took command. 'We had suffered 160 casualties . . . it was our only defeat in the whole campaign except for Hill 112,' wrote the Colonel. 'The formidable SS treated our wounded prisoners with every kindness.'

> Oh grim Wood of Hoven
> Now mined and silent lying
> Here men of Cornwall fought and died.

With Geilenkirchen taken Operation Clipper was formally called off and for the next fortnight the front from Birgden to Bruggerhof was held by successive Wyvern brigades.

Sgt. Wally Caines, 4th Dorsets, diary:

22 November. Weasels brought up rations, inc. baked beans, tinned foods and tea. Charlie Bolton brewed up tea every two hours, mug worth pounds in English money. TAC HQ shelled every few minutes, many times clutched the sides of our trenches, quietly kneeling and saying our prayers. Morale still high, we were all wet through, cold and filthy but hardly a man

failed to produce a smile. Casualties were piling up plus some sick with trench feet and severe influenza. Sgt. Manning and I gave the Signal Office boys a good stiff drink, mugs of whisky, gin and lemon warmed up, dry straw placed at bottom of trenches, slept like logs. 24 November. Rum was still being issued twice daily. 25 November. Some men evacuated with battle exhaustion, worn out dodging shells and bullets. Sitting in a trench is no good for the morale.

On 23 November 5th Wiltshires took over the village of Tripsrath but 104th Panzer Grenadier Regiment still tenaciously held the north-west area, indeed they reinforced their sector. So on the 26th a full-scale attack was put in as Ron Garner reports: 'At 1600 hrs the barrage of 5 Field Regts of 25-pdrs, a Medium regiment and 3 platoons of 3-in mortars started saturating the area. At 1640 hrs 'C' Coy reported that all the objectives had been taken together with fifty-five prisoners.' L/Cpl. Hoptroff with his PIAT, Pte. Kendall with his Bren, Sgt. Hall and Cpl. Barnett in 'C' Company, all performed nobly. Their prisoners decided that the Wyverns were truly a British SS Division because of their ferocity!

Gen. Horrocks wrote: 'The battle of Geilenkirchen is barely mentioned in most military histories, yet it was one of the hardest fought actions of the whole war at battalion, company and platoon level. This was warfare at its most beastly with continuous cold driving rain turning the ground into a sea of mud and constant counter-attacks from experienced German troops.'

40

WINTER CAMPAIGN –
DECEMBER

Lt.-Gen. Horrocks conjured up from thin air a new 'Services' battalion, mainly RASC and REME personnel with a sprinkling of HQ staff and gunners. They held a sector at Hatterath for some time and the hard-pressed infantry gained a period out of the line. The first snow fell on 9 December. Cpl. Doug Proctor, 4th SLI:

> We shared the woods with the Germans but our biggest enemy was the weather. It was cold and wet. Everywhere stank of death and desolation (in the Hoven woods). Our slit trenches were awash with water. We wore gas capes to try to keep our bodies dry, but were permanently wet from the knees down. We still managed to wash and shave each morning. Observation (of the enemy) was difficult, but movement in the thick undergrowth was instantly audible. We relied heavily on our sense of hearing. The dead of the Duke of Cornwalls still lay amongst the undergrowth, the corpses becoming more grotesque as each day passed.

Sartorial standards soon changed. Monty arrived for lunch at Divisional HQ carrying an umbrella, and Gen. Thomas sported a dark, long leather overcoat which made him look like a late Victorian stage villain. Monty also held an investiture for the Wyverns in the Trebeck Theatre at Rumpen, where many of the decorations awarded were posthumous.

In mid-December the 52nd Lowland Division relieved the Wyverns, who withdrew to an area north-east of Maastricht. Immense staff planning went on for Operation Shears, to resume the Corps offensive towards the Roer, but for a variety of reasons it was cancelled on the 12th; a few days before Rundstedt with great stealth hurled his 6th and 5th Panzer Armies against the Americans in the Ardennes. Monty, Horrocks and Thomas all put a brave face on over this startling new counter-attack which pushed 25 miles deep and 20 miles wide into the American defences. In freezing fog on the 19th and 20th the Wyverns concentrated between Hasselt and Liège (near Tongres) and a small task force – 43rd Recce Regiment, two companies of 7th Hampshires backed by 112th Field Regiment and two troops of 333rd A/Tank Battery – guarded three bridges over the Meuse. The Wyverns did not go into action during the Ardennes offensive, which was mainly resolved by the American gallantry at Bastogne, and the eventual clearer weather which gave both air forces scope for terrible destruction.

The 5th Cornwalls played football against the 7th Somersets and won 3–2. Many battalions sent an officer and jeep to Rheims to buy champagne to celebrate Christmas, and there were many officers' mess cocktail parties. A Christmas number of the Wyvern news-sheet and a divisional Christmas card were devised and circulated. A week before Christmas Sgt. Wally Caines's diary reports: 'At Hasselt, Cpl. Haines came running out of the Signal section: "Let me be the last to call you Sergeant and the first to call you Sir." I said "Thanks a lot". It was true. Sgt. Brown and I were confirmed as Commissioned Officers. The Adjutant said: "See the Tailor, get those stripes down and some pips up on your shoulders." In the Officers' Mess I was warmly greeted by my Christian name, made to feel at home.'

All units had made great preparations for Christmas Day. Cafés, halls and schools were requisitioned. Quartermasters, cooks and NAAFI all excelled themselves. The Recce Regiment had two Christmas dinners. 'A' and 'C' Squadrons had tinned turkey and plum pudding with the Americans on the Meuse and again on New Year's Eve. Maj. Ben Vigrass produced the NAAFI ration of 1 /2 bottles of whisky per officer and sergeant, plus half a bottle of gin and wine each. All ranks got two bottles of beer and seventy-five cigarettes each. 'RHQ had their Xmas dinner at Heerlen. I well remember after having dined and wined well, singing some very old songs, accompanied by the piano. "The man who broke the bank at Monte Carlo", "Down at the Old Bull and Bush", and my old favourite "A Stormy Night". Altogether a very enjoyable evening. 'B' Echelon had their main meal in a café with a dance, beer and sandwiches in the local in the evening.'

94th Field Regiment enjoyed oranges, apples, nuts, sweets, port, plum pudding, cigarettes, cigars, even some champagne as extras to the main meal. The CO visited ten different cookhouses and messes and survived.

The Somersets at Visé and Tongres – 'where possible we shared with our Belgian hosts who did the cooking' wrote Cpl. Doug Proctor, 'We took cigarettes, chocolate, various sweetmeats, mince pies and numerous bottles of beer back to our billets to share with our hosts. On the 27th moved back to Klimmen, near Hulsberg in Holland. 'D' and 'C' Companies combined to hold a dance. The battalion dance band got together for the evening and troops and civilians had a very enjoyable time.' Doug's Dutch hosts had a pretty daughter, who was lame. 'She was in great demand on the dance floor. The men behaved with tact and decorum but twice we had to rescue her from the unwelcome amorous attentions of junior officers.'

Eric Codling, 8th Middlesex, suffered a personal disaster:

A large jar of rum was smashed when the carrier slid about on the icy road, ran over the engine, the fumes arising rendered the occupants drunk. We couldn't get money from field cashier's office, so we flogged kit to raise funds, old boots, clothes sold in local café where the drink flowed freely. Charlie Scott our cook made a field oven (near Hasselt) of metal ammo box, bricks and clay. Meal of turkey, pork, beef, vegetables, Christmas pudding with rum sauce, a feast worthy of the best of cooks. Back at our Dutch farm for the New Year, pooled our booze. A pint of issue rum, bottle of white wine, bottle of Guinness warmed up in a kettle gave a third of a pint mug each. A potent brew and I passed out.

41

WINTER CAMPAIGN – JANUARY

Apart from New Year's Day, when the Luftwaffe had a field day and 110th LAA Regiment did too, by shooting down six aircraft including a jet which attacked the division area – the first two weeks of January were peaceful. A minimum of training, possibly coinciding with Gen. Thomas temporarily taking command of XXX Corps while Lt.-Gen. Horrocks returned home for leave and a medical check-up. Bill Garnham, 110th LAA: 'We were having more casualties from road accidents than from the Germans. Alternate frosts, snowfalls and thaws made all driving dangerous and 6th Guards Tank Brigade Churchills were "hors de combat" for a week or more.' BSM Fred Fowler's diary: '1 January. MEs and FW fly over our guns at zero. No incident. Heavy guns on our right shake the earth when they fire. Dehann finds a Jewish family in Putten. We visit them, they had had a pretty bad time. Scared to death Jerry will come back. 2 January. All leave has been drawn. I get number 108. Looks like I shall be home about June with luck. Snowed and thawed, an awful mess. In action in a ploughed field, had a bath today, first for a month.'

Brunssum was the centre of the division's social activities. NAAFI, ENSA, hot baths at the pitheads, and the Wyverns made many friends among the Dutch families. Snowball 'fights' were held with the children, whose consumption of NAAFI sweet rations was considerable. Many romantic attachments were made – some came back later to marry their girlfriends. Besides his visits to cinemas Stan Procter, 214th Brigade HQ, 'played cards and Monopoly with Heynens girls in Brunssum.'

The division relieved 52nd Lowland Division and was back in its earlier defensive position. There it stayed for the next two weeks on a very quiet front in bitter cold. Operation Blackcock was being planned. 12 Corps, which now included the Wyverns, the Desert Rats (7th Armoured) and 52nd Lowland, were given a key role in the plan to destroy the 183rd and 176th Divisions west of the Siegfried line in the River Roer triangle. 7th Armoured would be on the left flank, 52nd Lowland in the centre and the Wyverns on the right. Hart, Jug and Kettle were codenames for the three objectives. 130th Brigade was made responsible for Hart – the taking of Langbroich and Waldenrath – and for the second part of Jug; 129th Brigade was responsible for the first part of Jug – Wetterath – and 214th Brigade for Kettle – Randerath to the far eastern flank. A huge artillery programme with five to eight field regiments, three to six medium regiments and assorted heavy regiments, would possibly obliterate the unfortunate German defences. Despite postponements on 20 January 4th SLI captured Schummer Quartier and walked into Langbroich unopposed, and 5th Wiltshires took over Breberen from 52nd Lowland Division. The next morning at dawn it was 130th Brigade's turn and 4th Dorsets in Kangaroos of the 1st Canadian APC Regiments, moved against Schier Waldenrath. They were supported by tanks of the 4th Coldstream Guards and a troop of 79th Armoured Division's flails thrashing a way through the minefields. 2nd Lt. Wally Caines wrote: 'Our marvellous 477 Battery RA never failed to reply. Joe, our little Yellow Devil Mascot, had been killed in the signals No. 1 truck which got a direct hit from a shell.' Twelve prisoners were taken and many dead Germans on the ground proved the 'pepperpot' saturation fire was lethal. The attack next day was to be the attack on Putt and Waldenrath.

At 0500 hrs the Hampshires in white snow suits set off towards Gangelt. Lt.-Col. Talbot was temporarily brigadier of 129th Brigade, so Maj. D.B. Rooke commanded the Hampshires. Supported by two squadrons of Coldstream Guards in Churchills, Putt was taken by 0800 hrs with the capture of fifty POW. Maj. Viner led 'A' Company across 600 yds of mined open ground, mopping up enemy in trenches and haystacks. By midday, helped by flame-throwing Crocodiles under another 'pepperpot', Waldenrath was captured with another 200 prisoners taken. A German soldier drove his horse and cart into the village seemingly unaware of the shambles. It was full of canteen rations. The Hampshires suffered twenty-nine casualties and Maj. Viner and Rooke later received bars to their MCs. Phase Hart was over and the next day (23 January) 4th Wiltshires and 4th SLI took on Operation Jug.

From Birgden in Kangaroos came the Wiltshires, dressed in white to blend with the snow – painted gas capes, bed sheets and snow suits – on their way to take Straeten. The back up was now considerable – Crocodiles, flails, SP A/Tank guns of 235th A/Tank Battery and Churchills of the Grenadier Guards. Minefields at the exit from Waldenrath delayed the advance and 'D' Company was violently attacked by enemy SPs. The Kangaroos carried the infantry as far forward on the road as possible; then there was a single file attack on Waldenrath. This very successfully planned attack succeeded and over 200 POW were taken for a loss of eight KIA and thirty-two wounded.

From Waldenrath 4th SLI's task was to take Scheifendahl: 'a desolate area of farmland, featureless and covered with a thick carpet of frozen snow. 'Each section', wrote Cpl. Doug Proctor, 'was to have its own Kangaroo, but as usual, chaos reigned. Only sufficient arrived to transport one company. (Later) the Germans threw down their arms and surrendered.' By 1500 hrs with Scheifendahl taken, Maj. Brind with 'A' Company pushed on towards Erpen across 1500 yds of open country. Nearly 200 prisoners were taken and an assortment of guns. By nightfall the village was cleared and a determined counter-attack beaten off, as Sydney Jary reported: 'An extraordinary sight silhouetted by the setting sun on a ridge about 2,000 yds away was a long column of 150 Germans. Behind us a platoon of 8 Middlesex Vickers MGs firing special Mk VIII long range ammo engaged them. I could see the Germans scatter in panic.'

The following day, the 24th, 'C' Company of 4th SLI took Schleiden in the afternoon without much difficulty and 5th Wiltshires swept into Utterath easily. And on the 25th 5th Dorsets moved to Aphoven en route to clear Schafhausen, which they achieved with ease apart from two vehicles going up on mines. The ground in front of Schafhausen was a wide, flat valley through which the River Roer flowed. It became a no man's land occupied by snipers and night patrols. A Dorset patrol was ambushed and three were made prisoner. 4th Dorsets followed up and took Hullhoven and Grebben. Finally by dusk 7th Hampshires occupied Dremmen and moved on to Porseln with no opposition apart from minefields everywhere. 5th Wiltshires put in a classic attack on Utterath from Breberen on the 24th. There was the usual huge barrage and they were carried in Kangaroos. John McMath, their Signals Officer, described the action:

Together with the Bren carriers (and troop of Churchill tanks) there were over 100 armoured vehicles, surged forward over the flat open snow-covered fields, they looked like a mighty fleet of warships. At this fearful spectacle the enemy gave in at once. Utterath was captured, eighty prisoners taken and only one casualty suffered. Then the small villages of Baumen and Berg were taken. (Later) L/Cpl. Holloway with his section of Pioneers removed 126 Reigel mines from frozen ground in 1 /4 hours and on 26 January the enemy sent over pornographic propaganda leaflets in shells!

Brig. Essame's 214th Brigade in reserve prodded its way through minefields to Nirm, Kraudorf and Randerath without any trouble. Thus Operation Blackcock ended in a complete victory for the Wyverns. It could be argued that 183rd and 176th Divisions were not the crème de la crème, that they were attacked and bombarded on a huge terrifying scale but they were well dug in, had had plenty of time to prepare their defences and were surrounded by enormous minefields. Eric Codling: 'Typhoon and Tempests fired rockets, circling the battle area, then heading in our direction. Dropping to the bottom of the mortar pit and cowering in absolute terror, the sound of the aircraft's machine guns battered our eardrums. Bullets raked the parapet of our refuge.' Cpl. Don Linney of the Middlesex: 'We set up our Vickers machine guns for a really big barrage. Behind us was a troop of Welsh Guards, were treated to a rendition of beautiful choral singing with many of the Welsh favourites, ending with "Guide me, O thou great Jehovah" to the stirring tune Cwm Rhondda.'

On the 28th the division went back in reserve to the Brunssum area and the GOC, Gen. Thomas, returned to command his division, who without his iron control had done remarkably well clearing the Roer triangle.

Some changes of 'management' took place. Lt.-Col. Luce, CO 4th Wiltshires, left on 30 January to command 115th Infantry Brigade and was replaced by Maj. J.E.L. Corbyn, the Brigade Major of 214th Brigade, and Lt.-Col. H.A. Borradaile, CO 7th SLI, left on 22 January to take up a staff appointment at Corps. His successor, Maj. T.B. Elliott, was wounded and Lt.-Col. I.E. Reeves from 4th KSLI, took over command. After the 1st Worcesters lost Lt.-Col. Osborne-Smith wounded at Geilenkirchen, he was replaced by Lt.-Col. A.W.N.L. Vickers and shortly after by Lt.-Col. M.R.J. Hope-Thomson.

42

WINTER CAMPAIGN – FEBRUARY

Cleve and Goch

As part of a complex deception plan for the next massive operation – Veritable – 43rd Division reverted to XXX Corps, and moved on 2/3 February to the Herenthals area east of Antwerp. This city was out of bounds, being sorely battered by V1s and V2s. The Belgians were found to be extraordinarily friendly and hospitable. BSM Fred Fowler lodged in a café. 'I have my photo taken. Two cinemas and plenty of dances.'

The Wyvern and Guards Armoured Divisions were in reserve for XXX Corps' task of clearing the Reichswald, capturing the key towns of Cleve and Goch and sweeping right handed southeast to join up with the 9th US Army. Gen. Crerar's First Canadian Army at one stage controlled thirteen divisions, of which nine were British. The initial assault would be carried out from north to south by 3rd Canadian, 2nd Canadian, 15th Scottish, 53rd Welsh and 51st Highland. The huge forest of the Reichswald lies just west of the 8-mile north–south road between Cleve and Goch. South of Cleve are six villages, from west to east Notterden, Saalhof, Materborn, Hau, Bedburg and Moyland.

Gen. Horrocks, XXX Corps, wrote in his memoirs: 'Speed in capturing Cleve before the German reserves (7th Parachute Division) got established there was essential.' More than a thousand guns plus 1,000 fighters and fighter bombers were to provide close support. This included the complete destruction of the three vital towns of Cleve, Goch and Emmerich. 287 aircraft dropped 1,384 tons of bombs on Cleve alone!

15th Scottish Division were ordered to capture Kranenburg, breach the Siegfried line defences north of the Reichswald, capture the high ground at Nutterden and seize the Materborn feature and clear and hold Cleve. At 0500 hrs on 8 February the greatest artillery barrage of the war opened up. Peter Whately-Smith, 94th Field Regiment, wrote in his regimental history:

> On this occasion I was perched at the top of Groesbeek windmill, itself on high ground, and had a stupendous view of the assault. For three hours before Zero Hour a staggering bombardment rained down on the Boche lines. It became impossible to see more than half a mile ahead in the swirling eddies of the smoke that drifted over the battlefield. Then the khaki figures, Scots, Welsh and Canadians, filed out from the buildings below and advanced steadily behind the barrage and disappeared into the smoke towards the dark woods of the Reichswald.

Gen. Horrocks wrote: 'I unleashed my first reserve, the 43rd Wessex Div., which was to bypass through the 15th Scottish to burst out into the plain beyond and advance towards Goch. It was one of the worst traffic jams of the war. 15th Scottish forced their way into the shattered ruins of what had once been Cleve, followed by the 43rd, and after some very hard, almost hand to hand, fighting they succeeded in capturing the town.' Maj.-Gen. Fiebig, commanding 84th Division, plus 6th Para Division and tanks and SPs of 116th Panzer Division, made the Wyverns fight all the way.

Lt.-Col. Kenrick was acting brigade commander of 129th Brigade and ordered 4th Wiltshires to lead the column mounted 'quick lift' on Sherwood Ranger Shermans. At midnight on the 9th the ruins of Kranenburg were reached. The Germans had blown the Rhine's dykes to cause major problems. All roads were now awash, and heavy rain and sleet descended. After Nutterden was reached, the main road was found to be totally blocked by tanks, flails, Crocodiles, carriers and wheeled traffic of the 15th Scottish. Mounted thirteen on top of each Sherman, and tanks are completely blind in the dark, the Wiltshire's 'C' Company went into action along a minor road through the wood – it was a confused battle. At dawn they were in the south-east outskirts of Cleve, believed to have been cleared by the Scotsmen. The huge RAF-made bomb craters held up the advance. The one long line of tanks and infantry, like a skewer through a piece of meat, quickly dug in and cleared the neighbouring houses. They took seventy-five POW but a captured Sherman 'Trojan Horse' appeared. Fortunately 12 Platoon, 'B' Company spotted it was being followed by German infantry and opened fire. The other two battalions of 214th Brigade were ordered to move south down the road towards Goch, 5th Wiltshires on the right (west) and 4th SLI on the left (east). The fighting raged all day, with Tigers and Panthers roaming the bomb-shattered streets. Brigade HQ were caught up in the fighting and the GSO3, Capt. McGowan, was killed. 94th Field Regiment were deployed near Nutterden, right in the middle of the Siegfried line, a maze of slit trenches, barbed wire, and deeply constructed dugouts complete with electric light and bunks. All the houses were enemy strongpoints. The fighting was ferocious around the cemetery on the Materborn road and 4th SLI had a difficult day. Pte. Sweby, 'D' Company: 'Our bombers had destroyed nearly all the buildings. We advanced into the town, meeting fairly stiff resistance as we went, sniping mostly, occasional Spandau fire plus shelling and mortaring at times.' Lt. Sydney Jary:

> We went past strangely silent 15th Scottish troops on both sides of the road. None of their officers took the slightest notice of us, which as we were driving through their positions directly into the enemy's, was extraordinary. The whole column of 43rd Wessex was in the town before realising it was still held by the enemy. Behind us in the column a Panther tank and SP gun got within 25 yds of the column. Pte. Tipple of the carrier platoon engaged the tank with a PIAT, hit it, but it limped away. Groups of parachute troops attacked from both sides, sniped and engaged us with Spandaus from dozens of positions hidden in piles of rubble.

Pte. Robert Thornburrow, 4th SLI, noticed in Kranenburg a blue-capped CMP standing on top of a wooden crate, 3 ft above flood water, directing 'traffic'. Later in Cleve: 'We saw a familiar Defence Platoon corporal scrounging food from a cellar; ran into the road followed in hot pursuit by five German soldiers, shouting "Kamerad". They were trying hard to surrender to the fleeing corporal.' The next day near Bedburg Mental Hospital, Robert and Tom Fagan spent the night in a school. 'We heard a lot of squeaking, grunting and shouting coming from the rear of the building. Obviously an enemy patrol was infiltrating so we prostrated ourselves on the ground. It was a large white German pig being chased by the Defence Platoon.' During the savage fighting in Cleve Cpl. Doug Proctor was 'shocked to learn that "Bozzy" (Sgt. Les Bosworth) and all his A/Tank gun's crew had been killed, blown to smithereens by a German shell which landed among their own A/Tank shells. I'd played many piano duets with him to entertain the lads. There was nothing left of him or his crew.' In the confused fighting an enemy party of an officer and seventy-eight men was fought, cornered and then captured by an officer and twenty gunners of 59th A/Tank Regiment.

10 February was distinguished, as Brig. Essame put it, by 'a traffic jam of huge and bewildering proportions', as 15th Scottish and 43rd Division troops, transport, tanks and guns were entangled on the Cleve–Nijmegen road, mainly near Nutterden. The two GOCs tried their best to sort things out but there was still just the one main road. All communications with 129th Brigade, fighting in southern Cleve, had broken down.

The 5th Wiltshires had a traumatic battle in Cleve which raged non-stop for thirty-six hours. Maj. Hyde was temporarily CO. They were in the centre of the main attack with 4th Somersets on the right, 4th Wiltshires forming a defensive left flank. Held up at the junction of the Goch and Bedburg roads by huge bomb craters, 'A' Company was then attacked by SP guns. So 'B' Company swung right on the western outskirts of Cleve to be greeted also by SP guns which brewed up two Sherwood Ranger tanks, a jeep and a carrier. John McMath:

There advancing down the hill in front (of 'B' Company) were German infantry, a magnificent target. The enemy withdrew with heavy casualties. By now the noise of battle filled the air throughout the Bn column halted along the road. Everyone was fighting his own individual battle. German tanks and SP guns seemed to be everywhere. Absolute confusion reigned on both sides. Among the German prisoners taken were German Staff Officers, military policemen and others captured as they came into Cleve to draw their rations.

But later disaster struck. A single tank shell hit the Battalion Order Group. Maj. Field, the only rifle company commander left from Normandy, was killed. Capt. Rudd MC and bar, commanding 'D' Company, was mortally wounded and Maj. Henley, commanding 'B' Company, and Capt. Masterman, the Carrier officer, were both badly wounded. No one witnessed the scene, and stretcher-bearers from 4th Wiltshires took the wounded back to their RAP. 'At a vital crossroads by a cemetery "B" Coy were counter-attacked. The Sherwood Ranger tanks were knocked out and a platoon over-run. Pte. Tester took command and fought a withdrawal back to his company. Pte. Kennedy, a mortar man, grabbed a PIAT ran upstairs to a ladies boudoir,' John McMath recounts, 'knocked out a tank, engaged a second whose crew baled out and were shot.' Back at Battalion HQ near Brigade HQ RSM J.G. Smith organised signallers, cooks and drivers so effectively that twenty-nine dead Germans were counted in the back garden. In front of 'C' Company two enemy tried to surrender and were shot by their comrades. Many counter-attacks were made on 'C' during the afternoon, capturing a platoon commander and several men. There were many heroes; Pte. E.W.T. Green with his PIAT, Lt. J.C. Mitchell, and Pte. Brilliant, the company barber, who brewed up cups of tea. Cpl. Buckle lost his anti-tank gun but later took a carrier back under fire and retrieved it. In the morning of the 11th Lt. A. Fussey's 7th Platoon 'A' Company were counter-attacked. With Pte. Hodgetts firing their Bren gun the Wiltshires induced the attackers to take shelter in a quarry. John McMath: 'the fire brought panic to the Germans. Very soon they had had enough and came in with their hands up. One hundred and eighty paratroopers including eight officers was a good haul for a platoon.

'B' Squadron of 43rd Recce managed to probe south from Nutterden along a sandy track through the Reichswald. They contacted enemy near Materborn, but were firmly held at Saachof. The Cornwalls followed up as Col. George Taylor recounts: 'Our artillery and mortars softened up the opposition and then Maj. Lonsdale's "D" Company supported by tanks swept in to finish the job in house-to-house battles in the fading light. The Germans fell back into Materborn. Flanking attacks failed but "B" completed a 6,000-yd march south and as their wireless set failed eventually returned with fifteen prisoners.'

On the morning of 11 February fighting continued in Cleve. And the troops facing Sydney Jary, 4th SLI? 'In the end they departed, leaving us undisputed victors after a real Wild West shoot-out.' In the afternoon 214th Brigade put in a set-piece attack 2 miles south of Cleve directed first on Materborn, then on Hau. 'Our attack (1400 hrs) went like clockwork,' Col. George Taylor remembered. 'Covered by artillery fire and supported by the tanks of 4/7 Dragoon Guards we went forward in style. We quickly took half of the village (Materborn). Thirty prisoners were taken, we suffered few casualties.' Now 7th SLI poured through. Pte. Len Stokes:

> We had spent the whole night on the tanks, it was bitterly cold, icy rain and driving sleet. I could not find any footholds and could only just manage to hold on with my fingers. We could not sleep for fear of falling under the following tank. Breakfast consisted of one tin of self brewing soup divided between two men. I shared with the CSM. My hands and arms were useless, must have been in the last stages of frostbite. The CSM fed me. (Later) Orders were given for the Somersets to cross the start line at 1600 hrs to attack along the Goch road and capture the village of Hau. Delay because the crossroads was being shelled. The road was straight for hundreds of yards. Everyone was by now exhausted in the cold, wet and sleet and very dark between farms. 'B' Coy got into the cellar of a house where we rested for five minutes. (Len fell asleep standing up but) we reached our first objective, a farm at 0430 hrs following two nights on the road and thirteen hours of night fighting without sleep. During the rest of the night and all the next day, 12 February, we were heavily shelled and mortared. (At 1448 hrs 'B' Coy was counter-attacked by two companies of infantry supported by three Panther tanks. Radio was kaput so Len ran the gauntlet back to Bn HQ to get artillery support.)

'C' Company under Maj. Durie then advanced 1,000 yds. The crossroads to Cleve, Goch, Materborn and east was known as 'Tiger Corner' and was the scene of a tank battle with 'B' Squadron 4/7th Dragoon Guards saturating the enemy infantry with withering BESA fire. 'A' Company under Maj. Roberts swung right into Hau; and by dawn the village was taken. In the fifteen-day offensive 7th SLI had gained 8,000 yds, taken 800 POW in three tough battles and lost twenty-four KIA and seventy-six wounded. MCs were awarded to Majors Roberts and Durie, MMs to CSM Evans, Sgt. Chinnock and Pte. Bond. Cpl. Don Linney, 8th Middlesex, wrote: 'The small village of Hau was a bugger of a place and was nearly the undoing of us all. We fired over open sights at a visible target. The farm buildings behind us had been set alight by tracer. We only got out with the help of our infantry. We listened to the cries of the German wounded until their medics took them away.'

The Worcesters followed in the wake of 7th SLI, and at dawn

'D' Company advanced on Kukkuk, on the road to Bedburg, which was defended by 200 paratroopers and two SPs.

> Lt. Crossingham, 17 Platoon, was ordered to take a large building at the Kukkuk crossroads. Spandau fire and Very lights forced it to ground. Tracked vehicles were heard moving (recalls Lt. D.J. Pullen). It was my first experience of house clearing. We fired the contents of a Bren gun through windows, battering down the front door with a pickaxe and wandering through the house firing an occasional round just to lend colour to the situation. In the cellar a German paratrooper greeted Sgt. Lawler in perfect English. 'Hello, I've been waiting two hours for you!'

The Worcesters took three officers and eighty-seven ORs as POW but were subjected to incessant and heavy shellfire as they stayed in Kukkuk. Three counter-attacks were launched against 7th SLI but were held off with tank and artillery DF fire. On the morning of the 12th the Recce Regiment approached Niederdam level with Cleve Forest on the road to Goch. Lt. Joslin, 6th Troop, in the lead saw a German officer with a plate of breakfast in his hand. Bazookas opened up and knocked out three recce cars but Lt. Joslin brewed up a German halftrack with his 37-mm. An enemy SP knocked out all three of the 'friendly' tanks helping out, so 'B' Squadron was withdrawn. The last operation of the 12th was the taking of Bedberg by 4th SLI led by Maj. Cooke Hurle's 'D' Company. 'Freddie was a regular Somerset from an Indian cavalry regiment, a polo player, point to pointer, a kind, slightly built, strangely naïve new company commander,' recalls Sydney Jary. His 18 Platoon led and found Freudenberg Schloss empty, but Cpl. Doug Proctor was wounded in the groin by a Sten gun bullet. Cpl. Jim Kingston was searching a farmhouse when he stumbled and his Sten gun hit the floor. Most of the infantry reckoned the Sten was a wretched weapon, and that the German Schmeisser was far superior. 'Miracles do indeed happen,' thought Sydney Jary. On the outskirts of Bedburg a parachutist fired his Schmeisser at him from about 10 yds range. One bullet went through his beret, another under the jacket epaulette, grazing his right shoulder, another through his jacket, richocheting off the road and lodging in the palm of his right hand. 'The German looked at me in amazement, threw away his Schmeisser, shrugged his shoulders and surrendered. But L/Cpl.

Porteous was shot through the heart. 18 Platoon advanced 3 miles and took fifty-seven prisoners without armour or artillery support.'

Cleve had finally been taken by 15th Scottish with a great deal of help from the Wyverns. 130th Brigade now arrived from Nijmegen, temporarily lent to 53rd Welsh Division as a reserve in the Reichswald forest. The GOC had caught a severe chill and was confined to his caravan in the Cloister at Materborn, so employed Brig. Essame as his personal liaison officer. Morale was not high. Eric Codling, 8th Middlesex, spent the night on the straw covered floor of a café on the outskirts of Cleve. Unbearable itchiness from horse fleas resulted, as German army horses had recently been stabled in there. When the GOC recovered:

> we had a visit from Maj.-Gen. Thomas, complete with riding breeches, boots and large peaked cap. He presented the Military Medal won by Duggie Farnsworth and then explained to us (Cpls Eric Levy, Don Linney and the rest of 8th Middlesex) he was in the dog-house with Monty because the last job (the taking of Cleve) we did was a complete balls-up and he hoped we would make a better job of things next time. We almost felt sorry for him but at our level we did not know what he was on about. Apparently the Germans withdrew and the two brigades (both from 43rd) ended up firing at each other! Something must have gone horribly wrong for the General to come and commiserate with us!

The postponement of the US offensive from the Roer front meant that the Germans could reinforce the Siegfried line defences west of the Rhine. 116th Panzer and 15th Panzer Grenadier were going to defend the Fatherland at all costs.

13 February was a brutal bitter day for the Wiltshires. 129th Brigade were to advance towards Trippenberg, south-east of Bedburg on the Calcar road. In the morning 5th Wiltshires, as they advanced, were caught on the start line under intense shell fire which caused many casualties, but they gained the first vital ridge. In the afternoon 4th Wiltshires resumed the attack with heavy artillery support, and crossed the crossroads at Neuenhaus, but their tanks were stopped by mines and 88s. There was no cover on the bare waterlogged farmland, but under heavy shelling they took Trippenberg by 1500 hrs and captured fifty POW. The attack was helped by FOO Capt. A.J. Townsend, at 'A' Company

HQ, bringing down DF tasks and despite fourteen casualties, morale improved. The houses in the village were full of civilians, hams, boxes of eggs, even champagne from the cellar. Delicious suppers of eggs and bacon were served that night.

There was a vicious counter-attack at dawn on the 14th by the newly arrived 116th Panzer Division, backed by gun fire as heavy or even heavier and more concentrated than Hill 112. Two 17-pounders, some 6-pounder A/Tank guns and PIATs were knocked out by the shelling. The radios went dead. The war diary of 94th Field Regiment: '0957 hrs Capt. A Townsend (224 Bty) assumes command of 'A' Coy 4 Wilts.' Three platoon commanders were killed or wounded in hand-to-hand fighting in the houses as they tried to stalk with PIATs, the SP guns firing with great accuracy. Lt.-Col. Corbyn was awarded the DSO for the defence of Trippenberg, which cost fifty-one casualties. The advance by 5th Wiltshires was delayed until 1100 hrs. Savage hand-to-hand fighting with 15th Panzer Grenadiers backed by MG, mortars and SP, and the loss of all the senior officers, including Maj. Hyde, meant that the battalion had to dig in just to survive. Capt. John McMath then took over command until Maj. J.L. Brind, 4th SLI, arrived in the afternoon to be the new CO. He decided in the face of vicious machine gun fire to fight their way forward in the dark, reaching the key crossroads 400 yds east of the Cleve Forest. 5th Wiltshires had suffered 200 casualties in a few days. Eric Codling, 8th Middlesex, was there:

Next task to secure escarpment overlooking Goch from the north. A bitter struggle against a fanatical enemy. DF rained down and continued for what seemed an eternity. Soon the German fire shifted to the slowly advancing infantry, slowly advancing but much reduced (in numbers). Difficult to climb out of our refuge – a sure sign of 'bomb-happiness'. First real evidence of long-term effects of months of action whittling away the reserves of courage that we had enjoyed at the beginning of the campaign. The bank balance was running out.

John McMath in his battalion history wrote of the heroes of the attack on Bedburg: Lt. B.A. Tarrant who took over 'B' Company, Sgt. Norton who led 18 Platoon, Cpl. Lancey who was wounded but crawled forward to knock out a machine-gun with grenades. 'Many casualties were suffered and many wounded were left in No Man's Land. Wounds had to be dressed under heavy mortar, shell and MG fire. Stretcher-bearing jeeps had to be driven under the very nose of the enemy. Tirelessly and gallantly the stretcher-bearers worked on. L/Cpl. Hiett, Ptes Holmes, Bigrigg, Hancock and O'Connor are but some of those who did so well on that memorable St Valentine's Day.'

On the 15th it was 130 Brigade's turn to face Battle Group Hutze with 4th Dorsets leading the attack. Wally Caines:

I leaned against the wall of the remains of a house in Bedburg and quietly prayed. It was like hell let loose for about an hour. We took over from the Wiltshires. Their signal officer sadly informed me all lines had been shattered by heavy shelling. 15 February. 1000 hrs objective three small villages on a crest overlooking the outskirts of Goch. The German paras opened up with all they had. Spandaus and every sort of weapon. They had dug into the ground floor of the houses in the first village, concealed themselves excellently. Shells and mortars rained down and both company COs, Maj. Symonds and Gill were wounded. 'A' lost twenty-four killed and numerous bodies had been wounded. I was operator in the Scout car with Capt. Richards acting as Adjutant. At 1300 hrs CO sent me to Brigade HQ for further instructions. 'B' Coy were ordered to carry out the second phase. By now Jerry was falling back. Very few prisoners were taken. The boys had no intentions over worrying about that. . . .

And Maj. Joe Symonds:

Never before or since been the object of such concentrated shelling whilst forming up for the attack. (Later) Lt. Girardot with No. 2 Platoon (in my 'A' Company) was wounded, Sgt. Gregory killed. No. 1 Platoon assaulted with splendid courage under Lt. Pope but was badly shot up by the German paras. I launched another assault with the rest of 3 Platoon, remainder of Nos 1 and 2, supported by 3 Shermans. Went well. The Germans ran out of the rear of the houses as we rushed in through the front gardens. . . . At 1220 hrs much depleted, consolidated as did 'C' Coy (under Capt. John Kirkwood) for similar reasons.

Col. W.G. Roberts: 'A vivid picture of tall figure of Maj. Joe Symonds standing up blowing his whistle and bowling his steel helmet in the direction of the Germans.' At 1530 hrs 7th Royal Hampshires came through under Maj. D.B. Rooke, as their CO was temporarily commanding 130th Brigade. Maj. Morgan led 'B' Company against Van der Heydte's parachute group and despite the heaviest shelling and mortaring encountered by the regiment in the campaign, reached Berkhofel. Then Maj. Mumford took 'D' Company through to a small hamlet 800 yds on. In furious house-to-house and trench clearing they took sixty POW, but fighting continued through the night and 'D' was reduced to a strength of thirty-five. Since 15th Scottish on the left flank attacking in Moyland wood had had an equally torrid time, Brig. Essame wrote: 'No sign of a break in the German morale. It seemed as if a deadlock had been reached. For the 16th the outlook on both Divisional fronts seemed black indeed.' But the GOC now threw 214th Brigade plus 4th SLI, under a huge supporting fire plan, into an ambitious attack due south towards Goch, starting in the hamlets of Blacknik and Berkhovel. Four villages were the main objectives – Pfalzdorf, Imigshof, Bermanshof and Schroenshof – and then the cutting of the main road from Goch north-east to Calcar. The CRA, Brig. Mackay Lewis, described how 'the drive towards the Goch escarpment was a CRA's nightmare, a protracted right wheel with range rather than switch being the governing factor in deployment.' First of all 5th Dorsets had to clear the start line for 214th Brigade. Skirting Berkhovel, still held by the enemy, they fought their way towards Blacknik. 'A' Company (Maj. H.C. Allen) suffered severe casualties. Both 'A' and 'C' were shelled at close range by SP guns. Thoroughly exhausted by their hard fighting they lost two more officers killed that evening as 'B' Company moved forward.

Col. George Taylor explained: 'A four battalion attack, 1 Worcester would go in on the right, and 7 Somerset on the left. The 5 DCLI and 4 Somersets would exploit southwards to get on to the high ground overlooking Goch.' Both attacks were delayed until about mid-afternoon. The Worcesters fought their way from Bedburg to Blacknik and despite sixteen casualties captured three officers and 120 ORs with Lt. Pullen of 'D' Company taking a farm stronghold at bayonet point. 'As we got closer to the village,' wrote William Gould, 'the Germans sent up Very lights, illuminated the whole area. We could see plainly the depressions on the grass verges where mines were laid. I had to borrow a rifleman to help with the line-laying. We then had a wonderful view of Goch immediately below us.'

Helped by 4/7th Dragoon Guards' tanks, the 7th SLI advanced 3,000 yds south. Despite severe punishment, at dusk the Somersets had taken 413 prisoners and reached all their objectives. 'We advanced in five armoured columns of tanks and Kangaroo armoured troop carriers with a carrier and Jeep column coming up behind, 100 armoured vehicles moving in a solid phalanx. "D" Coy's objective was Schresshof, and "B" the hamlet of Bergmanshof, then "C" would take a small rise called "Kidney Ridge". The artillery fire plan worked out with Lt.-Col. Wyldbore-Smith, 179 Field Reg CO, of "prophylactic fire" short concentrations on buildings and orchards on the outer and inner flanks and in front of each company column,' wrote George Taylor. 'The night was ours. More than 50 of the enemy had been killed, 100 prisoners taken, our booty included two 88 guns, a pompom and assorted vehicles. Our own losses totalled three including our Provost Sgt. Barret, a mighty puncher, killed by a shell, and Maj. Hutchins wounded by a shell splinter.'

The final masterstroke of this exciting day for the Wyverns was Lt.-Col. 'Lippy' Lipscombe's night attack with the 4th SLI to occupy the escarpment dominating Goch. It was a silent attack starting east of Pfalzdorf at 0300 hrs. 'The enemy were taken completely by surprise. They had all gone to ground to avoid the shelling,' recalls Maj. Beckhurst, 'and no less than three officers and sixty-eight ORs were taken prisoner. The German CO spoke good English, said that in his six years of soldiering he had never known the British to attack by night. It was most unfair. I told him he still had a lot to learn.'

The unrelenting push by Gen. Horrocks's corps continued. The Welsh 53rd Division were now out of the Reichswald Forest and were west of the Cleve–Goch railway line, while the Canadians were battering the enemy round Moyland, 2 miles to the east. In his memoirs Horrocks wrote: 'I must mention the 43rd Wessex Div. who having fought their way through Cleve, on 16 February carried out a brilliant 8,000-yd advance which enabled them to occupy the escarpment overlooking the fortified town of Goch. This proved the turning point of the battle.'

The Cleve forest on the east of the Cleve–Goch road was now cleared quite easily by 4th Dorsets. Col. Roberts:

A large piece of shrapnel struck a wall near the IO, Lt. John Adams and the Mortar Officer, Capt. Gordon Perring. The look on their faces was encouraging! We were arranging another

'Canadian Mattress' for the benefit of the Forest of Cleve on our exposed right flank. That night Brig. Aubrey Coad visited Bn HQ with a large and good-looking bottle with a fascinating label that promised nectar to a very tired team of officers, signallers, Intelligence personnel and sappers. The Adjutant Tony Cottle opened it to toast the regiment. It contained malt vinegar! The QM produced our rum ration.

After seven days of continuous action, on the 17th the Worcesters and 7th SLI side by side, aided by 4/7th Dragoon Guards, spent the day fighting through a maze of houses, trenches, wire, farm buildings and strongpoints to reach the western part of the escarpment at Imigshof overlooking Goch and the River Niers.

The Worcesters had to contend with 15th Panzer Grenadier Division defending every inch of ground with ferocity – they stood or they perished, armed with Spandau, MG, SPs, A/Tank guns and every type of artillery. Lt. Pullen of 'D' Company had a difficult time:

To reach the road a mile of open country under enemy observation had to be crossed, swept by long range small arms fire and nebelwerfers. 17 platoon was slightly disorganised, constantly going to ground. Within five minutes Lt. Crossingham and three section leaders of my platoon were wounded. I sent my sergeant back to bring his platoon forward. In one large hole excavated by the Germans he found ten of his men sheltering. He instructed them to move, received replies 'Got it in the leg, Sarge'; 'Got it in the arm, Sarge'; 'Got a Blighty in my foot, Sarge'. I had not realised what dire state the platoon had come to.

Nevertheless ninety prisoners were taken for the Worcesters' seventy-two casualties. William Gould described the 'Canadian Carpet' fired from the back of a large vehicle, belching forth staggered bursts of rockets over a large area. The divisional artillery now started to saturate the defences of Goch, covering the seven bridge crossings over a 20-ft deep anti-tank ditch outside Goch. Goch was now surrounded by 15th Scottish, 51st Division, 53rd Welsh and by the Wyverns. The pivot of the Siegfried Line was doomed. In ten days the division had taken 2,472 prisoners and advanced 10,000 yds down the Siegfried line. Horrocks wrote: 'Goch was subsequently captured by the Jocks of the 51st and 15th Scottish after some very bitter fighting. Clearing these frontier towns was a costly business in casualties because each house had to be dealt with separately. The Germans were almost immune to artillery fire and could sweep the road with fire through the loopholes in the reinforced cellars.' Hobart's 'Funnies' – petard mortars mounted on AVREs – were used successfully against pillboxes where some diehard Nazis were roasted alive.

On 20 February 4th SLI had one final battle before being pulled out of the line, as described by their neighbour Col. George Taylor:

The 4 Somersets now moved through us to the east to attack Halvanboon (500 yds south of the Calcar road) using 'our' tank squadron and some of the Kangaroos. Unfortunately Spandaus caught one of the companies ('C') dismounting from the Kangaroos and mortar and artillery fire inflicted forty casualties. But the village was taken. The fighting had been bitter and the Somersets had lost many men in a hail of shell and mortar fire including their 'C' Coy CO, Maj. Mallalieu. Maj. David Richards of 4/7 Dragoon Guards rose to the occasion magnificently, leading both the Somersets and tanks until Halvanboon was taken. Mallalieu had been in the forefront of the battle since Normandy.

43

WINTER CAMPAIGN

Clearing the West Bank of the Rhine

Three well-earned days of rest now followed in devastated Cleve for 129th and 214th Brigades. There were still many ground-floor rooms and cellars to provide sleep and warmth. The stoutly built houses provided quite snug billets and mobile baths and cinema shows appeared. On the 23rd the floods on the Roer subsided enough for the 9th US Army to launch the offensive Grenade. The Wyverns were placed under command of Lt.-Gen. Simonds' II Canadian Corps, with the task of breaching another defensive line of the Hochwald and the Calcar–KerhumMarrenbaum–Xanten road and railway lines. 130th Brigade had now joined the Navy! They took over from 8th Canadian Brigade a 5-mile stretch of inland sea created by the Roer flooding between Emmerich and Milligen. Both Dorset battalions sailed in buffaloes along the Cleve canal north-east to Grithausen, Killen and Milligen. 5th Dorsets lost their CO, posted back to the UK, and he was replaced by Lt.-Col. A.E.C. Bredin, known as 'Speedy' for his track prowess. A factory on the River Rhine ruined by the RAF, was used as an OP; indeed 'Speedy' got a drenching as he inspected the site and a welcoming salvo fell in the water beside him. The LAA Regiment deployed to fire against ground targets, as did the Recce Regiment. 2nd/Lt. Wally Caines, 4th Dorsets:

. . . everything completely under water; one could see for miles only the tops of trees and houses. Several Buffaloes were knocked out by mines washed up around them. We packed all the line kit into a dinghy, all wearing rubber and waterproofed equipment laying lines to the forward companies. 22 February. French, Polish, Russians, hundreds of German slave labour began to return to their houses abandoned during the flooding, overjoyed they were now free and could roam around. 27 February. Gen. Thomas and Brig. Coad 130 Brigade paid us a visit to see possibilities of crossing the Rhine in this sector.

On the 24th 129th Brigade had returned into the line south of Moyland to free 6th Canadian Brigade for their next attack eastwards, and the Recce Regiment probed vigorously out of Kennen, 2 miles north-east of Cleve, into Grieth, Wissel and Honnepel. 'I was FOO with Maj. Blood and "B" Sqn,' wrote Capt. Hancock, 94th Field Regiment. 'He was a thruster and spent far more time with the leading armoured cars than at his HQ.

The Canadians struggled to clear the large Hochwald forest halfway between Calcar and Xanten. The GOC decided 214th Brigade should attack and capture the villages of Kehrum, Marienbaum, Vynen and Wardt, south-east of Calcar. Capt. George Searle, Recce Regiment, had the duties of 'sort of camp commandant, Movements and Radio. I was given the task to hold a bridge at Calcar with an armoured car section to stop infiltration from the direction of the Rhine by troops, civilians or cattle! The first day Gen. Thomas came through. He stopped and asked me my job. Then he said "Oh, Horatio". Each morning afterwards it was "Good morning Horatio". He was human after all!'

By 4 March 7th SLI, then the Cornwalls and the Worcesters, helped considerably by the sappers of 204th Field Company, had mopped up all of the west bank of the Rhine except for the important town of Xanten.

129 Brigade were given the task of taking Xanten and Luttingen. 2nd Canadian Division at the same time would seize the western section of Xanten and the high ground to the south. The fields around both objectives were waterlogged, minefields everywhere, and a deep anti-tank ditch protected the perimeter. It was a daunting prospect. 4th SLI were given Xanten and 5th Wiltshires, Luttingen as their objectives. Both attacks started at 0500 hrs on 8 March. Bombadier Hillier of 'A' Troop 94th Field Regiment with Gunners Iles and Bleach, formed an OP party with 4th Somersets:

We had a 22 set converted to a pack set and an 18 set for communication with the infantry. At a quarter minute to four the dark sky behind us was lit with a mass of leaping, flickering flashes followed by the thunder of 300 guns, the tearing whistle of shells overhead and the crash as they exploded beyond us Promptly at 0405 hrs the leading company ('B' under Maj. Mike Hutchinson) began to file off in the darkness towards the red glare of bursting shells. We passed an enormous structure or the road – a partly assembled Bailey bridge mounted on skids – towed by a Churchill tank (destined to block the 90-ft wide anti-tank ditch. Eventually they reached the start line.) 70 yds past the start line we were greeted by a hail of Spandau, including tracer zipping and whistling up the road, ricocheting off the trees and houses. We went to ground. Maj. Hutchinson put in a perfect Battle Drill 'left flanking', which after a bit more shooting by the Hun dislodged twenty-two young paratroopers, who came out at the double hands in air. The tanks put a scissors bridge across the ditch and over went the flame-throwing Crocodiles. One got bogged down, but the other two put an end to the resistance.

Over a hundred sullen young paratroopers were captured; even more lay dead in the ruins. Cpl. Grant won the DCM for destroying a Spandau team with a grenade. Sydney Jary, 'D' Company: 'We advanced across those open fields stonked by a battery of 105mms, accurate and intensely noisy. The street-fighting continued against Schmeissers and panzerfaust but the Germans withdrew after a token defence. Hutch won a bar to his MC, Brian Innes a MC and L/Cpl. White a MM.'

The taking of Luttingen, just north of Xanten, was an all-Wiltshire affair. The 5th Battalion started from Wardt and had to attack across 1,500 yds of flat open ground along two tracks leading to Luttingen, held by paratroops. On the left runs a high embankment, protection against flood waters from the Rhine. Slightly in front and to the right of Luttingen was a square copse. 'A' Company started at 0500 hrs under the usual barrage but withering fire came from the copse wounding Lt. Fussey and Maj. Lang. Scooping out shallow trenches in the wet and soggy ground was the only cover. John McMath:

On the right 8 Platoon were fighting a lone battle, but encountered fire from no less than fifteen light machine-guns. Lt. Massey showed magnificent leadership with a one-man bayonet charge against the nearest MG. He killed both occupants, shouted loudly in fluent German, demanded the surrender of the enemy in the neighbouring trenches. Nine Germans promptly gave themselves up. (Later) The next day after the battle was won, forty-seven dead Germans were counted in those trenches. But 'C' Coy attacking the village on the left met equally fanatical resistance. Thanks to some training in the correct battle drill for house-clearing, forty Paratroop prisoners were taken.

After several hours of fighting 'C' Company were surrounded, and defending houses turned into strongpoints. A huge stonk descended on the village from the divisional artillery, but the Wiltshires were safe in their fortified cellars and 'D' Company arrived to break the siege. The enemy in the copse defended themselves stoutly and it took three attacks by 'B' Company to subdue them. Pte. Horton drove his carrier with Wiltshire wounded in it, shepherding a posse of captured paratroopers in front. The final attack, led by Capt. Mottram and Lt. Fisher, was successful, and the copse taken. During the taking of Luttingen seventy-nine casualties were sustained.

Pte. R. Gladman had just joined 4th Wiltshires from 1st Royal Hampshires:

The attack on Xanten – the heavy barrage of fire lasted from 4 a.m. to 6 a.m. We went forward right through the town stopping at the very last building. It was a heavy barrage 25-pdrs, rocket guns even heavy MGs. We went down the road in file. (Later) We heard a single shot, found our Captain slumped against the side wall shot in the stomach. Bill helped him with a field dressing. He had just ordered up a Bren gun carrier with flame thrower equipment (a WASP) to fire this last house.

The 4th Wiltshires mopped up on the morning of the 9th in Xanten and Luttingen. The German High Command had ordered a general withdrawal across the Rhine on 6 March which was largely completed by the 10th. To protect their bridgehead at Wesel it was essential for the ruined town of Xanten to hold out as long as possible.

Veritable was over for the Wyverns. The battle of the Rhineland was over. On 13 March the division handed over to the 3rd British Division and went back to the banks of the Maas.

Brig. Joe Vandeleur wrote in his memoirs:

The first phase of our attack on Xanten went badly. Our left flank was screened by a persistent smoke screen. The Divisional Engineers with great gallantry helped the rolling Bailey bridge into position and our armour including flame throwers crossed. Soon after dawn the 4th Somersets under their wonderful commander 'Lippy' Lipscomb had fought their way into the town but had suffered heavy casualties. The Germans had some Tiger tanks dug in in the town centre equipped with infra-red sights. They succeeded in knocking out several of our tanks in pitch darkness at a range of 200 yds. . . . The German garrison of Xanten were very gallant men.

44

OPERATION PLUNDER

For nearly two weeks the Wyverns were out of action on the east bank of the River Maas near Gennep, Afferden and Well. 'We were billeted in the small village of Hayan, part of the Germans' front line, through that bitter winter of 1944/5. It was like a left-over scene from the Great War of a quarter of a century before: the houses stood in ruins, victims of continuous Allied bombardment. . . . Here we stayed (the Cornwalls under Col. George Taylor) enjoying the early spring weather as we honed ourselves and equipment to a new sharpness for Operation Plunder, the crossing of the Rhine and the final thrust into the Nazi heart.' 129th Brigade held a sports meeting, new reinforcements were integrated. Gordon Reinhold returned to his old unit, 1st Worcesters, from being Brigade Major 130th Brigade. 'The unit by this time was something of a hotchpotch. The CO Vickers was ex-KOYLI, and CO Tim Hope-Thomson was ex-Royal Scots Fusiliers. The men were a mixed bunch including a number of maritime AA. But morale was good. The Bn was in sound battle order.'

The Recce Regiment maintained OPs along the Rhine until 12 March when they moved back to Weeze. Newly arrived Daimler heavy armoured cars replaced most of their well-tried Humbers. Those crews who had had the same car since the long ago pre-invasion days were sorry to part with their Humbers. Mobile baths, ENSA and cinema shows were available. The quality of food reached a new high with the discovery that every German household's cellar was crammed with goodies – hams, preserved fruits, vegetables and bottles of wine. 2nd/Lt. Wally Caines's diary noted that on the 15th: 'Our Dutch interpreter's brother reported wine was buried in some trenches near Cleve. Capt. Richards and a party of 'diggers' excavated 1,600 bottles of Cognac and with superlative honesty it was distributed throughout 130 Brigade!' An investiture was held on the 18th at Afferden and among other awards were the DSO to Maj. John Ricketts and the MM to Sgt. Edwards and Pte. Day of the Worcesters. The next day their CO left for England to get married and Gordon Reinhold took over command. Peter Hall had a strange encounter in a fortified manor house. Two Germans approached his Company HQ under flag of truce to evacuate and exchange the captured wounded of each side. Two badly wounded Dorset officers were being held. For two hours Peter talked to his friend Hauptman Gerhart Milner about hockey tactics from pre-war encounters! And Cpl. William Gould burst into verse:

> Our army has been doing fine
> We've crossed the Seine and reached the Rhine
> And now we wait to make our move
> Our courage and our strength to prove.

and:

> When shells are bursting on the deck
> The house next door is just a wreck
> The place of refuge for a fellah
> Is down the stairs and in the cellar.

The thirty-five verses contained references to 'Dosey' Denby, 'Busty' Bowen (bald as a coot), the Brummie Morgan (a taste for GI Jive Music), Sgt. Jim Norton and his platoon commander, Lt. 'Sally' Gray.

Lt. Sydney Jary and 18 Platoon of 4th SLI gave a sophisticated dinner party – written invitations, tablecloths, candlesticks, cutlery, glasses, many assorted bottles. Predictably the menu consisted of a roasted German porker, vegetables and bottled fruit. A 'borrowed' Mercedes with pigskin upholstery collected and delivered guests – up until midnight! Pte. Robert Thornburrow drew a one week's Blighty leave. He departed in old German railway rolling stock of six or seven carriages hauled by an ancient steam engine from a station west of Wesel. The locos were changed at each border crossing, and trundled along briskly at 25 mph. At Armentières Robert's breakfast was bacon, sausage, beans, two slices of bread and marge and a mess tin of hot tea.

Soon all ranks of Wyverns were told by Monty: 'Having crossed the Rhine we will crack about in the plains of Northern Germany chasing the enemy from pillar to post. . . . May the lord mighty in battle give us victory.' Presumably 15th Panzer Grenadier Division and 116th PZ Division on the other side of the Rhine were saying much the same thing.

We Brigadiers (wrote 'Joe' Vandeleur) had to work very hard. Our Commander was in the habit of making outline plans to meet every contingency. We had not only to plan the battles we were fighting but in between engagements we had to study in detail alternative lines of action. At Liège, for example, we not only planned the defence of the city but countless other courses, such as counter-attacks, backstop positions, alternative positions, etc. My caravan was piled high with aeroplane photographs, overprints, fire plans and so forth. Battle planning is not a matter purely of tactics but the whole logistical plan of supply and movement had to be carefully discussed with the Brigade staff. Personally I found the times in battle were restful compared to those when we were in reserve. This alternative planning reaped great dividends as we were always one jump ahead of the Germans. Gen. Ivo Thomas taught me a great deal about soldiering and I am most grateful to him.

Indeed, multiply Vandeleur's brigade planning fifty times over to get some idea of the complexity of the preparations for the Rhine crossing. Vast dumps of 25-pounder and medium shells, engineering, pontoon rafts and other bridging equipment, hundreds of Buffaloes and Weasels appeared. At Kevelaer huge ration collection points were set up. The RASC as always were the unsung heroes, under Lt.-Col. E.H. Reeder. Lt.-Gen. Horrocks had under command of XXX Corps, 43rd Division, 3rd British, 51st Highland, Guards Armoured and 8th Armoured Brigade. The Highlanders were charged with the amphibious assault crossing. The Rhine was very swollen and almost twice its normal size. Their objectives were the capture of Rees and Haldern. Once out of the bridgehead 51st Highland would continue on the right flank, the Wyverns in the centre, with 3rd Canadian Division on their left. The order of crossing within the division was to be 130th, 129th, then 214th Brigade directed on Anholt and Aalten. On 21 March the GOC organised a dress rehearsal on the River Maas, and on the same day the Corps Commander briefed all senior officers in the village hall at Pfalzdorf near Goch.

The divisional artillery moved opposite Rees on the 22nd to join the seventeen field regiments, ten medium, two heavy regiments and two super-heavy batteries, to support the crossing. On their left at Honnepol 8th Middlesex arrived to take part in the Rhine crossing barrage. Cpl. Eric Levy:

The battalion dug in on the crest of the high bank of the river amidst the smoke screen that was laid down to conceal our presence. What a bombardment that was! I believe it was the biggest of the war. The machine gunners' job was to fire so many taps each way and then raise our dial sight 50 yds every so often as the crossing was calculated to progress. The German counter-bombardment was very heavy. I got caught in the blast of their shell explosions and lost my hearing completely in both ears. It was the end of the war for me. Only six of the original platoon were left of those who landed in Normandy.

At 1900 hrs on the 23rd after darkness had fallen the 400 guns concealed behind the river from 40-mm Bofors to the 240-mm heavies with half ton shells deluged the Boche positions (wrote Peter Whately-Smith, 94th Field Regiment). Overhead came the (227) heavy bombers of the RAF who went in to obliterate the town of Wesel. Then at 2100 hrs the men of the Highland Division crept down to the river bank, clambered into their Buffaloes and assault boats, surged across the 500 yds of water and fought for the bridgehead at Rees. (Later) With the dawn came the Dakotas of the two airborne divisions flying 200 or 300 ft overhead to drop their paratroops and land their gliders behind the Germans at Wesel.

Over 4,000 Dakotas, Stirlings, Halifaxes, Lancasters, Fortresses and Liberators, protected by 1,200 fighters, took part in this incredible 'armada'. But despite the bombardment there were very considerable losses due to heavy AA fire. On the night of the 24th the division's OP parties joined up with their battalions.

Capt. C.N.B. Hancock, 94th Field Regiment: 'I buffaloed across at about 0700 hrs on the morning of the 25th moving with Col. Lipscombe and the 4 Somersets. While on the water I noticed that the sappers had parts of a Class 40 bridge running out from both banks and only about 40 yds apart, while a Class 9 bridge was already completed. Twenty-six sappers were killed, they put up a first class show. Here and there were marks of a less successful crossing where the aerial masts and turrets of some tanks stuck out above the water.' The Luftwaffe bombed the bridges at night and a near miss damaged one bridge, which was quickly repaired. The Royal Navy deployed a small naval tug complete with White Ensign, which busily steamed up and down the river hauling sections of the bridges into position.

The Germans to their credit fought like demons. If the Rhine was carried they were done for and Monty's crack armoured divisions, 11th Black Bull, 7th Desert Rats and Guards Armoured, were champing in the wings 'to crack about'. The airborne drop took three important bridges over the River Ijssel on 12 Corps front and then linked up with 15th Scottish Division. Bitter fighting went on however in Rees, Bienen and Speldrop for two days.

The first fighting Wessex Wyverns ashore were 5th Dorsets, directed with the rest of 130th Brigade to take Millingen, a mile north-east of Bienen. Cpl. Les Hart: 'On reaching the other side we found only shell holes for ½ mile. The first humans, about fifty women and children were all shell shocked, being looked after by a Padre in an underground bunker.' On their way 5th Dorsets took Androp by a midnight attack and occupied Speldrop, while 4th Dorsets continued. 2nd/Lt. Wally Caines:

26 March 0015 hrs. The Buffaloes took us over, had a tot of whisky with Maj. Joe Symonds, wished each other good luck for the battles lying ahead. We all crossed by 0300 hrs. 'O' Group to attack village of Millingen, 3,000 yds in front. Typhoons had rocketed the village with shells, as 'A' Coy (Joe Symonds) led off at 1400 hrs with 7 Hampshires attacking on our right, 5 Dorsets guarding right flank. Hundreds of worn-out and bomb happy Germans taken prisoner, many of them running at the double. (Wally was sent forward in semi darkness and) found Maj. Guy Matthews, 'D' Coy CO, asleep in an armchair in a house. He came out and met 'B' Coy who were just about to attack. 'Christ, we are about to attack that area.' Oh well things happen like that in war. (Col. Roberts was pleased.) . . . battle went entirely according to plan. 4 Dorsets took the village with 190 POW and with no fatal casualties. Sound junior leadership and a fair knowledge of street fighting techniques by officers, NCOs and men were responsible for this success.

The Colonel received a bar to his DSO for this operation.

On the 26th 129th Brigade had crossed in Buffaloes and on the next day 214th Brigade marched across the two bridges (Class 9 and Class 15) and by the morning of the 27th both brigades were huddled together around Esserden – unshelled, unstrafed, which was a minor miracle. The next objective was a partly constructed autobahn between Millingen and Anholt and 129th Brigade were ordered to secure it. Both Wiltshire regiments came under heavy shelling and mortaring as they neared the autobahn. 15th Panzer Grenadiers were strongly entrenched among the hedges, trees and houses along the autobahn, backed up by SP guns. So it was decided that 214th Brigade would attack. It was a complicated battle. The 4/7th Dragoon Guards' tanks were bogged down, but on the extreme right the Worcesters fought their way tenaciously and were dug in by nightfall on their objectives.

The autobahn was a heaped-up embankment for a road still under construction occupied by elite parachutists backed by skilled enemy artillery and well-sited MF positions (wrote Peter Hall). 1 Worcs would attack on the right, 7 SLI on the left. On our right the 51st Highland Div would attack at the same time. 'D' Coy on the left (Brian Elder) and 'A' Coy on the right (mine). H-hour was 1145 hrs . . . things started to go wrong. We had to advance 1,000 yds over flat open country with no cover. The ground was sodden and muddy, impossible for tank movement, but my supporting troop of 13/18 Hussars gave ferocious firepower. By 1700 hrs we were on objective, and Brian Elder and my comrades in 'D' Coy by dark. There were thirty Germans dead and the same number, some badly wounded, surrendered to us. A triumphant but also a very sad day. We paid a heavy price for the Battle of the Autobahn.

On the left 7th SLI also had a difficult time. Lt.-Col. Ivor Rees, the CO, was badly wounded with a shattered shoulder, but twenty men from Maj. K.J. Whitehead's 'B' Company reached the concrete fly-over buttress of the autobahn. Here Cpl. Comm won the DCM in this bitter battle. The use of WASPS, carrier-mounted flame-throwers, helped settle the issue. The Cornwalls now continued with a night attack on Meghelen. In a wet mist, across 8-ft dykes, fighting all the way, by 0400 hrs 'B' Company led, having taken ninety-four prisoners. 'The village was like a disturbed beehive with Germans in various stages of undress rushing to man their trenches,' recalls Col. George Taylor. With the help of Lothian's Horse flame-throwing tanks, 'in a short time the enemy surrendered. Thus the terror weapons saved both British and German lives. Maj. Kitchen received his third wound of the campaign – in the leg' – and later gained a DSO. The inhabitants from the cellars went mad with joy, the Wyverns had fought their way back into Holland!

Since crossing the Rhine over 150 paratroopers had been taken prisoner and over 400 had been killed fighting against an avalanche of armour, artillery power, RAF bombing and Typhoons, and of course infantry mopping up, as always. Anholt on the River Ijssel – back in Germany – was the next objective. Brig. Coad's 130th Brigade moved up on the evening of the 28th to force a crossing at Landfort, which was captured by 4th Dorsets. Lt.-Col. 'Speedy' Bredin with 5th Dorsets was ordered to make a night assault across the river. All went well. Sgt. Foster of 'D' won his MM for house clearance. The Pioneers built a light bridge and anti-tank guns were towed across by jeep. 'We were standing on a road while "Speedy" Bredin was briefing me on a patrol,' recalls Canloan Bill Hudson, 'when I heard incoming shells and went for the ditch. The shells landed while he remained on the road. His comment was "Hudson, what are you doing down there?"' 4th Dorsets then rapidly took Anholt and 5th Dorsets pushed a bridgehead over the River Eisle. The Hampshires took Dinxperlo and 4th Wiltshires pushed the bridgehead out to the line of the Priesterbeek. 'Turnscrew' was part of Operation Plunder and the Wyverns were turning the screw with a vengeance. Col. George Taylor wrote:

> The advance was to be sustained by day and by night. Every division of XXX Corps would move forward on a one-brigade front with each brigade fighting its way out of trouble if encountered. Then the next brigade would move up to keep the momentum going. The leading battalion usually moved behind a screen of armoured cars and carriers of the Recce Regiment with a mixed company group of a troop of tanks, ten armoured Kangaroos, carrying infantry sections, 3-in mortars and anti-tank guns. The long armoured column clattered and clanked its way like some centipede across the Dutch–German border. It was exhilarating stuff.

Forrard On was the next operation.

45

'FORRARD ON'

The Wyverns were given the task of left flank protection and keeping open 'Club Route', due north from Anholt into Holland to the Twente Canal at Lochem. Then to move due east to Hengelo, re-enter the Reich, cross the River Vechte at Nordhorn and capture Lingen on the Dortmund–Ems Canal. Gen. Thomas now created an Armoured Thrust Group similar to that of 7th, 11th or Guards Armoured Divisions. 8th Armoured Brigade, who had been closely linked to the Wyverns, were interspersed in the huge column. Next came the Follow Up Group of 129th, 214th and 130th Brigades. With limited road centre lines available, wet and boggy fields unsuitable for armour, it only needed a determined paratrooper with a panzerfaust to hold up the column. On Good Friday morning, 30 March, there was a monumental traffic jam from Anholt, extending 5 miles to the village of Sinderen. 4th SLI cleared the village and by 1900 hrs their armoured group were in the outskirts of Varsseveld.

Lt. Sydney Jary, 18 Platoon, recalls:

It was Bank Holiday spirit until the leading Sherwood Rangers tank encountered the first enemy roadblock covered by 88mm guns or SPs or two or three Spandau teams. We had three nasty little battles at Sinderen, Lochem and Osterlinden. The Padre John Williams took me for a short stroll and chat, sent by the Adjutant Tim Watson to see what shape I was in! In Sinderen 5 miles east of the Rhine the leading Sherman was brewed up by a Mk IV SP hidden in a haystack. Its passengers were killed by Brens but twenty Germans charged us with bayonets shouting. Brave lads, they didn't stand a chance. My only order was 'Cease Fire'. An unarmed German stretcher-bearer with a huge Red Cross flag emerged from the village, collected our dead and wounded. The German MO then saluted the Somersets!

By 1900 hrs the Somersets were close to Varsseveld and were fired on by SPs. Maj. Beckwith, OC 'A' Company, was ordered to make a night attack at 0115 hrs. 'Lt. May with 8 Platoon encountered numerous wire obstacles which L/Sgt. Ford cut in several places. 30 yds short of the enemy gun positions 8 Platoon charged. Hell was then let loose as they accounted for every member of the gun crew. I found a swarm of enemy prisoners being searched, so many that our men had difficulty dealing with them in the dark. Lt. May was busy clearing slit trenches on his own some 25 yds in advance of his platoon, poking his Sten into one trench after another kicking the Germans back to the rear.' 'D' Company made for the Slingerbeek to the north-east, but both bridges were blown. 5th Wiltshires then crossed to cover a bridge to be made by 260th Field Company. 'C' Company 4th SLI resumed the hunt and, riding on the 4/7th Dragoon Guards' tanks, barged ahead towards Ruurlo, 10 miles away, in pitch darkness. On the way Sgt. Hayman, commanding the Pioneers, bravely neutralised a 500-lb aerial bomb lying in the middle of a bridge. With two 'volunteers' he cut the vital fuse and then rolled the bomb clear, thus earning a bar to his MM. In Ruurlo there was another brisk scrap in the darkness and a further sixty POW were taken. The indomitable Somersets kept up the charge that same morning of 1 April via Bauchem to Lochem as Maj. Beckwith relates: 'Maj. Hutchinson, 'B' Coy CO and I (OC 'A' Coy) would made a concerted attack, dodging from house to house in some cases entailing a run of 100–150 yds, section by section. Capt. B. Lock leading his forward section lost five out of their nine men but captured thirty prisoners. The tanks gave us every support but the German slit trenches were cunningly concealed. One Sherman was hit by a panzerfaust, but the other sent back another large batch of prisoners to us.'

The Recce Regiment often bore the first brunt of the German defences. Sgt. Barraclough near Millingen, Lt. Jackson near Mechelen, Sgt. Hall near Sinderen, Lt. Lindsay Baker near Hengelo, were all either blown up, wounded or killed. The regiment took over 100 prisoners. Trooper Eddy, 9th Troop's DR, taking shelter from shelling in Anholt, opened the door of a house and saw thirteen paratroopers in the hall. He closed the door hastily, then opened it again and fired in a burst of Sten. At once twelve men came out with their hands up, but the thirteenth and unlucky one made a run for it out of the back door. He was spotted and shot down by Brengunner L/Cpl. Teasdale.

Capt. Hancock, FOO with the Somersets:

As the leading tanks were entering Ruurlo, 6 miles short of
Lochem, they were fired upon by Panzerfausts and Spandaus
and two of them were hit and burst into flames. The only
building nearby bore a large red cross. It was immediately
treated to concentrated fire from BESAs and 17-pdrs. Out of it
came one German officer and fifty-six soldiers. It was the Flak
HQ of the area, contained much transport and six 20mm guns.
We reached Lochem by 1000 hrs on 1 April. The road between
Ruurlo and Lochem was littered with shot-up trucks, dead
horses and waggons, assorted staff cars, some with their bullet-
riddled occupants still sitting as they were when the RAF caught
them fleeing to the rear.

1 April was not only All Fools' Day but also Easter Sunday and
the Dutch – war notwithstanding – were in the streets in their
churchgoing best suits. Guards Armoured took the large town of
Enschede followed by 3rd British Division, and Lt.-Gen. Horrocks
ordered the Wyverns to secure the left flank of the advance at
Hengelo. During 2 and 3 April the division closed up on the line
of the Twente Kanaale. At 0900 hrs on the 3rd 5th Dorsets
started the assault on Hengelo, 6 miles north-west of Enschede,
while the Hampshires took a wider sweep and came in from the
north-east. Despite mines and mortars, the town was soon taken
and 100 POW taken. 'D' Company captured a factory which made
the latest type of AA predictor, still on the secret list. The Dorsets
received a rapturous welcome from the Dutch for their liberation,
and all the billets were luxurious. Canloan Lt. W.I. Smith, in
Hengelo with 4th Wiltshires:

We were likely to move at midnight. I tried to get the lads to
sleep in the loft of the barn except for sentries. It was
impossible. The Dutch family in the house were overjoyed at
being liberated. There were two or three nuns in the house.
When I returned from Coy HQ I found the Dutch – boys, girls,
even old men and women as well as the nuns with British
troops of all ranks hand in hand dancing in a ring and singing
Dutch and English songs. I have rarely, if ever, seen such pure
delight as was shown by these Dutch people.

After our slight dilemma at Winterswijk (4th SLI) pushed on
again giving the Germans no respite whatsoever. Through
Groenlo, Ruurlo on to Lochem where we met a strong pocket of

resistance near the Berkel river and canal there of the 23rd SS 'Freiwilligen' Panzer Grenadier Division (Netherland). Some of these Dutch towns and villages looked very innocent but sometimes there were nasty surprises waiting for us. Then to Diepenheim to the NE, Delden and to the industrial centre of Hengelo where we had some well-earned rest (wrote Pte. S.G. Sweby). Scores of us made friends in Hengelo and kept in touch for years to come.

Brig. Coad then sent 4th Dorsets off to take Borne, 3 miles ahead, which fell quickly. The enthusiastic Dutch pulled Col. Roberts and the 2 i/c Maj. Lonsdale all round the town in a cart and named the town's main square Dorset Square. Brig. Essame wrote: 'It must be admitted that Lt.-Gen. Erdmann conducted the withdrawal (of the German Army) to Bremen with great professional skill. Travelling in a captured jeep he raked together the remants of many formations into battle groups which still fought on.'

Because all the main canal and river bridges had been blown and were well defended, the Wyverns' advance continued with 7th SLI in Kangaroos plus 13/18th Hussars and they pushed down the main road to Bremen through the traffic jams. The Recce Regiment, having changed its khaki berets for black ones in Hengelo, led from Nordhorn and Lingen towards Bawinkel, where in a determined action against bazooka teams, Maj. Bindon Blood won the MC and Sgt. H.G.W. Drake the DCM. Road blocks were so strongly built that petards had to be fired at them to blast them to pieces. 'C' Squadron raced ahead towards Buckelte, where the bridge was blown and its defenders caught on the hop – sunbathing! The Adjutant Capt. J.A.H. Clark, 7th SLI, takes up the story:

What I mainly remember about the battle of Buckelte–Hamm was that it was a very hot fine day. Off we went, Kangaroos, tank, TCVs, appendages of every sort. 'D' Coy in front through this thick wooded country along a straight track with many intersections. Frequent halts while forward recce was made. Flank recce? None. We got out of our vehicles. I went to sleep in the sun. Even the wireless dozed. The track became looser and narrower – a fine surface for tanks and TCVs! So we motored into Buckelte which was a charming village in the sunshine – daffodils, forsythia, tulips, jonquils, fat farms and blossom. The bridge was blown of course, a dozen sunbathing Germans were captured. (Later) River crossing with boats. It was 4 o'clock. It was like any exercise in England. Tea and bread and butter were being got ready in the kitchen. 'O' Group at five. . . . All went well and by midnight Hamm had fallen, and a river bridge called Jellalabah was built by the Pioneers in one hour. At 2015 hrs 'A' Coy in assault boats crossed so quickly ahead of fire plan that by 0130 hrs 9 April Hamm was captured with a number of young Nazis hastily changing into civvies.

The next town of Haselunne was bombarded.

'Our set-piece infantry attack was made across a large field, 400 yds of dead flat terrain. Smoke was laid down before the attack,' wrote William Gould, 'and two companies (of Worcesters) moved forward in open formation followed by my intrepid section of line-layers.' Haselunne was not defended and William established his Signal Office in a photographer's domestic premises. 'The retreating German artillery then shelled us extensively, caused many casualties, including our well-respected MO. The very friendly residents offered us bottles of Schnapps.' Indeed two gin distilleries were taken over and Col. Alabaster, the Corps Welfare Officer, took over the stocks for NAAFI to sell. The Cornwalls put in a feint attack on Haselunne and pushed on to Eltern. On the way Capt. John Rabet's 'D' Company cleared woods successfully, but while outflanking a massive roadblock 'things went tragically wrong, trying to skirt a minefield. A blinding flash lit up the night followed by the roar of an exploding mine. Cries of wounded men rent the air,' was Col. George Taylor's description. Rabet and Lt. Wheeler were killed, Lt. Bacon and several men wounded.

The advance towards Cloppenburg was resumed on 'Heart Route', the curious name for the division's centre line, as 5th Wiltshires led on 10 April. Despite defended road blocks and mines, by dawn on the 11th they had reached Holte, 4 miles north of Herzlake. The advance continued another 10 miles to Loningen, where 4th Dorsets outfought a battalion of Gross Deutschland Brigade of young officer cadets.

On the northern centre line, the villages of Herssom and Vinner fell to 4th Wiltshires and by dusk, after covering 12 miles in the day fighting all the way, they reached Wachtum, where mines and an enormous road block held them up.

Pte. R. Gladman, 4th Wiltshires: 'We carried on through

Germany, sometimes walking, sometimes in a TCV. If the road was blocked by fallen trees, vehicles would have to go round through the grass. To avoid land mines, we crawled in line probing with bayonets but a problem with anti-personnel mines. Our officer said to step on one would mean the loss of your wedding tackle, a cause of problems on your honeymoon.' On the 12th 5th Dorsets were held up 6 miles on at Lastrup where an imposing display of firepower persuaded the defenders to scarper and repeat the process a few miles further on. 94th Field Regiment deployed their guns in Vinen, Wachtum, Lindern and Osterlinden. BSM Fred Fowler's diary for the 13th read: 'We moved to a flank to Ermke and have CP in a pub. Just outside are seven dead civvies blown up by German mines by a road block. A little boy is killed since we arrived.'

On Friday 13th Brig. Coad pushed the Hampshires towards the important town of Cloppenburg, as Lt.-Col. Talbot wrote in his war diary:

It was the last battle of the war. The plan was to capture two bridges over the river in the town, then clear the rest of the town on the far bank. 'B' and 'D' Coys led with 'B' (Maj. Morgan) on the right, advanced into the mined town, found main bridge demolished. They forced their way across, but the leading platoon was pinned down by heavy small arms fire and bazookas used as mortars. The next plan was to work round the left flank, infiltrate over the river, under cover of smoke and covering fire from our Sherwood Ranger Yeomanry tanks. The third platoon of 'B' followed and established a bridgehead. Maj. Morgan earned his MC here. On the left flank Maj. Mumford's 'D' Coy had to cross 200 yds of open ground to get to the other bridge, still standing. Boggy ground held up the SRY and the first two platoons were pinned down by heavy MMG. Another fireplan and smokescreen and a bridgehead was established and a hospital cleared. Several MMs for gallantry were earned by Cpl. Alan Carter and others. But two enemy SPs blasted at pointblank range as Maj. Game's 'A' Coy plunged into confused close quarter battle amongst the houses. Lt. R.A. Daniels was seriously wounded and CSM Greenyer died of wounds. Fighting raged in the streets all night. At midnight thirty enemy over-ran one of the Bn's anti-tank guns. At first light 5th DCLI passed through the smoking town and the

Hampshires' hard-won position. Although 100 prisoners of the officer-cadet Grossdeutschland were taken, and double that number killed or wounded, the Hampshires lost many men themselves.

The Cornwalls then spent eight hours painfully mopping up the northern suburbs of Cloppenburg and 'D' Company captured a complete enemy company.

Although the end of the war was obviously very close, Adolf Hitler would have been proud of the incredible defensive battles fought by the young officer cadets in front of the Wessex Wyverns and a few miles further east at Ibbenburen by the middle-aged officer cadets who with courageous ferocity defied 11th and 7th Armoured Division for almost a week. It was pointless, pure Wagnerian Gotterdammerung! But it still cost the lives of Wyverns.

Petards and armoured bulldozers were used to demolish the many strong intricately built roadblocks, clear the debris and fill in the RAF bomb craters. The main road went through the dense forest of Cloppenburg, planted with dark and gloomy spruce and pine trees. By the afternoon of the 14th the line of the River Leithe, 2,000 yds short of the Ahlhorn crossroads, was reached. As Maj. Peter Hall recalls:

Brian Elder, CO 'D' Coy, found the vanguard company's job frustrating and hazardous hard work. Along this single axis, they had to contend with mines, road blocks, booby traps and periodic mortaring and occasional sniping for good measure. They reached the river Leithe, 20 yds wide, with steep banks and the bridge was blown. (On the 15th) about 0545 hrs there was a tremendous artillery thunder on my forward platoon positions, followed by a massive enemy infantry and tank assault. From my Coy HQ I saw our forward platoon soldiers running back hastily. I organised new forward positions. My two signallers were killed. The wireless was destroyed. The only link was through the Regimental wireless network of 13/18 Hussars. We were on our own! For the next two hours the battle raged through the woods. This was one of the last serious counter-attacks of the war. We took numerous prisoners, between 400 and 600 enemy dead and one Royal Tiger Tank out of action. My forward platoon commander Lt. 'Smudger' Smith gave his life amongst others. The Germans included Luftwaffe, Panzer units, Waffen SS and Wehrmacht troops.

Peter Hall also persuaded the cooks to fire their rifles in the confused wood battles!

'Maj. B.N.R. Elder had been wounded so I (Percy Huxter was 2 i/c 'D' Company) returned to Coy HQ. A tank fired a shell straight through the room. Covered in dust from head to foot we dashed outside firing machine guns and two PIATs. The tank then withdrew. Everything was now quiet and about forty to fifty Germans gave themselves up. A German officer said to me in perfect English "Where do you live in England? I spent five years at Oxford before the war." My reply was unprintable!'

At 1730 hrs the 7th SLI and Worcesters made a final assault on Ahlhorn crossroads which led to Oldenburg and Wilhelmshaven. It was a classic attack, a rolling artillery barrage, 'pepper-potting' by the LAA, MMGs and supporting tanks of 13/18th Hussars. Sgt.-Maj. Clarke, 7th SLI, said: 'It was the only time in the whole campaign when I saw everything work exactly as in "Battle Drill". Sgt. H. Carroll of 7 platoon captured the telephone exchange and had a fluent three word conversation with his opposite number, who answered "Hier ist Bremen".'

The die-hard Nazis – and this was almost their last aggressive battle – lost sixty prisoners and as many killed or wounded against the Worcesters, and 120 against the 7th SLI, including two immaculate and polite Luftwaffe officers.

For the next week the division regrouped and even retrained for the final assault on Bremen. Large numbers of Allied prisoners straggled along the roads and they had to be collected and checked before being sent back. Minefields were a great danger. In three consecutive days 94th Field Regiment lost a sapper jeep, Maj. Bill Comyns was killed in his jeep leading a recce party, and Capt. Hadow's carrier also went up on a mine, but luckily he escaped with burst eardrums.

The Recce Regiment were the busiest unit in the division. Every day their Daimlers scurried round the German countryside, testing defences, checking out roads, fighting small battles and always reporting back to Divisional HQ. Every battalion was effectively in action every day mopping up and wood clearing.

46

THE LAST LAP

Bremen and Cuxhaven

Bremen was the next key objective, a city of half a million inhabitants, with most of it north of the River Weser. The remains of the German parachute army had now reinforced the garrison and the task of taking Bremen was given to Lt.-Gen. Horrocks. His XXX Corps was to be deployed with two divisions (51st Highland and 3rd British) attacking from the west side, and two more (52nd Lowland and 43rd Wessex) from the east. Gen. Thomas was almost certainly not a happy man. On 19 April 130th Brigade was loaned out to 52nd Lowland Division to provide fire support from the west bank of the River Weser and on 22 April 129th Brigade was lent to 51st Highland Division. 214th Brigade was left behind to mop up German pockets of resistance in the woods east of Ahlhorn, and moved towards the Weser.

The siege and capture of Bremen was to take six days, by which time the city was an utter ruin. The Wyverns' first action came on 23 April, started by 130th Brigade now safely back in the fold, who moved into the area of Verden on the south bank of the River Weser. The Hampshires cleared endless woods north of Welle and took 236 POW for the loss of five casualties. After a brisk encounter 5th Dorsets captured Ahausen, where L/Cpl. Watkins won his MM, taking eighty prisoners. At night 4th Dorsets moved forward several miles as 2nd/Lt. Wally Caines reported:

> 1000 hrs attack Hellwegge, nr Bremen. Troops carried on tanks: battle for a while was like hell let loose as 'A' Coy went into the assault. The CO of tanks ran from tank to tank pointing out enemy guns 'There they are – Jerry guns – fire!' Only a few prisoners taken, main body literally slaughtered. TAC HQ was near the crossroads. We had no cover whatsoever and nothing to do other than to trust in the Lord above. Shells rained down on us for several seconds. Shells burst all round us. I thought it

was all up. The Col. (Roberts) lay on the ground with his legs wounded. I lit a cigarette and stuffed it in the Colonel's mouth. This left Maj. Joe Symonds in command.

480th Division were prepared to fight on but abandoned a medium and some A/Tank guns. 4th Dorsets captured Bloediek and Ellem after a stiff fight for a bridge crossing.

It was the turn of 214th Brigade the next day to clear an area through Achim and the autobahn 6 miles to the north. 7th SLI and the Cornwalls started their advance at midnight. 'I decided on a short sharp fire plan on the line of the autobahn to shield the initial attack,' wrote Col. George Taylor. "A" Coy went in covered by artillery fire and Middlesex MGs. Only resistance spasmodic fire from 88s and mortars.'

The Wyverns' main assault started on the 25th. 130th Brigade motored over to Oyten and on to the autobahn, 2 miles east of Bremen. The Dorsets captured Sagehorn and Rockwinkel, taking 100 prisoners, over-running two German hospitals and capturing a number of 88-mm and 20-mm guns. They also liberated a trainload of Allied POW. Newly liberated 'slave' labourers, particularly Yugoslavs, were drinking and looting and had to be restrained. The Hampshires consolidated on a crossing of the autobahn, captured 150 POW, one hospital and several 88-mm AA guns. The brigade stayed here for another day and the POW haul was then over 100, plus fifty AA guns.

The XXX Corps battle plan was for 51st Highland Division to make a feint attack on Delmenhorst on the west side of the city. 3rd British Division in Buffaloes would put in a surprise attack across flooded country from the south-west, while 52nd and 43rd attacked the main part of the city from the south-east. Gen. Becker intended to fight to the last, but many of his troops had already surrendered tamely. The Wyverns captured merchant seamen, civil police, flak gunners, U-boat crews and German female ATS in uniform. Brig. Essame wrote: 'They were treated with the utmost correctness. Besides, they were very plain.' Bomber Command kept up their relentless attack on Bremen – for five hours continuously on the 24th, when 52nd Lowland Division had made a 2-mile penetration into the town's defences. The GOC was now more cheerful. 51st Highland Division released 129th Brigade, and the Wyverns were at full strength for their last battle.

Brig. J.O.E. Vandeleur wrote:

The attack upon Bremen was the last big battle in which we were engaged. My 129th Brigade was to capture the Burgher Park, a stronghold on the eastern side of the city. The 3rd British Division were to cross the river in Buffaloes and the 52nd Lowland Division were to capture the U-boat yards. We approached Bremen cautiously two up; right 4th Wilts, left 5th Wilts. I kept the Somerset LI in reserve. Our opponents were German marines who were lusty fighters. I had been instructed not only to capture the Burgher Park but also the Army, Naval and Luftwaffe commanders. When darkness fell I decided to launch the 4th Somersets under Col. Lipscomb and smash our way into the big bunkers where the German HQ and core of their defences were situated.

'Joe' Vandeleur was reluctant to use Crocodile flame-throwers but offers of surrender were rejected by the German garrison, so in they went. From their start line in the suburb of Rockwinkel both Wiltshire battalions met little resistance from dawn until 1400 hrs when they reached their objectives. 4th Wiltshires lost twelve men attacking a German barracks, Maj. Colverson of 'C' Company was killed by a Spandau, and their CO, Lt.-Col. Corbyn, was wounded.

Burgher Park was described as the Hyde Park Corner of Bremen, a junction of six roads. Capt. C.N.B. Hancock, 94th Field Regiment, wrote:

I was FOO with the Somersets. Darkness had fallen and the Crocodiles were put to work on a couple of large houses which were giving a lot of trouble. It was a grand sight to watch them belching great tongues of flame, 70 or 80 yds long and in a short time both houses were burning furiously. The Boche inside had an unpleasant choice, the flames within or the waiting machine guns of our infantry and tanks outside. The roads were littered with branches of trees and smashed buses and civilian cars destroyed in the preliminary bombardment. The battle was now well under control with the tanks, crocodiles and infantry providing mutual covering fire as together they assaulted house after house.

Col. Lipscomb, the CO, brought Brig. Vandeleur up to a corner to watch. 'The Brigadier who is an Irishman found the thirst for battle almost too much for him. I had great difficulty in restraining him from joining the attacking company's leading section.' Capt. Hancock: 'Eventually the bunker was reached and Maj. Beckhurst (and Maj. Pope OC 'D' Coy 4th Wilts) went inside to take the surrender of Maj.-Gen. Siber, the Garrison Commander and many other senior officers. I assisted the greatly outnumbered Somersets' section in relieving the Nazis of their automatics and Zeiss binoculars. There were thirty officers inside the bunker sitting round wooden tables with empty champagne bottles.' But 'C' Company of 5th Wiltshires had a furious one-hour battle before the tanks of the Sherwood Foresters destroyed most of the enemy MG nests. The CRA organised every gun in the area including mediums and heavies to bombard the main bunkers.

At daybreak on the 27th 4th Wiltshires 'B' Company crossed the canal and Maj. Pope captured Lt.-Gen. Fritz Becker, C.-in-C. Bremen defence, plus a Vice-Admiral and the Nazi Bishop of Bremen. Within thirty-six hours the Wiltshires had taken two generals, forty officers and 600 POW. The divisional bag was 2,500 all told. 2nd/Lt. Wally Caines, 4th Dorsets, made a recce to the village of Lehe, 2 miles east of Bremen: 'Brigade HQ was established in a large mansion in a park, with two large grand pianos, beautiful paintings, with jewellery littering the place.' And Capt. John Meredith gave a vivid description of Bremen at the end of April 1945:

A shambles of tangled tram wires, cratered gas mains and fallen buildings. Open sewers gaped and smelt. The devastation of the factories and docks was indescribable. Mountains of rubble later removed by armoured bulldozers. Emergency wells prevented a water famine. In a prosperous shipbuilder's house was a copy of *Mein Kampf* on a round coffee table. The Brigadier wrote on the flyleaf: 'This illuminating volume is left to you by courtesy of the British Liberation Army. If you can believe it, you can believe anything. It is left in the hope that you will study its follies in the years to come.'

Pte. Robert Thornburrow, 4th SLI, witnessed the bizarre scene in the Nazi HQ. The Gauleiter and his wife had committed suicide, with a bullet hole in each other's temples, a Luger pistol and a brandy bottle beside them.

Maj. Gordon Reinhold back with his Worcesters: 'Down by the docks there was an interesting sight. Sections of a U-boat were waiting to be assembled. Clearly constructed elsewhere, brought to the port in three large sections to be put together and launched. Very astute and enterprising!' Brig. Essame wrote:

> All day on the 27th prisoners streamed into the Divisional cage. By nightfall 2,771 including 94 officers and 831 hospital cases had been taken in this forty-eight hours. . . . The people were broken spirited and lifeless, docile, bewildered and hopeless. Fighting, rape and open murder broke out among the thousands of released slave labourers. We handed over this charnel house, once a civilised city, to 52nd Lowland Division and moved out into the clean air of the Cuxhaven peninsula on the morning of the 28th.

The final task given the Wyverns was the clearance of the Cuxhaven peninsula, a large square area bounded on three sides by the River Elbe, Bremerhaven 40 miles north-west and Cuxhaven some 60 miles due north. The Wyverns were directed on the western centre line after the sappers had reconstructed the bridges over the Wumme and Ottersbrug. Late on the evening of the 28th the GOC directed the Recce Regiment to lead from Bassen through Quelkhorn, Tarmstedt and Breddorf, across the marshlands to Kuhstedt. 5th Dorsets and the Sherwood Rangers were to follow up with the rest of 130th Brigade, despite Nebelwerfers, snipers and aerial-mine booby traps, since each village was defended. As Capt. John McMath, 5th Wiltshires, wrote: 'At Tarmstedt a heavy stonk of moaning minnies crashed down among the houses. The enemy was certainly dying hard. A complete section of 5th Dorsets were blown to smithereens when a Kangaroo encountered a sea mine with a vibration fuse buried beneath the road.' Capt. John Fletcher, 112th Field Regiment, and his carrier crew suffered the same fate, as did Sgt. Whiting and Lt. Caulkin's Humber cars in the Recce Regiment. In many places WASP flame-throwers were used to clear Tarmstedt and other hamlets. It was a vile, cold day with drenching rain and the rearguard of 15th Panzer Grenadier Division were still fighting bitterly.

Late on the 29th 214th Brigade were brought up to clear the country up to the line of the Bremen–Tarmstedt road, as Col. George Taylor recalls:

> The Cornwalls were on the right (directed on Grasburg) and the 7th Somersets on the left (directed on Truppermoor). The low

boggy country was intersected by dykes and streams. The opposition was light consisting mainly of a screen of Spandaus and Nebelwerfer mortars manned by teams of instructors from the Nebelwerfer school. Their fire at all times was deadly accurate. (Later) We had taken seventy-four prisoners in this final operation. A new sense of self-preservation had now entered our lives. The end of our long ordeal was now in sight. A deep feeling of gratitude to my officers and men. I looked upon them as my sons. They had never failed.

Capt. George Searle with the Recce Regiment: 'From Wildstedt the CO went ahead and I brought up RHQ travelling in the Staff car. As I entered the village I heard the scream of Nebelwerfer mortars and saw tank crews diving for cover under their vehicles. My driver and I sat tight in our softskin car and got away with it. Sadly so near the end our Provost Sergeant Ernie Mayle was killed instantly as he was placing more 41 Signs out. There was a tear in many an eye that day.' 170th Field Regiment had to bring down fire on the Nebelwerfer school to subdue them. By the 30th 7th SLI had advanced 5 miles in the night but were held up by 10-ft deep ditches and bomb craters. However the following day they reached the Artists Colony on a wooded hill at Worpswede. The next two days were mainly taken up by bridging craters and very carefully making safe the deadly aerial mines. 4th Dorsets took Hepstedt, the Hampshires Breddorf and 5th Dorsets Rhade, usually under fire as enemy SPs were still active. On 3 May 4th Dorsets took Glinstedt and the Hampshires Augustendrof and Gnarrenburg. The enemy was still falling back but the division was ordered not to continue in hot pursuit. At 2000 hrs on the 4th the GOC returned in his Ark to Westertimke, which also happened to be 214th Brigade HQ, and started to brief Brig. Essame on his plans for the capture of Bremerhaven. The Brigade-Major intruded at 2040 hrs and politely informed his audience: 'The BBC have just announced the unconditional surrender of the German Forces opposing Field Marshal Montgomery in NW Europe.' True to form, back came the answer: 'I take the orders from the Corps Commander, not the BBC.' Rather later the intrepid Maj. W.J. Chalmers tried again with a signal message to hand. 'A personal message to you, Sir, from the Corps Commander timed 2115 hrs.' 'Read it.' 'The German forces surrendered unconditionally at 1820 hrs. Hostilities on all Second Army Fronts will cease at 0800 hrs tomorrow 5 May '45. No – repeat No – advance beyond present front line without further orders from me.' Brig. Essame, who was there at the time, recalls: 'He walked over in silence to his ark, 20 yds away, turned and said "The troops have done us damn well."'

2nd/Lt. Wally Caines, 4th Dorsets: 'I cannot express in words the joy that met our hearts on hearing the great news. It did not seem possible that the war for us had ended after eleven months of hell and horror which had been endured by us veterans from the Beaches of Normandy to Germany. I could only thank God that I had been spared to hear this longed for announcement.' And Eric Codling, 8th Middlesex:

Forty men drawn together by fate landed in Normandy. Almost a year later less than half are present to witness the story's end. With hoarded rum we toasted absent fallen comrades. Rum flowed free. Outside it was almost as noisy as a battle of the past, signal and parachute flares soared, tracer bullets marked their graceful arcs in the sky and plastic grenades exploded. It sounded quite dangerous. By the early hours we were unconscious to be woken by our two officers with tea in time to witness the magical 8 a.m. ceasefire. The war was over in Europe.

And two unusual stories to end the saga of the Fighting Wessex Wyverns. Maj. Gordon Viner returned to the Hampshires after being wounded on his left cheek. His CSM had discovered a black tin box tucked away in 'A' Echelon, crammed full of worthless Reichsmarks, retained as a curiosity. Just after the end of hostilities, stationed at Winsen, the old BA Forces notes were withdrawn and Reichsmarks approved. With his 'fortune' Maj. Viner purchased LIFE membership for 320 other ranks of the battalion in the Regimental Association.

The last word must go to the intrepid, brutal, demanding, controversial GOC. Gen. Ivo Thomas, a day or so after the news of the end of the war was broadcast, said to his ADC, Pat Spencer Moore: 'We could cut through those Russians like a knife through butter.' And he would have done.

47

THE 43RD (WESSEX) DIVISION ORDER OF BATTLE

6 June 1944 to 5 May 1945

HQ   43 (Wessex) Infantry
      Division
HQ   129 Infantry Brigade
      4 Somerset Light
      Infantry
      4 Wiltshire
      5 Wiltshire
HQ   130 Infantry Brigade
      7 Royal Hampshire
      4 Dorsets
      5 Dorsets
HQ   214 Infantry Brigade
      7 Somerset Light Infantry
      1 Worcestershire
      5 Duke of Cornwall's Light
      Infantry

RECONNAISSANCE
      43 Reconnaissance
      Regiment (The
      Gloucestershire
      Regiment)

MACHINE-GUN BATTALION
      8 Middlesex

RA
      94 Field Regiment
      112 Field Regiment
      179 Field Regiment

      59 Anti-Tank Regiment
      110 L.A.A. Regiment
RE
      204 Field Company
      260 Field Company
      553 Field Company
      207 Field Park Company

SIGNALS
      43 Wessex Divisional
      Signals

RASC
      504 Company
      505 Company
      54 Company
      506 Company

RAMC
      129 Field Ambulance
      130 Field Ambulance
      213 Field Ambulance
      14 Field Dressing Station
      15 Field Dressing Station
      38 Field Hygiene Section

RAOC
      43 Ordance Field Park
      306 Mobile Laundry and
      Bath Unit

REME

    129 Infantry Brigade
        Workshop
    130 Infantry Brigade
        Workshop
    214 Infantry Brigade
        Workshop

PROVOST

    43 Wessex Division Provost
        Company R.C.M.P.

FIELD SECURITY

    57 Field Security Section

POSTAL UNIT

48

THE BUTCHER'S BILL

The official figures of casualties suffered by the Wessex Wyverns in the north-west Europe campaign (24 June 1944 to 5 May 1945) were 12,484, of which 1,587 were killed, 8,292 wounded and 2,603 missing.

Unfortunately many of those posted as missing were in fact killed, and many of those wounded later died of their wounds. The full strength of a battalion was usually thirty-six officers and about eight hundred men. The individual battalion histories record these sad unforgettable casualty figures (alphabetically).

5th Duke of Cornwall's Light Infantry – 300 KIA, inc. 12 officers

4th Dorsets – 266 KIA, inc. 7 officers

5th Dorsets – 218 KIA, inc. 11 officers

43rd Recce (5th Glosters) – 180 at sea and 61 KIA, inc. 11 officers

7th Royal Hampshires (estimated) – 270 KIA, inc. 20 officers

4th Somerset Light Infantry – 229 KIA, inc. 13 officers (1,313 casualties)

7th Somerset Light Infantry – 239 KIA, inc. 17 officers (1,180 casualties)

4th Wiltshires – 232 KIA, inc. 19 officers

5th Wiltshires – 334 KIA, inc. 21 officers (1,277 casualties)

1st Worcesters – 264 KIA, inc. 23 officers (1,177 casualties)

8th Middlesex, 94th Field Regt. RA – 38 KIA; 112 Field Regt., 179 Field Regt. – 37 KIA; 59th A/Tank Regt., 110 LAA Regt., Royal Engineers, Royal Signals, RASC, REME, ADMS, APM, RAOC – estimated 270–300 KIA.

The Fighting Wessex Wyverns were certainly led from the front.

One brigadier and twelve battalion or regimental commanders were killed in action and another seven wounded.

I have a rendezvous with Death,
At some disputed barricade
I have a rendezvous with Death,
On some scarred slope of battered hill
But I've a rendezvous with Death,
At midnight in some flaming town.

Alan Seeger's words seem appropriate for the Fighting Wessex Wyverns.

INDEX

Note: major entries are in chronological order, where appropriate.